Christian
Integrity

CHRISTIAN INTEGRITY

R. B. THIEME, JR.

EDITED BY
WAYNE F. HILL

R. B. THIEME, JR., BIBLE MINISTRIES
HOUSTON, TEXAS

FINANCIAL POLICY

No price appears on any material from R. B. Thieme, Jr., Bible Ministries. Anyone who desires Bible teaching can receive our books and tapes without charge or obligation. God provides Bible doctrine. We wish to reflect His grace.

R. B. Thieme, Jr., Bible Ministries operates entirely on voluntary contributions. There is no price list for books or tapes. No money is requested. When gratitude for the Word of God motivates a believer to give, he has the privilege of contributing to the dissemination of Bible doctrine.

This book is edited from the lectures and unpublished notes of R. B. Thieme, Jr.

A catalog of available tapes and publications will be provided upon request

R. B. Thieme, Jr., Bible Ministries
5139 West Alabama, Houston, Texas 77056

©1990 by R. B. Thieme, Jr. All rights reserved
First Edition published 1984. Second Edition 1990

Printed in the United States of America

ISBN 1-55764-040-8

Contents

Chapter III   Gate Two, Basic Christian Modus Operandi

Chapter IV   Gate Three, Teachability

Chapter V   Gate Four, Spiritual Momentum

Chapter VI   Gates Five and Six, Motivational and Functional Virtue

Chapter VII   Gate Seven, Momentum Testing

Chapter VIII   Gate Eight, The Winner's Gate

Chapter IX A New Approach to Christology

Indexes

Preface

Before you begin your Bible study, be sure that, as a believer in the Lord Jesus Christ, you have named your known sins privately to God (1 John 1:9). You will then be in fellowship with God, under the control of the indwelling Holy Spirit, and ready to learn doctrine from the Word of God.

If you are an unbeliever, the issue is not naming your sins. The issue is faith in Christ:

> He who believes in the Son has eternal life; but he who does not obey [the command to believe in] the Son shall not see life, but the wrath of God abides on him. (John 3:36)

I
God's Game Plan

THE SYSTEM THAT SUSTAINED CHRIST

GOD THE FATHER DESIGNED A SOURCE OF STRENGTH for the humanity of Christ. Jesus stated repeatedly that He was sent by the Father, that He revealed the Father, that He obeyed the Father's will (Matt. 11:27; Luke 22:42; John 14:10). Christ did not come to glorify Himself or carry out His own program. Since the Father planned Christ's mission, the Father also provided Him with powerful resources to execute that mission.

Loyalty to the Father's plan resulted in the supreme success in all history: Christ fulfilled His destiny to be the Savior of mankind.

The assets God provided for the humanity of Christ functioned together as a system of power and love. This system proved so effective that Christ could say in the midst of human suffering, "My yoke is easy, and My burden is light" (Matt. 11:30). He could endure the cross with "the already demonstrated happiness" that He found during His life in the divine system (Heb. 12:2). The Father's provisions enabled the humanity of Christ to handle the "burden" of His first advent, which was far heavier than any load we will ever need to carry (Heb. 2:7-9). Before He departed, Christ gave the divine support system to us (John 15:9, 10).

The same divine system that sustained Jesus Christ now belongs to each believer.

Christian integrity comes from loyalty to the divine system. When we study Christian integrity, therefore, we are studying Christ. He is the "author and perfecter of our faith" (Heb. 12:2). Because Christ set the precedent for our lives in the divine system, we discover facets of His character not only in His life and death but also in the divine commands addressed to us.

By drawing upon the source of Christ's inner strength, we fulfill the general mandate to "grow in grace and in the knowledge of our Lord and Savior Jesus Christ" (2 Pet. 3:18). In learning to thrive under the provisions of God's grace, we are also learning about Christ, for He lived inside the same system that the Bible mandates for us. As demonstrated by the humanity of Christ, spiritual growth from this divine source of strength enables each believer to fulfill his personal destiny.

> For begin thinking of such a Person [Jesus Christ], having
> endured such opposition by sinners against Himself, in order
> that you do not become exhausted, fainting in your souls.
> (Heb. 12:3)[1]

Christ is the model of confidence and effectiveness under maximum stress. He encourages us when we face pressure. His example inspires us to look beyond ourselves and our immediate problems and see Him, to "begin thinking of such a Person." As we reflect on Him and His achievements, the theme of this book becomes emphatic: Jesus Christ has given us access to the very system that sustained Him throughout His first advent. His life on earth is proof that the system works. There is no fainting in the soul when residing inside the divine sphere of power and love.

> But in all these things [pressure, persecution, economic
> depression, deprivation, danger, violence in crime or war]
> we win the supreme victory through Him who loves us.
> (Rom. 8:37)

Christ is our "most important love" (Rev. 2:4). We come to know Him by living within the system in which He lived. We think His thoughts, for the "mind of Christ" is Bible doctrine (1 Cor. 2:16). We have the same attitude that governed His life (Phil. 2:5). His inner dynamics are generated within us (John 16:13-15; Gal. 5:16; Eph. 5:18). Eventually, His virtues become our virtues, His great capacity for life and happiness becomes our capacity, His integrity becomes our integrity (John 15:11; 1 Pet. 2:9b). If we continue to learn, think about, and apply Bible doctrine, the divine system will produce this spiritual growth in us (Matt. 6:33; Luke 2:52). This is the very purpose for which God keeps us alive (Rom. 12:2; Eph. 4:13-16).

> For of His fullness we have all received, and grace upon
> grace. (John 1:16, NASV)

---

1. Unless indicated, Scripture quotations are my translations of the Hebrew and Greek texts. References marked AV are quoted from the Authorized Version (King James); those marked NASV, from the New American Standard Version. Bracketed commentary correlates the quotation with its context or the discussion at hand.

Christ has passed down to us the heritage of His daily life on earth, when God "was made flesh and dwelt among us . . . full of grace and truth" (John 1:14). The divine system, with all its parts functioning in proper balance, gives the Christian a life of grace and truth. By understanding God's plan as a system, we can adhere to all God's mandates for us. We can avoid distortions of the Christian way of life that come from taking favorite biblical principles out of context. No part or parts of God's system will function effectively if isolated from the system as a whole. God desires to bless us to the maximum, "infinitely more than that which we could ask or imagine" (Eph. 3:20). His complete system is designed to accomplish this purpose.

INNOVATION WITHIN A SYSTEM

God's plan is analogous to the game plan of a championship athletic team. A skillful football coach wins consistently not just because he has shrewd instincts for the game but because he follows a winning system. Without a system he has no standards, no coordination, no performance, no effectiveness. Success demands a system. A system is a coordinated plan that unifies and directs the efforts of all the diverse individuals in the organization. No coach can innovate on the playing field without a cohesive system of organization, authority, training, and discipline.

Innovation without a system is disastrous in any realm—athletics, business, politics, economics, the military, social life, spiritual life. We as believers in Christ cannot successfully innovate in our lives, exercising wisdom and common sense in the challenges that confront us, unless we live in the system God has ordained. Each life is unique; the system establishes protocol for all. God does not tell us precisely what to think and do in each situation; He gives us freedom to apply the correct doctrine in our own lives. But innovation and practical application must be within His system. Each believer must learn God's game plan just as a professional athlete learns the playbook.

One of the most effective systems in professional football forbids the quarterback to call the plays. The coach personally directs every play from the sidelines. He is the one who does the thinking and plans the strategy. The players execute the game plan with confidence because they know the system works. No quarterback under pressure on the field can outthink the coach.

Every successful system has a *purpose, policy,* and structure of *authority.* On a football team the coach's purpose is to win; his policies promote winning; and his structure of authority takes the talented, the arrogant, the strong, the weak, the lazy, the insouciant, teaches them to concentrate under pressure, and transforms them into one of the finest teams in professional football. The smart coach devises his system to be greater than any of its component parts, greater than any individual player. The system enables his organization to establish a consistent winning record over the years regardless of who is on the team. It does not matter who executes the plays, as long as he does it the coach's way.

God's perfect system—the Christian way of life—is greater than any human system or individual Christian. God's plan works in every generation, for anyone who will follow its mandates. The divine system transforms all kinds of believers into mature Christians, winners in the devil's world (John 12:31; 14:30; 16:11; Eph. 2:1-8; 1 John 2:13, 14). In God's system the *purpose* is to glorify Jesus Christ; the *policy* is grace; the *authority* is the sovereignty of God. Christ is glorified by the salvation of unbelievers and the imputation of blessings to believers; the policy of grace is delineated in Bible doctrine; divine authority is embodied in the Word of God (Rom. 1:16) and delegated as temporal authority under the divine laws of establishment (Rom. 13:1-7).[2] Like the coach, God has done the thinking, planned the strategy, and called the plays. As believers our responsibility is to execute His plan.

MANY COMMANDS, ONE DYNASPHERE

God has issued hundreds of commands throughout the New Testament. We are instructed to be filled with the Spirit, to confess our sins, to love the brethren, to rest in the Lord, to maintain humility, to learn and apply the Word of God, to love God and be occupied with Christ, to acquire virtue, to resist evil, to achieve spiritual maturity. These imperatives are not isolated mandates unrelated to one another; all these diverse commandments for the believer combine to form the perfect divine system.

> If you keep My mandates, you shall reside in the sphere of
> My love. (John 15:10*a*)

God's system is designated the "sphere of love" or love complex to emphasize love as the supreme Christian virtue (1 Cor. 13:13). The New Testament commands us to love, but no one can obey these commands without understanding that love is an entire sphere, a complex of interrelated elements, a system of power. I have coined a term for this divine system from the Greek nouns *dunamis,* "power," and *sphaia,* "sphere": the "divine *dynasphere.*" This descriptive synonym emphasizes the efficacy and sustaining strength of the love complex.

---

2. See Thieme, *Divine Establishment* (Houston: R. B. Thieme, Jr., Bible Ministries, 1976).

In the future, keep on being strong [*dunamai*, the cognate verb of *dunamis*] in the Lord, even by means of the inner rule of His endowed power [the divine dynasphere]. Wear for yourselves the full armor from God [the divine dynasphere] that you may be able [*dunamai*] to hold your ground against the tactics of the devil. (Eph. 6:10, 11)

In Ephesians 6:13-17, Paul illustrates the Christian way of life through an analogy to the Roman soldier's uniform—his belt, breastplate, sandals, shield, helmet, and sword. The panoply of God consists of separate items of spiritual armor and weaponry, each of which contributes to the believer's victory in spiritual combat. Just as the directive to "don the full armor of God" requires you to skillfully wield an array of offensive and defensive weapons against the enemy, so also the commands to reside in the divine dynasphere demand obedience to an entire system of divine imperatives. The divine dynasphere coordinates every legitimate temporal and spiritual activity in life. By consistently living in this power system, the believer obeys all God's mandates.

THE GATES OF THE SYSTEM

Since divine mandates can be organized into eight categories, the divine dynasphere has eight "gates."

1. *THE POWER GATE:* the filling of the Holy Spirit.
2. *OBJECTIVITY:* basic Christian modus operandi.
3. *TEACHABILITY:* enforced and genuine humility.
4. *SPIRITUAL MOMENTUM:* perception and application of Bible doctrine.
5. *MOTIVATIONAL VIRTUE:* personal love for God.
6. *FUNCTIONAL VIRTUE:* impersonal love for mankind.[3]
7. *MOMENTUM TESTING:* acceleration of spiritual growth.
8. *THE WINNER'S GATE:* spiritual maturity, sharing the happiness of God.

Because all eight gates are engaged as one dynamic unity, I also designate the love complex as the "interlocking system of love." A diagram of the system shows the coalescence of the gates.

---

3. The distinction between personal and impersonal love, which depend on each other, will be developed in gates two, five, and six.

Gates one, two, and three interlock to provide the power, objectivity, and receptivity needed for learning and applying the Word of God at gate four. Gate four is the momentum gate. All spiritual momentum in the Christian life is fueled by *knowledge* of Bible doctrine and accelerated by proper *application* of doctrine. Spiritual momentum carries the believer to maturity. Gates one through three constitute motivation essential for concentration on doctrine, whereas gates five through eight are result gates, the results of spiritual momentum.

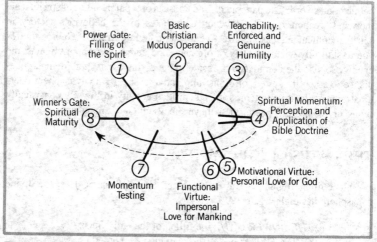

THE DIVINE DYNASPHERE (OR LOVE COMPLEX, OR INTERLOCKING SYSTEM OF LOVE)

Gates five and six form a double gate that expresses the most vital concept in experiential Christianity: integrity precedes love. In dealing with mankind, God's integrity always comes before His love; the essence of God establishes the precedent for the Christian way of life.[4] We, too, must possess integrity before we have capacity to love God or man. This is the doctrine of virtue-love.

The first four gates of the system build Christian virtue, honor, and integrity; love pervades the system at gates five and six. The virtues in gate five directed toward God motivate the functional virtues in gate six directed toward man and circumstances. These motivational and functional virtues stand or fall together.

---

4. See Thieme, *The Integrity of God* (1979).

Gate seven provides divine solutions to resolve the problems of life as the believer's spiritual momentum is repeatedly challenged. Passing these tests accelerates spiritual growth. Gate eight, the objective, is spiritual maturity.

MATURITY AND INTEGRITY

Maturity, the goal of the Christian's life, is achieved through steadfastness in the divine dynasphere, where the believer acquires capacity for life, for love, for happiness, for "greater grace" or supergrace (James 4:6) beyond God's faithful sustenance of all believers. The believer in gate eight has become a spiritual aristocrat invested with the title "Friend of God" (James 2:23). Through his tenacity to reside and function in the love complex, he has attained an honorable status in his soul that glorifies the Lord Jesus Christ.

The superior quality of the mature believer's life is a testimony to divine grace; all the mature Christian has and is depends entirely on Christ's saving work and His gift of the divine dynasphere. God can prosper the mature believer with a maximum expression of grace because he has capacity to appreciate God's blessings without forgetting their source. In gate eight the believer recognizes the giver, God Himself, in every gift received.

The mature believer approaches life from the divine viewpoint, which is manifested in discernment, thoughtfulness toward people, and the ability to astutely interpret current trends of history. Stabilized by his love for truth, he is distinguished by his spiritual common sense. He maintains his poise in all circumstances, sustained by the unseen reality of his love for God. In the strength of the divine dynasphere, the mature believer has constructed an edifice in his soul (1 Cor. 3:9-17; Eph. 4:12b), an inner structure I call the "edification complex," with a penthouse that represents the happiness of God.[5] True happiness is achieved only in the divine dynasphere. Happiness depends on virtue, honor, and integrity.

Integrity is a state or quality of being complete; an unimpaired state of honesty and purity; a soundness of moral principle; the character of uncorrupted virtue, especially in relation to truth and fair dealing. Integrity is uprightness of character; probity; candor; uncompromising adherence to a code of moral or professional values; the avoidance of deception, expediency, artificiality, or shallowness of any kind.[6]

Reduced to essentials, *integrity is loyalty to truth*. Truth exists in three categories: the divine laws of establishment, the Gospel, and Bible doctrine. Our

---

5. See below, pp. 183-88.

6. *Oxford English Dictionary* and *Webster's Third New International Dictionary*, s. v. "integrity."

residence in the sphere of God's power is our loyalty to the absolute truth of His design. In mandates that form part of Bible doctrine, He has prescribed for us this complete, interlocking structure for developing integrity so that, from His own integrity, He may share His happiness with us both now and forever.

PAUL'S PRAYERS CONCERNING THE DIVINE DYNASPHERE

The divine dynasphere is the subject of two apostolic prayers by Paul, the man who exploited God's power and advanced farther in spiritual maturity than any other believer. The apostle Paul is the greatest of all believers (2 Pet. 3:15, 16).

> For this reason, I [Paul], too, having heard about your faith in the Lord Jesus and the love toward all the saints [functional virtue, impersonal love toward all believers, gate six] do not cease giving thanks for you while mentioning you in my prayers, that the God of our Lord Jesus Christ, the Father of glory, may give you a Spirit of wisdom and of revelation [the filling and teaching ministry of the Holy Spirit, gate one] in the full knowledge of Him [perception and application of Bible doctrine, the Mind of Christ, gate four, resulting in personal love for God, gate five], that the eyes of your heart [the thinking portion of the soul] may be enlightened [perceptive ability based on the first four gates of the system] so that you may know what is the hope of His election [know the objective of the system] and what are the riches of the glory of His inheritance in the saints [temporal and eternal blessings to believers who live in the system], and what is the surpassing greatness of His power [spiritual victory from living in the divine dynasphere] toward us who believe. These are according to the standard of the operational power [the function of the divine system] of His inner power [Bible doctrine, gate four], which power [the divine dynasphere] has been operational in Christ [the humanity of Christ living in the prototype divine dynasphere throughout the First Advent] when He [the Father] raised Him from the dead and seated Him at the right hand in the heavenlies [Christ's strategic victory over Satan through death, burial, resurrection, ascension, and session]. (Eph. 1:15-20)

The second apostolic prayer expresses Paul's exhortation that believers "become strong by means of His power [the divine dynasphere] through His Spirit [the Holy Spirit, gate one] in the inner man" and that they "may be filled with all the fullness of God," a synonym for spiritual maturity in gate eight of the divine system (Eph. 3:16, 19). This second prayer concludes:

> Now to the One [God the Father] Himself being able [*dunamai*, referring to divine omnipotence] far beyond all things to do infinitely more than that which we could ask or imagine, according to the power [*dunamis*, the divine dynasphere] being itself effective in us, to Him be the glory in the Church and in Christ Jesus with reference to all generations forever and ever. Amen. (Eph. 3:20, 21)

SPIRITUAL ARISTOCRACY

The love complex is unique to the Church Age, that period of human history from the day of Pentecost, circa A.D. 30, to the resurrection or Rapture of the Church, which is yet future (Acts 1:5; 2:1; 1 Cor. 15:51-53; 1 Thess. 4:13-17). We possess the entire divine dynasphere, a privilege never extended to believers of other dispensations.

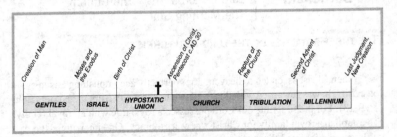

HUMAN HISTORY FROM GOD'S VIEWPOINT – THE DISPENSATIONS

The Holy Spirit as the power of the system "was not yet given" prior to the Church Age "because Jesus was not yet glorified" (John 7:39). The divine dynasphere was designed for Jesus Christ. This system of power could not be given to believers until Christ had proven the system throughout His life, accomplishing His mission for the First Advent, earning the glory of a new royal title, founding a new royal dynasty to which He could bequeath His system of power and love.

During the Church Age, Jesus Christ as glorified royalty is seated at the right hand of God the Father in heaven, while the Father forms on earth a royal family for Him. We are the new royal family.

Jesus Christ retains three titles of royalty, each with a royal family. As *God*, our Lord is divine royalty, the "Son of God," and His royal family is the Trinity. As *man*, Jesus is Jewish royalty, the "Son of David," and His royal family is the line of King David. As the *God-Man*, the Lord Jesus Christ won the strategic victory over Satan at the Cross and earned a third series of royal titles, "King of Kings and Lord of Lords" and "The Morning Star" (1 Tim. 6:15; Rev. 19:16; 22:16). These last titles signify His battlefield royalty, His strategic victory over Satan.[7]

	Royal Title	Royal Family
Divine	Son of God	God the Father God the Holy Spirit
Jewish	Son of David	The Davidic Dynasty
Battlefield	King of Kings Lord of Lords The Morning Star	The Church

THE THREE ROYALTIES OF THE LORD JESUS CHRIST

When Christ ascended to heaven, after perfectly accomplishing His mission on earth, He was rewarded with this third patent of royalty from the Father (Eph. 1:20-23). For the first time our Lord possessed a royal title with no royal family. To establish a royal family for Christ's new aristocracy, God interrupted the Age of Israel and inserted the Age of the Church. Designated the "body of Christ" (Eph. 1:22, 23; 4:12), the "bride of Christ" (2 Cor. 11:2; Eph. 5:25-27; Rev. 19:6-8), and implied in the vocatives "beloved" and "brethren," the Church is His third royal family. Everyone who believes in Christ during the Church Age simultaneously becomes a member of the royal family of God forever and has access to the complete divine dynasphere.

The divine dynasphere did not exist until the incarnation of Jesus Christ. As a man Jesus required divine support, which He received in such abundance that His human life reflected the character of God.

---

7. See below, note 11.

> And the Word became flesh and dwelt among us, and we
> beheld His glory [manifestation of the divine dynasphere],
> glory as the unique Son of the Father, full of grace and truth.
> (John 1:14)

As a demonstration of love for the Son, God the Father invented the divine dynasphere to sustain the humanity of Christ who, from the virgin birth until His ascension to heaven, would face continuous opposition in the devil's world. God combined certain divine principles into a unique system. He took impersonal love and personal love—patterned after His own divine attribute of love—and added the ministry of God the Holy Spirit as the power to support our Lord during his earthly ministry. Given at the virgin birth (Isa. 11:1, 2; 61:1; John 3:34, 35; Col. 1:19) the divine dynasphere was the original Christmas present from the Father to Jesus Christ. Christ in His humanity lived perpetually inside the prototype of the same divine dynasphere in which we are commanded to live (Luke 2:40).

Ten days after our Lord ascended and was seated in heaven, the Church Age began, and the divine dynasphere was the first blessing given to each member of the royal family. On the night He was betrayed, fifty days before the Church Age began, our Lord prophesied to His disciples that they would receive the same system of divine power that had sustained and blessed Him throughout the First Advent. He taught them that His love in the prototype divine dynasphere was patterned after the love of God. Genuine human love is based on divine love.

> Just as the Father loves Me, so also have I loved you.
> (John 15:9*a*)

As the original recipient of the love complex, the Lord Jesus Christ bequeathed to the royal family this unique gift designed for Him by God the Father.

> Reside [remain, persist] in My love [the love complex]. If
> you keep [observe, fulfill] My mandates, you shall reside in
> the sphere of My love, just as I have fulfilled the mandates
> of My Father and I reside in the sphere of His love [the pro-
> totype divine dynasphere]. (John 15:9*b*, 10)

Christ lived and functioned for thirty-three years in the very system in which we are now commanded to live. He succeeded in fulfilling perfectly God's plan, not in His own power but in the power of the Holy Spirit, gate one in the divine dynasphere. This same divine power is now available to us; we too can fulfill the plan of God. We cannot be sinless, as was the humanity of Christ, but with the rebound provision, which enables us to recover instantly from the control of the sin nature, we can execute God's game plan for our lives.[8]

The Bible describes the believer who resides and functions in the divine dynasphere.

> If we walk in the light [the divine dynasphere] as He is in the light [the prototype divine dynasphere], we have fellowship with each other [impersonal love, gates two, six, and seven] and the blood of Jesus Christ [the basis for rebound] cleanses us from all sin.[9] (1 John 1:7)

The believer inside the divine dynasphere is also described as "filled with the Spirit" (Eph. 5:18); he "walks by means of the Spirit" (Gal. 5:16); and he is said to be "cleansed" (1 John 1:9). He has "put on Christ" (Rom. 13:14) because Christ lived in the original system. The believer in the love complex is "walking in love" (Eph. 5:2), "loving one another" (1 John 3:23), and, as we have seen, "residing in the love [complex]" (John 15:9, 10). He is "holding his ground" in the full armor of God (Eph. 6:11). Each phrase emphasizes a different aspect of our royal way of life.

Aristocracy means achievement. Christ achieved strategic victory in the angelic conflict and established a new and unique dynasty of spiritual nobility. As His eternal royal family we depend entirely on Christ and therefore must emulate the integrity He possessed in the prototype divine dynasphere. He gave us the system by which we can in our temporal lives manifest the superiority of our eternal position. Integrity perpetuates nobility. Royalty lives by a superior code of honor, and as members of spiritual aristocracy, we fulfill the royal family honor code and create Christian integrity by functioning in the divine dynasphere.[10]

CHARACTERISTICS AND PRIORITIES

In summary, God's game plan, the divine dynasphere, has the following general characteristics:

---

8. See below, pp. 22-24, 34-35. See Also Thieme, *Rebound and Keep Moving* (1973). The old sin nature is fallen man's inherent, genetic weakness to commit sin, human good, and evil; idem, *Integrity of God*, pp. 57-77.

9. See Thieme, *The Blood of Christ* (1977).

10. See below, pp. 129-32.

A purpose: glorification of the Lord Jesus Christ in time. The believer's tactical victory exploits our Lord's strategic victory over Satan in the angelic conflict.[11]

An objective: spiritual maturity. Momentum toward spiritual maturity is possible only inside the divine dynasphere.

A policy: grace. Grace is always the policy of God in the administration of His plan for sinful man.

A protocol: obedience to divine mandates. Believers and elect angels in heaven observe divine protocol; happiness on earth is based on the precisely correct procedure of the divine dynasphere.

A system: virtue first. The foundational virtue of humility, which is directed toward authority, lays the groundwork for motivational virtue toward God and functional virtue toward man and circumstances.

A point of reference: the justice of God. The holiness or integrity of God is composed of His absolute righteousness and perfect justice. Our point of contact with God is His integrity, not His sovereignty, as taught by hypercalvinists, nor His omnipotence, as alleged by so-called divine healers, nor His love, as presumed by overly emotional fundamentalists, nor His omnipresence, as believed by pantheists.

An authority: the Word of God. Bible doctrine reveals the essence of God to man and embodies the absolute authority of divine sovereignty.

A result: good decisions from a position of strength in the divine system, control of your life, and a personal sense of destiny.

An enemy: the cosmic system of Satan.[12]

These nine characteristics will become meaningful in the study we are about to begin. We can translate these axioms into a set of priorities, which provide a framework for organizing your life and applying doctrine under all circumstances.

---

11.   The angelic conflict is the unseen warfare between God and Satan, ignited by Satan's prehistoric revolution. When God sentenced Satan to eternal judgment, Satan appealed the sentence, accusing God of injustice; God responded by creating the human race to resolve the angelic conflict, demonstrating His perfect integrity and grace in human history despite satanic opposition. The Cross was the strategic victory over Satan. A strategic victory creates advantageous conditions for tactical victory in combat with the enemy. See below, pp. 175-77.

12.   See below, pp. 158-70.

In God's plan the priority is *Mandates first*.
In God's system, *Virtue first*.
In God's purpose, *Christ first*.
In God's policy, *Grace first*.
In God's objective, *Momentum first*.
In God's authority, *Doctrine first*.

These six priorities represent one superior way of life, one system of power and love, the divine dynasphere, with different emphasis as the believer continues to grow. As we approach all eight gates of the divine dynasphere, you will learn that these priorities enable you to make good decisions from a position of strength, take control of your life, and acquire a personal sense of destiny within God's game plan.

II
Gate One, The Power Gate

THE SOURCE OF ENERGY

Just as the Holy Spirit sustained the earthly ministry of Jesus (Matt. 12:18; John 3:34), the filling of the Spirit provides the power for our lives. On the eve of His crucifixion, fifty days before the feast of Pentecost when the Holy Spirit would be given and the Church Age would begin, Christ Himself prophesied the advent of the Spirit in the new love complex.

> And when the Energizer comes [the Holy Spirit as the power source in the divine dynasphere] whom I will send from the Father, that is, the Spirit of Truth [a functional title for the Holy Spirit] who proceeds from the Father, that one [the Spirit] will give evidence [make a deposition, testify] concerning Me. (John 15:26)

The Greek noun *parakletos*, which I have translated "Energizer," is used in the Bible only by the Apostle John, referring once to Christ (1 John 2:1) but generally to the Holy Spirit (John 14:16, 26; 15:26; 16:7). This title for God is translated "Comforter" in the King James Version and "Helper" in the New American Standard Version.

In the classical Greek a *parakletos* was someone called to the aid of another, particularly in the legal process; hence, an advisor, intercessor, or mediator in court. In Roman times, when the official Greek language of the eastern empire was translated into the official Latin of the west, the Latin equivalent for *parakletos* was *advocatus*, from which we derive the English word "advocate" or lawyer.

A *parakletos* was a professional legal advisor, sometimes a defense attorney. The word connotes ability, aid, and assistance, rather than assuagement of pain or distress, as the translation "comforter" suggests. Certainly comfort is implied; the one being aided by a powerful helper is relieved and encouraged. But eternal God, the third Person of the Trinity, does not come to the royal family to say, "There, there, everything will be all right." Instead, He was sent by the Father (John 15:26b) to empower, help, and sustain the humanity of Christ against all the forces of evil Satan could hurl against Him.

This same omnipotent Member of the Godhead was in turn sent by the Father and the Son (John 14:26; 15:26a) to be the power source for the new royal family. The Holy Spirit reproduces in us the virtues of Christ when we advance in the divine dynasphere (Eph. 5:1, 2; Gal. 5:22, 23; Rom. 13:14). The Spirit's title, *Parakletos*, must be understood in terms of power within the divine system, in which we, like the humanity of Christ, must live in the devil's world.

Christ's final words on earth before ascending into heaven prophesied the coming of the Holy Spirit, the Energizer of the divine dynasphere. The divine power system would motivate growing believers to spread the Gospel of Christ throughout the world.

> But you shall receive power [the divine dynasphere] when
> the Holy Spirit has come upon you; and you shall be My
> witnesses both in Jerusalem and Samaria, and even to the
> remotest part of the earth. (Acts 1:8, NASV)

God the Energizer has two basic ministries to the royal family, one of which is indicated by His functional title in John 15:26, "Spirit of Truth, or Doctrine."[13] He provides the spiritual IQ for learning Bible doctrine, which itself is the power of God (Rom. 1:16). Thus the filling of the Spirit at gate one and the perception and application of doctrine at gate four interlock with each other (1 Cor. 2:9-16). The Word and the Spirit join forces to form the greatest power system ever offered to any dispensation in the history of mankind.

> And my message and my preaching [Bible doctrine] were
> not in persuasive words of wisdom, but in demonstration of
> the Spirit and of power [the divine dynasphere], that your
> faith should not rest on the wisdom of men, but on the power
> of God [the divine dynasphere]. (1 Cor. 2:4, 5, NASV)

---

13. At salvation the Holy Spirit has five permanent ministries and one temporary ministry. *Permanent:* regeneration, baptism, indwelling, sealing, and distribution of spiritual gifts. *Temporary:* filling. The Spirit's role in teaching doctrine and aiding the believer's function in the divine dynasphere are aspects of His *filling* ministry. See Thieme, *Integrity of God,* pp. 105-17.

[handwritten margin notes:]
Sun. 1-2 -12 12:35 PM
Energizer Comforter Advocate
The HS Works on Case By Case (Individual) Making Recommendations for How Best to Work Gods Good Into shit Happens for the Believer the HS Works with all Fore knowledge Because He Knows best and Only Pleys the Father As If He Hired the HS to Help

This Would Get Riel of Salen Argument of Things Would Be Different If Omni God Did Every thing. Unlike Job when we Go through life we have HS

pleroo -research
We Are to Walk By Means of the HS
Ps 23 2nd Post two Mandate

...IQ for *perception* of the written Word of God in
...upplies energy for the believer's *function* in the
..., 22, 23). At all gates of the divine system, the
...ian life with an unseen power that surpasses any
...ement of man. We have an inexhaustible supply
...of the divine dynasphere; with this power we can
...ive divine blessings beyond imagination. Apart
...irit there is no spiritual life.

...ministry to believers of Old Testament dispen-
...of believers changed dramatically when the
...*ed* certain believers of the past; He *indwells*
...John 14:17). We have a superior system,
...e Old Testament believers did not possess.
...en commanded to ''be filled with the Spirit''
...s of the Spirit'' (Gal. 5:16).

...TES

The first of these two mandates commands the Church Age believer to *reside* in the divine dynasphere.

> Stop being intoxicated with wine, which is dissipation, but be filled with the Spirit. (Eph. 5:18)

The Greek verb *plerŏo*, translated ''be filled,'' conveys a wealth of related meanings. Each of its four basic definitions applies to the ministry of the Holy Spirit.

"Fill up a deficiency": Outside the divine dynasphere we possess no ability to learn or apply Bible doctrine or resist the influence of Satan (Col. 1:25; 1 John 4:4).

"Be fully possessed": God the Holy Spirit, who indwells the body of every Church Age believer (1 Cor. 6:19), controls the soul of the believer residing in the divine dynasphere (1 Cor. 6:20).

"Be fully influenced": The divine dynasphere, with the Holy Spirit as the power source, is a comprehensive system that influences every facet of the believer's life.

"Be filled with a certain quality": The ministry of the Holy
Spirit in the divine dynasphere leads the believer to spiritual
maturity (Eph. 3:19; 4:10; Phil. 1:11; Rev. 3:2; 1 John 1:4)

This mandate to "be filled with the Spirit" orders us to enter the divine
dynasphere at gate one.

Pleroö indicates that the filling of the Spirit is an absolute. Either you are inside the divine dynasphere or you are not; there is no middle ground for the
believer. Under His filling ministry, the Holy Spirit fully energizes the believer
and fully controls his soul. Although the Spirit fully *controls* the believer
whenever he resides in the divine dynasphere, the *manifestations* of the filling of
the Spirit increase with maturity. In the immature Christian the Spirit has little
Bible doctrine to use as raw material for producing the "fruit of the Spirit" (Gal.
5:22, 23). In the mature believer He can use the Mind of Christ (1 Cor. 2:16)
to reproduce the virtues of Christ (1 Pet. 2:9).

Ephesians 5:18 teaches that the filling of the Spirit is the opposite of
drunkenness. As the believer's IQ for "spiritually discerning" the truth of Bible
doctrine (1 Cor. 2:14, 15), the filling of the Spirit contributes to concentration
and mental *focus*, not to dissipation. Imbibing too much alcohol depresses the
mentality, releasing uninhibited *emotion*; the filling of the Spirit supports lucid
thinking and is indetectable, behind the scenes, and unrelated to emotion. The
mission of the Holy Spirit to the royal family is not to make a name for Himself
by interjecting ecstatic experiences but to reveal the Lord Jesus Christ (John
16:13, 14). The so-called charismatics and other denominations that exaggerate
the function of the third Person of the Trinity distort God's game plan. Their
emotionalism is "dissipation," not the ministry of God the Holy Spirit to
spiritual aristocracy.

This first mandate regarding the Holy Spirit contributes to the integrity of
the entire divine system. Christians who lack the complete doctrine of the divine
dynasphere assume that the filling of the Spirit is an end in itself when actually
the power of the Spirit is a means to an end. The ultimate objective is the consistent, coordinated function of all eight gates of the system, which result in
phenomenal blessing for the believer and maximum glorification of the Lord
Jesus Christ.

The spiritual momentum required to reach this objective is commanded in
the second positive mandate concerning the Holy Spirit, the mandate to *function*
in the divine dynasphere.

Keep walking by means of the Spirit. (Gal. 5:16)

God never coerces your volition. He designed you and knows what is best
for you at each moment of your life. He has established clear policies for you to

follow so that you may fulfill His perfect plan for your prosperity and happiness. You can accept His authority and obey His mandates, or revolt and disobey. God's sovereign authority cannot prosper you without your consent.

The filling of the Holy Spirit alone is not the entire thrust of the Christian way of life. Gate one, the filling of the Spirit, functions as part of a *system* in conjunction with our volition. After we have entered gate one, we must by our own decisions enter the other gates of the complex; this is "walking by means of the Spirit."

While filled with the Spirit, we claim promises, resist temptations to sin, and maintain the objectivity of basic impersonal love in gate two. We remain teachable through enforced and genuine humility in gate three. We establish the habit of doctrinal perception in gate four, where we also maintain a constant alertness in the application of doctrine to circumstances. Thousands of positive decisions in these first four gates of the divine dynasphere comprise our Christian walk, resulting in personal love for God in gate five, the integrity of impersonal love in gate six, stability under testing in gate seven, and the happiness of Christian maturity in gate eight. The filling of the Holy Spirit is the *principle* of the Christian life; walking by means of the Spirit is the *function* of the Christian life.

TWO NEGATIVE MANDATES

Two additional mandates define the power struggle in which the Church Age believer must rely on the Holy Spirit. God commands us to resist the power and influence of Satan.

> And stop grieving the Holy Spirit from God. (Eph. 4:30*a*)

> Do not quench the Spirit. (1 Thess. 5:19)

These two mandates warn us that, when we sin, we cut off the power of the divine dynasphere, permitting the old sin nature to seize control of the soul. The divine dynasphere and Satan's cosmic system are mutually exclusive. We always reside in one or the other: if not in God's system, we live in Satan's power system. We "grieve" the Spirit when we enter Satan's system of *arrogance*; we "quench" the Spirit when we live in Satan's system of *antagonism* toward God, truth, and the divine plan.[14]

Both of these negative mandates describe the Holy Spirit in terms of anthropopathisms. Grieving and quenching are language of accommodation,

---

14. See below, pp. 160-63.

describing God in human terms to make His infinite functions perspicuous to finite man.[15] Perfect happiness belongs eternally to the essence of God. The third Person of the Trinity cannot suffer grief, nor can His infinite power be quenched. He is always omnipotent.

By negative volition we refuse to benefit from the plan of God so that the attributes of God do not have their intended function in our lives. We may reject the grace provisions of God's power system, but we cannot jeopardize the essence of God. God will always have His way; He will be glorified with us or without us. Our blessings accrue through obedience to the positive and negative mandates concerning the Energizer of the divine system.

OPPOSITION THROUGH DISTORTION

So effective is our power source that we are not surprised that Satan would mount a concentrated assault against this divine provision. With insidious cunning he has distorted the doctrines pertaining to the Holy Spirit by counterfeiting bona fide functions of the past and linking them to human emotion and arrogance to consolidate his evil sedition. Satanic doctrines influence people to vie for spiritual status by claiming to speak in tongues, hear voices, see visions, perform miracles, heal the sick—all in a welter of emotionalism. The Church Age ministry of God the Holy Spirit has nothing to do with such practices (Rom. 16:17, 18; Phil. 3:19a).

The pursuit of such ecstatic experiences in the name of spirituality obscures the truth and blasphemes against God. Christianity is a system of thinking—thinking the truth—and the Holy Spirit provides the power that, first, aids our concentration in learning doctrine and, second, enhances our ability to apply in all the gates the doctrines we know.

A period of transition existed between the beginning of the Church Age in A.D. 30 and the completion of the written canon of Scripture in A.D. 96, when the Apostle John wrote Revelation. During this time spectacular but temporary spiritual gifts facilitated the change from the now-interrupted Age of Israel into the new dispensation of the Church. Miracles and healings were performed to focus attention upon the divine authority of the apostles and to authenticate their new message (Acts 19:11-20). The Spirit inspired the apostles to write the New Testament canon, including the doctrines of the Church Age, the "mystery" that had not been revealed in the Old Testament but was now pertinent to the royal family (John 14:26; Eph. 3:2-6). The gift of tongues was a bona fide ministry for the first forty years of the Church Age as a warning sign to Israel of her approaching national destruction, which occurred in A.D. 70 (Isa. 28:11,

15. See Thieme, Integrity of God, pp. 1-11.

12; Acts 2:39, 40).[16] In that precanon transition period of the Church Age, the coming of the Holy Spirit as the power for the divine dynasphere was accompanied by unusual and now defunct manifestations.

On the day the Church Age began, temporary gifts accompanied the divine dynasphere; initially the ministry of the Spirit included functions that have since ceased to legitimately exist (1 Cor. 13:8; Phil. 2:27; 2 Tim. 4:20). In the Scriptures we must distinguish these overt, temporary ministries of the Spirit from His invisible, permanent ministries if we are to avoid the trap of emotional arrogance. We must "rightly divide the Word of truth" in order to execute God's game plan for our lives (2 Tim. 2:15).

THE DIVINE DYNASPHERE AT SALVATION

Christ received the prototype divine dynasphere at His virgin birth; the apostles and others received it on the day of Pentecost; we receive the divine dynasphere at the new birth.

> At the moment when anyone is born from God [the moment of salvation through faith in Christ], he is not sinning [it is impossible to sin inside the divine dynasphere], because His seed [the believer] keeps residing in it [the divine dynasphere]. Furthermore, he is not able to sin [inside the divine dynasphere] because he has been born of God. (1 John 3:9)

The Greek personal pronoun *autos* takes the same form in both the neuter and masculine genders. The context determines whether this pronoun is translated "it" or "him." In 1 John 3:9 *autos* can be rendered by the neuter, "keeps residing in *it*," the divine dynasphere. The power of the Holy Spirit regenerates the believer (John 3:6; Titus 3:5), making him God's "seed" or son or heir. The same power functions in the divine dynasphere to empower the believer's Christian life. This verse indicates that the divine dynasphere is received at salvation.

The Spirit indwells the body as of salvation (1 Cor. 6:19, 20; Gal. 3:2; 4:6). He opposes the old sin nature and seeks to fill, empower, and control the believer's soul (Eph. 5:18). The Christian is permanently *indwelt* by the Spirit, even when he sins (Rom. 8:9), but he is *filled* with the Spirit only when he resides in the divine dynasphere. Controlled by the infinite power of the Holy Spirit, the believer cannot sin inside the divine dynasphere, a condition that occurs first in the moment of regeneration.

---

16. See Thieme, *Tongues* (1974).

When anyone believes in Christ during the Church Age, he receives simultaneously—entirely unfelt and undetected—the baptism of the Holy Spirit, the indwelling of the Holy Spirit, and the filling of the Holy Spirit. The *baptism* of the Spirit places us into union with Christ so that we share all He is and all He has; this union makes us members of the royal family. Unique among believers in all dispensations, we are "in Christ," identified with Christ forever (Rom. 16:7; 2 Cor. 5:17).

Like the baptism of the Spirit, which has eternal repercussions, the *indwelling* of the Spirit is also permanent. Never before has the Holy Spirit resided in the body of any believer, but from the moment of salvation, God the third Person perpetually indwells the body of each member of the royal family. A sign of our royal status, the indwelling of the Spirit is described as anointing (1 John 2:20, 27). The worst believers, the finest believers, and all believers in between, are beneficiaries of this aspect of gate one of the divine dynasphere: the body of every Christian is the temple of the Holy Spirit (1 Cor. 6:19), just as in the prototype divine dynasphere our Lord described His body as a temple (John 2:19-21).

LEAVING AND REENTERING THE DIVINE SYSTEM

The baptism and indwelling of the Spirit cannot be lost, but we close down the *filling* of the Spirit each time we succumb to temptation and decide to sin.

> And this is the message which we have heard from Him [Jesus Christ] and communicated to you, that God is light and in Him darkness does not exist [no compromise of God's system with Satan's system]. If we contend [claim, assert, maintain] that we have fellowship with Him [God] and keep walking in darkness [exiting the divine dynasphere through sin, followed by continued function in Satan's system], we lie and do not practice the truth. . . . If we contend that we have no sin [no sin nature, the source of temptation], we are deceiving ourselves and the truth [the doctrine of sin or hamartiology] is not in us. . . . If we contend [when we have sinned] that we have not sinned [have not succumbed to temptation, have not exited the divine dynasphere], we keep making Him [God] a liar, and His Word is not in us. (1 John 1:5, 6, 8, 10)

Under His filling ministry the Holy Spirit controls and empowers only when we reside in the divine dynasphere. We begin our Christian lives filled with the

Spirit, but that initial filling is short-lived because we still possess volition and the old sin nature still resides in our bodies (Rom. 6:16-22; 7:7-25; 1 John 1:8).

As the resident antagonist against the indwelling Holy Spirit, the old sin nature is Satan's inside agent for distracting us from God's game plan (Gal. 5:17). The sin nature is the source of temptation, but our volition is the source of sin. When the sin nature tempts us to commit a sin, we can resist the temptation and remain filled with the Spirit inside the divine dynasphere. The Biblical mandates to resist temptation are incorporated into the love complex at gate one.

> Submit therefore to God [execute the divine game plan].
> Resist the devil [in the power of the divine dynasphere], and
> he will flee from you. (James 4:7)

> No testing has caught up with you except the human kind;
> moreover, God is faithful who will not allow you to be tested
> beyond your capabilities, but with the testing He will also
> provide [through Bible doctrine] the way of escape so that
> you may be able [in the power of the divine dynasphere] to
> endure it. (1 Cor. 10:13)

We can choose to resist temptation and remain in the love complex, or we can acquiesce to temptation and eject ourselves from God's power system. Because no one can sin inside the divine dynasphere, we exit when we choose to sin. We are still saved, still in the royal family of God, still in union with Christ, still indwelled by the Spirit, but we must return to God's system. Outside the love complex we can reenter through gate one just as we first entered at salvation. God has given us the rebound technique, which restores us to the divine dynasphere after we have sinned.

> If we acknowledge [name, admit, confess] our sins, He
> [God the Father] is faithful and just so that He forgives us
> our sins [known sins] and also cleanses us from all unright-
> eousness [unknown sins]. (1 John 1:9)

By acknowledging our sins privately to God, we restore the filling of the Spirit and once again reside in the sphere of divine power. All Biblical mandates to recover from sin and resume our fellowship with God pertain to gate one of the divine dynasphere. These commands are variously phrased to emphasize different facets of the doctrine. We are commanded to "acknowledge our sins" (Jer. 3:13), "yield" ourselves to God (Rom. 6:13), "judge ourselves" (1 Cor. 11:31), "lay aside every weight" (Heb. 12:1), "put aside all filthiness" (James 1:21), "be in subjection to the Father" (Heb. 12:9), "put off the old man'' (Eph. 4:22), ''present our bodies'' (Rom. 12:1), ''make straight paths'' (Matt. 3:3; Heb. 12:13), ''stand up again from out of deaths'' (Eph. 5:14), and ''lift up the hands that hang down'' (Heb.12:12).

Once we reenter the divine dynasphere through rebound, the pertinent mandate then becomes ''walk by means of the Spirit'' (Gal. 5:16), the command to advance spiritually in the other gates of the system powered by the Energizer.

III
Gate Two, Basic Christian Modus Operandi

THE BELIEVER'S OBJECTIVITY

Early in his Christian life the believer must learn the basics of God's game plan. He must practice and master certain rudimentary skills until they become second nature to him. The new believer may not understand the system, but God has issued basic mandates and the believer must obey them. The Christian way of life begins with *obedience*, not with perfect understanding.

Gate two represents the routine procedure of the Christian way of life. Obedience to basic techniques of daily life in God's system creates and maintains objectivity. Gate two, the objectivity gate, is mandatory for the function of the other gates of the love complex (2 Tim. 1:7). The techniques of gate two are designed to sustain the daily discipline of living in the Word of God.

The basic techniques of gate two go beyond rebound to include claiming divine promises and exercising impersonal love. I will summarize the principle of claiming promises[17] then define impersonal love, which is essential to the dynamics of Christian integrity.

Claiming the promises that God has given us eliminates fear, worry, and anxiety—sins that cut off thinking. The immature believer can cling to promises until he can learn enough Bible doctrine to fully understand God's plan for his life.

---

17. See Thieme, *The Faith-Rest Life* (1961).

Trust in the Lord with all your heart,
And do not lean on your own understanding.
In all your ways acknowledge Him,
And He will make your paths straight [accurate].
(Prov. 3:5, 6; NASV)

And the Lord is the one who goes ahead of you; He will be
with you. He will not fail you or forsake you. Do not fear or
be dismayed. (Deut. 31:8, NASV)

Therefore, the Lord waits to be gracious to you,
And therefore He waits on high to have compassion on you.
For the Lord is a God of justice;
How blessed are all those who wait for Him. (Isa. 30:18,
NASV)

Humble yourselves, therefore, under the mighty hand of
God, that He may exalt you at the proper time, casting all
your cares on Him, because He cares for you. (1 Pet. 5:6, 7;
NASV)

Promises enable the growing believer to enter the "peace of God which
passes all understanding" (Phil. 4:7). In this peace or "rest" (Heb. 4:1–3), he
possesses the objectivity required to think clearly and function in the other gates
of the divine dynasphere.

Relying on the promises of God is only the first step of the faith-rest drill,
a three-step technique for applying doctrine to life.[18] A believer acquires the
ability to utilize the entire faith-rest drill as he grows in doctrine, but from the
beginning of his Christian life he can latch on to divine promises and stabilize
himself under pressure.

The practice of impersonal love also contributes to the new believer's objectivity. An entire gate, gate six, is devoted to the virtue of impersonal love, but
at this point in gate two, impersonal love becomes an issue and must be
developed as a category of doctrine.

SPIRITUAL PRODUCTION AND
THE SUPREME CHRISTIAN VIRTUE

In John 15, where our Lord prophesied the coming of the divine
dynasphere, He also identified spiritual growth and maturity as the objective of

---

18. See below, pp. 102-109.

the divine plan. He emphasized that properly motivated Christian production *results* from spiritual advance. Impersonal love is a category of spiritual production and is essential for further growth.

> You did not choose Me [God, not man, initiates grace], but I have chosen you [selected you for special privilege, including the divine dynasphere] and I have appointed you [to be placed in the love complex] that you should go [spiritual advance] and that you might produce fruit [maturity as the result of spiritual advance] and that your fruit [mature production inside the divine dynasphere] might persist [continued function in the divine dynasphere after reaching maturity]. (John 15:16a)

To illustrate mature production, Christ described effective prayer as the mature believer's tremendous privilege to engage divine power in personal or historical circumstances.[19] Prayer is a weapon for the strong, not an expedient for the weak. Except for the rebound prayer, which restores the believer to the divine power system, all effective prayer must be offered inside the divine dynasphere. Because the Father is the author of the divine plan and designer of the divine dynasphere, all prayer is addressed to Him in the name of Christ, who won our salvation and pioneered the Christian way of life.

> That whatever you might ask of the Father in My name, He may give to you. (John 15:16b)

God's commands for the royal family are classified as mandates for either residence or function. *Residence* in the divine dynasphere is exploited through *function* in the divine dynasphere. Rebound fulfills the mandate to "reside in love" (John 15:9); then in the strength of gate one, we generate Christian production as we "walk by means of love" (Eph. 5:2), obeying the functional mandates. Prayer is an example of a functional responsibility of every believer (1 Thess. 5:17): in the power of the Holy Spirit (Rom. 8:26, 27), the believer is given the privilege of bringing gratitude, intercessions, and personal petitions before the throne of grace (Heb. 4:16).

A further definition of the "fruit" mentioned by our Lord in John 15:16 is found in Galatians 5:22, 23.

> The fruit of the Spirit is love, happiness, prosperity, steadfastness, integrity, generosity, doctrinal confidence, humility, self-discipline. (Gal. 5:22, 23a)

---

19. See Thieme, *Prayer (1975).*

From these two verses we learn that the believer's production encompasses far more than just the overt fulfillment of Christian responsibilities—giving, prayer, witnessing, service in the local church. These legitimate demonstrations of Christian service, when properly motivated, are the *result* of spiritual growth, not the *cause*. Integrity comes first; service demands integrity. True thinking creates true motivation; true motivation creates true action. Christian production is the coordinated, interlocking function of all the gates in the divine dynasphere empowered by God the Holy Spirit (2 Thess. 1:11).

FAITH, HOPE, AND LOVE

Heading the list in Galatians 5:22, love receives top billing because it is the title of God's game plan. First Corinthians 13 shows that love is a *system* and states that love is the supreme Christian virtue.

> Now remain [temporary spiritual gifts are excluded] faith,
> hope, and love, these three, and the greatest of these [is]
> love. (1 Cor. 13:13)

Given to only a few believers in the precanon period of the Church Age, temporary spiritual gifts are gone; only the superior virtues remain, which are available to all. The virtues of faith, hope, and love are part of our permanent heritage as spiritual aristocracy.

Translated "faith," the Greek noun *pistis* has a dual connotation. In its objective sense *pistis* means "what is believed," Bible doctrine. Never in any previous dispensation has Bible doctrine been committed to writing in a completed canon of Scripture. *Pistis* also refers, as here, to the believer's application of doctrine to experience, the faith-rest technique.

Just as "faith" represents an entire system of applying the Word of God, so also "hope" is a system, which is derived from knowledge of doctrine.[20] Hope is absolute confidence in future divine provisions and blessings (Rom. 8:24, 25). At each stage of a person's life, he not only can enjoy the blessings he has but also can anticipate with assurance or "hope for" the blessings that will come with the next stage of growth. Thus, there are three hopes; together they trace an individual's advance from being an unbeliever who anticipates salvation, to becoming an immature believer who looks forward to supergrace blessings, to becoming a mature believer who eagerly awaits the eternal rewards of heaven. The fulfillment of each hope lays the foundation for the next hope. No matter how much God blesses us, we can always anticipate more.

---

20. See Thieme, *Integrity of God*, pp. 142-46, 165-72.

Both faith-rest and hope are subordinate systems that function within the larger sphere, the love complex. A believer can apply doctrine and advance from hope to hope to hope only inside the divine dynasphere. Faith and hope depend on the divine system, which empowers us to learn doctrine and sustain our spiritual momentum. Love is superior to either faith or hope because love is the characteristic virtue of the entire divine system. We will develop the full significance of this virtue when we study the doctrine of virtue-love in connection with gates five and six of the love complex.

Even before the Church Age began, Christ encapsulated the entire Mosaic Law in two commandments: to love God and to love man (Matt. 22:37–40). In the divine dynasphere nearly every gate involves a specific category of love. In order to describe the basic exercise of impersonal love in gate two, we must define the overall concept of love. We must understand why love is the highest Christian virtue and the Biblical designation for the Christian way of life.

IMPERSONAL AND PERSONAL HUMAN LOVE

In English as well as the Greek, "love" is a transitive verb; love takes both a subject and an object. The subject is the one who loves; the object is the one loved, the recipient of love. In the sentence *I love you,* "I" is the subject, and "you" is the object.

This distinction between subject and object explains the two basic types of genuine love that exist between members of the human race. I have designated these two categories "impersonal love" and "personal love." Impersonal love emphasizes the subject; personal love emphasizes the object. Impersonal love depends on the honor and integrity of the one who loves; personal love depends on the attractiveness, capacity, and response of the one who is loved.

By "impersonal" I mean that this love does not require intimacy, friendliness, or even acquaintance with the object of love. A close relationship between subject and object may exist but is not necessary; impersonal love is simply the consistent function of your own integrity toward other people. Impersonal love can be directed toward friends, enemies, loved ones, strangers—in fact, toward the entire human race. In contrast, personal love requires that you know the object with some degree of intimacy. The object of personal love must be attractive to you, share basic values with you, and have capacity to love you in return. Only a select few people qualify as objects of your personal love, whereas all mankind can be the object of your impersonal love. Personal love, is designed for interaction with a few; impersonal love is designed to benefit the human race. Personal love is highly discriminating; impersonal love is non-discriminating. Personal love is conditional; impersonal love is unconditional.

I	Love	You
IMPERSONAL LOVE		**PERSONAL LOVE**
Emphasizes subject		Emphasizes object
Demands integrity in subject		Demands attractiveness in object
Requires no personal acquaintance		Requires personal acquaintance
Directed toward all		Directed toward few
Unconditional		Conditional
Virtue		Virtue dependent
Strong		Vulnerable
Stable		Volatile
Variables under control		Uncontrollable variables
Depends on Bible doctrine		Depends on impersonal love
Problem solver		Problem maker
Mandatory		Optional

IMPERSONAL AND PERSONAL LOVE

Personal love creates weaknesses. You bring your own problems into any personal relationship, but so does the one you love. The problems, shortcomings, and faults of two people are combined and multiplied by personal love. Your vulnerability to the influence of the one you love can spawn subjectivity and the mental attitude sins of jealousy, self-pity, and bitterness. Personal love in the human race is highly volatile, emotionally charged, and complicated with variables and unpredictables that personal love cannot control. Often turbulent and frustrating, personal love is never stronger than the integrity of those involved. An enduring personal love depends on impersonal love.

Impersonal love is the integrity that alone can strengthen, stabilize, and perpetuate personal love. The only variable in impersonal love remains under your control: your own mental attitude. Whereas personal love may lead to compromise of true norms and standards, impersonal love never compromises virtue or integrity. Impersonal love for mankind is a result of your relationship with God; personal love is often a distraction from what is most important, Bible doctrine. Impersonal love is a problem-solver; personal love can be a problem.

In 1 Corinthians 13:13 impersonal love, not personal love, is proclaimed the ultimate Christian virtue. Impersonal love, not personal love, furnishes the environment for faith and hope. Impersonal love is mandatory; personal love is optional. Certainly personal love is legitimate and potentially wonderful, but it is virtue-dependent, hinging on the virtue of impersonal love, which represents the highest degree of integrity the soul can attain.

LOVE AND INDEPENDENCE

A believer with impersonal love does not rely on the object of his love for strength and support; he is sustained by Bible doctrine in his own soul. No variables or unpredictables are involved except those controlled by his own self-determination. Based on his own right decisions over an extended period of time to learn and apply doctrine, he can solve or cope with the problems of personal love and maintain a marvelous relationship with another person, or he can be content alone. He functions consistently whether faced with hostility or admiration, antagonism or personal love. His attitude of impersonal love does not depend on emotional stimulation, reciprocation, or attraction. He cannot be manipulated by flattery or approbation. This is the genuine and honorable independence of the believer who is spiritually self-sustaining. He does not depend on the advice of others or on a pastor's counseling; Bible doctrine in his own soul gives him the strength and wisdom to live his own life before the Lord. Although genuinely humble and teachable, he is not controlled by what anyone else thinks, says, or does. Impersonal love, generated in the believer's soul no matter whom he encounters, is the only category of love that can fulfill the divine mandates to love all believers.

> I [Jesus Christ] give you [believers] a new mandate, that you love one another; just as I have loved you [in the prototype divine dynasphere], you also love [impersonal love] one another. (John 13:34)

Some Christians are admirable, but then again others are among the most arrogant, self-righteous, boorish, obnoxious people on the face of the earth. Even a wonderful, mature believer can have a personality, background, life-style, or combination of interests that makes him utterly incompatible with you. According to divine mandates you must love all these believers. Obviously your exclusive personal love cannot be granted to rude, arrogant believers or to those with whom you have no rapport. Nor should you burn up your nervous energy trying to do the impossible—*personally* love all Christians.

The only love you can possess for most individuals is based, not on their weaknesses, idiosyncrasies, or incompatibility with you, but on the strength of your own character. Through impersonal love your attitude toward everyone will be basically the same, manifested in courtesy, thoughtfulness, sensitivity to the feelings of others, tolerance, and flexibility in nonessential areas of disagreement or dispute. Such attitudes can be consistently maintained toward any believer, regardless of how incompatible your personalities or modus vivendi may be. Christian love is not condescending, hypocritical, or self-righteous.

> Your love must be nonhypocritical. (Rom. 12:9a)

Impersonal love is not a stoic, artificial, emotionless facade, but rather a gracious attitude consistent with the doctrine in your soul. The policy of impersonal love is simply this: integrity toward all, no matter who or what they are. Through this attitude your spiritual aristocracy is revealed as you honorably represent Christ in the devil's world.

Impersonal love must be directed not just toward other believers but toward unbelievers as well. You need not determine that a person is a Christian before you exhibit Christian love. This explains God's commands that you love your neighbors—everyone in your periphery—and even your enemies.

> You shall love your neighbor as yourself [from your own integrity]. (Mark 12:31b)

> You have heard that it was said, You shall love your neighbor and hate your enemy, but I say to you, love your enemies, and pray for those who persecute you; in order that you may show yourselves to be sons of your Father [the author of the divine dynasphere] who is in heaven; for He causes His sun to rise on the evil and the good, and sends rain on the righteous and the unrighteous. For if you love those who love you [personal love], what reward have you? Do not even the tax-gatherers do the same? (Matt. 5:43–46, NASV)

Personal love for another member of the human race is not a virtue in itself but must rely on the true virtue of impersonal love. The divine mandates to love all mankind command us to develop integrity and, in all our relationships with other people, to live by our own honor.

REBOUND AND THE RELAXED MENTAL ATTITUDE

In contrast to the mature integrity of the advanced believer, basic impersonal love at gate two of the divine dynasphere is simply a relaxed mental attitude. Basic impersonal love is the absence of mental attitude sins toward those you know or do not know, toward friends or enemies.

> But I say to you who hear, love your enemies, do good to
> those who hate you, bless those who curse you, pray for
> those who mistreat you. (Luke 6:27, 28; NASV)

The believer who utilizes rebound to reenter gate one after he has sinned, but who then becomes arrogant, jealous, angry, petty, vindictive, afraid, or filled with self-pity or guilt, has again removed himself from the divine dynasphere. He has been tempted to sin and has acquiesced. This problem of chain sinning is solved by rebound and an immediate interlock with gate two. The relaxed mental attitude of basic impersonal love insulates the believer against the temptations of the old sin nature.

When Galatians 5:22 states that "the fruit of the Spirit is love," some believers expect the fruit of the Spirit to appear, as if by magic, as soon as they rebound and regain the filling of the Spirit. When a feeling of love for all mankind does not materialize instantaneously, they assume that something is wrong with the rebound technique. They then resort to remorse, penance, self-effacement, or self-reproach in an attempt to *deserve* God's forgiveness and *feel* restored to fellowship with Him. This common practice among immature Christians is an exercise in futility.

First, God forgives us because He is perfect justice (1 John 1:9); the sin we confess in rebound was judged on the Cross. Second, we cannot earn forgiveness. Restoration to fellowship was earned for us by the only one who is qualified to earn it, the Lord Jesus Christ, the one who gave us His own divine dynasphere. Human works added to the work of Christ are blasphemous (Eph. 2:8, 9). Third, we are instantly restored to fellowship, but the ministry of the Holy Spirit in the Church Age is not related to feelings or emotion. We may feel wonderful or wretched and still be filled with the Spirit, just as we may have felt wonderful or wretched when we first believed in Christ yet were still saved. Emotion is never the criterion of spiritual status (Rom. 16:18).

Fourth, the love designated as the fruit of the Spirit is impersonal love, not personal love. We need not feel any kind of special inner warmth to manifest the fruit of the Spirit. We must, however, avoid mental attitude sins in order to fulfill the divine mandate to "love one another." Finally, even freedom from mental attitude sins is not automatic with rebound. God is faithful (1 John 1:9); rebound always works; we are always forgiven, cleansed, and free from mental attitude sins when we rebound. But our restoration to fellowship with God may last only a split second. We possess free will, and as soon as we rebound we can choose to sin again. At all times we are solely responsible for our own state of mind. We must interlock gate one with gate two as soon as we rebound, or we will be out of the divine dynasphere again. Consistent impersonal love as the fruit of the Spirit requires us to be continually filled with the Spirit.

APPLYING DOCTRINE IN REBOUND

Only our volition can resolve the problem of chain sinning. With rebound, the filling of the Spirit, and the application of Bible doctrine, God has given us the power to break the momentum of consecutive sinning. Upon rebounding we must use doctrine to resist the temptation to follow one sin with another. Hence, rebound has three stages.

> First, we claim God's rebound promises by naming our already-judged sins to Him.

> Second, we remember the doctrine that, because of the Cross, we are completely restored to fellowship inside the divine dynasphere.

> Third, we take control of the situation by forgetting that sin and moving on in the plan of God.

Claiming promises, recalling a logical rationale, and reaching doctrinal conclusions that enable us to take control of the situation constitute the three stages of the faith-rest drill. Faith-rest, which we will develop in greater detail in our study of gate four of the divine dynasphere, is an essential technique that adapts to rebound or any other practical application of God's Word.

The ability to avoid mental attitude sins comes from self-discipline in applying the doctrine we know. There is a pertinent doctrine to neutralize every mental attitude sin. Vindictiveness and implacability are dispelled by taking God at His word when He says, "Vengeance is Mine; I will repay" (Rom. 12:19). Fear is removed by the doctrine that "if God is for us, who can be against us?" (Rom. 8:31). Arrogance and self-righteousness are excluded when we remember that we are not appointed to judge other people (Matt. 7:1, 2; Luke 6:37; Rom. 2:1). And we are left with no cause for jealousy since our own blessings are sufficient and perfectly timed for our maximum benefit: we must concentrate on what we have, not on what we have not. (Matt. 6:25–34).

> Your love must be nonhypocritical; despise the evil [including mental attitude sins], adhere to the good [the plan of God for your own life]; with regard to your brotherly love [impersonal love], be devoted to each other. (Rom. 12:9, 10)

In place of mental attitude sins, impersonal love insures the serenity of mind that lays the foundation for toleration, flexibility, courtesy, thoughtfulness, and discretion. These manifestations of integrity, demanded by the royal family honor code, become stronger and more constant as the believer advances in learning Bible doctrine under the power of the Holy Spirit (1 Cor. 2). Doctrine in the soul is the raw material from which the Spirit manufactures the fruit of the Spirit. If you are negative toward doctrinal teaching and refuse to store up God's Word in your soul, the filling of the Spirit will be intermittent and will not produce the characteristics of maturity. In the absence of doctrine, the old sin nature dominates the inner, spiritual conflict for control of the soul. By giving doctrine first priority in your life, you rise above the pettiness that engenders mental attitude sins, and you establish yourself in gate two of the love complex. Bible doctrine strengthens objectivity and sustains the relaxed mental attitude.

JESUS CHRIST'S IMPERSONAL LOVE

The perfect example of impersonal love was the Lord Jesus Christ living in the original divine dynasphere. Since sin is impossible inside the love complex (1 John 3:9) and Christ remained in the love complex throughout His Incarnation (John 15:10*b*), our Lord never committed a mental attitude sin. He never departed from His impersonal love for all mankind, not even when being ridiculed by arrogant scribes and Pharisees. In addition to being our unique Savior, Jesus was also a man of matchless grace, courage, thoughtfulness, honor, and integrity toward people and circumstances. He possessed a resolute, stabilized mental attitude. Indeed, He reached maturity sometime before twelve years of age (Luke 2:42–52) so that His impersonal love rapidly exceeded the basic modus operandi of gate two of the love complex and became the functional virtue of gate six.

During His life on earth, the ultimate demonstration of Christ's impersonal love was His stalwart attitude throughout His trials and crucifixion. Certainly no one can duplicate His saving work, but Christ enjoins us to emulate toward others the attitude He sustained toward all of us when He acquiesced to the ordeal of unjust and prejudiced treatment at the hands of evil men.

> When anyone loves father or mother [personal love] more than Me [personal love for Christ, which motivates impersonal love for mankind], he is not worthy of Me [he is not living in the divine dynasphere as Christ lived in the prototype]. . . . And when anyone does not take up his cross [impersonal love] and follow Me [in the love complex], he is not worthy of Me. (Matt. 10:37, 38)

Christ does not suggest we stop loving our parents, exhort us to endure literal crucifixion, or teach us to place a premium on suffering. Only His suffering was efficacious; the self-flagellation of religion is an abomination. Instead, our Lord commands us to obey the plan of God for our lives, setting aside every distraction. For Him the plan of God required death on the Cross; for us the plan of God secures maximum blessing in the power of the divine dynasphere. The growing believer's impersonal love establishes his inner strength and separates him from people, organizations, and activities that would clutter his mind with false concepts, dissipate his time and energy, and interfere with his spiritual progress. Taking up one's cross occurs in the soul; it is mental separation from the influences of Satan's world.

THE EXAMPLE OF THE CROSS

Christ had been tortured and abused throughout the night in Jewish and Roman courts, but when He staggered from the Praetorium carrying that beam of wood on His lacerated back, He was neither a Jewish nor a Roman criminal. He was the perfect God-Man, the unique Person of the universe. He had been beaten and condemned to death by men who did not deserve to touch the hem of His robe. Throughout His seven trials He refused to execrate or rail against His cruel and unfair treatment. When scourged, He "opened not His mouth," refusing even to show pain (Acts 8:32). Our Lord's valiant courage under the most agonizing pressure is proof that the power of impersonal love in the divine dynasphere does triumph over evil.

As Christ was nailed to the Cross, He saw around Him wicked men gloating over their apparent victory. Yet He did not lower Himself to their level by denouncing them. He functioned on His own honor and integrity. He did not react to their dishonor (Luke 23:32–46).

Christ remained free from all mental attitude sins even when God the Father, who loved Him and whom He loved, imputed to Him the sins of mankind and became His judge. The pain of spiritual death was so excruciating to our perfect Savior that He screamed and kept screaming (Ps. 22:1). He had the power to end His ordeal at any moment, yet He remained on the Cross and bore the punishment until every human sin was paid for in full.

When Christ was bearing our sins, no member of the human race deserved to be the object of His personal love. Only Christ was impeccable; everyone else is a sinner and contributed to His agony on the Cross. Personal rapport with anyone was impossible, and He endured the Cross alone, in the strength of His own perfect integrity, the quintessence of impersonal love. When He took up His Cross, He switched from personal to impersonal love, mentally separating Himself from the entire human race, including those He had personally loved during the Incarnation (John 19:25–27). Under divine judgment Christ concentrated exclusively on the Bible doctrine in His soul, and He commands us to emulate His concentration on God's Word, to remember Him and follow His example in the divine dynasphere.

In the Communion service, or Eucharist, we focus our minds on Jesus Christ in a tribute, an *auld lang syne,* to the One we love (Luke 22:19). The bread represents the Person of Christ; the cup, His work of salvation on the Cross. As we partake of the bread, we remember the personal love of Christ: His love for the Father that motivated Him to obey God's plan in every detail "unto death, even the death of the Cross" (Phil. 2:8). As we partake of the cup, we concentrate on His impersonal love: His integrity as He "endured the Cross, having disregarded the shame" of being imputed with the sins of mankind and judged by the Father in our place (Heb. 12:2).

Impersonal love is far stronger than personal love. Impersonal love, not personal love, enabled Jesus to remain undaunted against those who were reviling and taunting Him, those who would never appreciate His saving work on their behalf, who would live out their lives in unbelief, die, and spend eternity in the Lake of Fire. He was fully aware of their arrogant, intransigent hostility against Him, yet He died in their place without harboring a single mental attitude sin, without succumbing to the temptation to retaliate (1 John 2:2; 1 Pet. 2:22, 23). Christ demonstrated a perfectly relaxed mental attitude as He operated on His inner resources of Bible doctrine even when the sins of Judas Iscariot, Pontius Pilate, Herod, and the priests of the Sanhedrin came up for judgment on the Cross. Perhaps more startling to us, when the sins of Hitler, Stalin, and Mao Tse-tung were imputed to Him and judged, Christ's impersonal love kept Him on the Cross without deprecation.

SEPARATION AND IMPERSONAL LOVE

When our Lord commands, "Take up your cross and follow Me," He means, "Develop impersonal love. Live on the basis of your own integrity from the Bible doctrine in your own soul. Do not let the pressures of life distract you from living according to God's game plan." By the injunction "take up your cross," Christ is not advocating a martyr complex or self-sacrifice, as some Christians assume; He is advocating personal integrity. This is the true doctrine of separation.

As members of the royal family of God, we are *in* the world but not *of* the world. Our spiritual heritage is heavenly, not earthly, yet God preserves us alive in the devil's world after salvation to represent the absent Christ. God does not totally separate us from the devil's kingdom but intends that we advance to spiritual maturity and become imitators of God and ambassadors of Christ in whatever circumstances we find ourselves (Eph. 5:1; 2 Cor. 5:20). God is glorified by our lives in the devil's world when we can be prospered with phenomenal blessings of supergrace in the midst of the failures, pseudo-blessings, pseudo-happiness, and misery that characterize Satan's counterfeit systems.

The devil's world has a pull greater than any force of gravity to draw the believer away from the divine dynasphere. Regardless of our dedication or altruism, we cannot improve Satan's evil system; we can only avoid his influence by opting for the power of God's perfect system. God alone can successfully oppose evil. He will eradicate evil in His perfect time, but our human good contributes nothing to the divine plan (Isa. 64:6). Indeed, Satan sponsors human good, and the old sin nature produces human good. We must depend on divine power, which alone produces intrinsic good (Rom. 8:28).

God's purpose for our lives on earth requires that we mentally separate ourselves unto Him. As we grow in grace and in the knowledge of our Lord Jesus Christ, we renew our minds with the Mind of Christ (2 Pet. 1:2; Rom. 12:2; 1 Cor. 2:16). Simultaneously we separate ourselves from satanic distractions that would swerve us away from God's plan. Impersonal love, which depends on the subject, never the object, is the requisite attitude toward anyone or anything that would prevent us from fulfilling our spiritual destiny. Impersonal love obeys the divine commands to avoid reversionism (2 Thess. 3:6, 14; 2 Tim. 3:5; Heb. 13:13),[21] perversion (1 Cor. 5:10), emotionalism (Rom. 16:17), negative volition (Matt. 10:34–40; 1 John 2:15–17), marriage to an unbeliever (2 Cor. 6:14), idolatry (2 Cor. 6:15, 16), distracting social life (1 Pet. 4:3, 4), and crime (Prov. 1:10–19).

We must separate ourselves from Satan's nefarious, multifaceted systems, but always our emphasis must be separation *unto* God, not separation *from* the world. Each believer must stress the function of Bible doctrine in his own soul and his own Christian integrity, not the object he wishes to avoid. We must focus on doctrine, not on the evils we purport to leave behind. In this manner we avoid the arrogance of self-righteous crusading, which itself is a subtle satanic trap.[22] The proper spiritual priority places doctrine before the influence of any personal relationship, even beneficial relationships built on doctrine (Matt. 10:37; Rom. 12:1–3). As a result of spiritual growth, we leave behind entanglements that would impede our continued advance. Loyalty to the truth supersedes but does not eliminate loyalty to people and organizations.

---

21. Reversionism is spiritual retrogression rather than spiritual growth. This progressive maladjustment to the justice of God results from prolonged residence in the cosmic system. See Thieme, *Integrity of God,* p. 9.

22. See below, p. 164.

Separation means, first, to avoid distractions by switching from personal to impersonal love in mental separation. Then, only if necessary and if possible, physical separation is a drastic measure to avoid satanic influence by removing yourself from a relationship. In most cases mental separation is sufficient without the unwarranted major surgery of abruptly removing yourself from those who were once close friends, loved ones, or associates. If you retreat from every situation that puts pressure on you, you will be continually running from one problem to another without making any progress in the Christian life. Often pressure is designed to teach, and you accelerate your spiritual growth by remaining under pressure, exercising impersonal love, and waiting on the Lord.

Impersonal love insulates you from false influences, even when you are in their presence, while also eliminating instability, bitterness, hostility, malice, subjectivity, revenge, and arrogance. Impersonal love is not swayed by any relationship but continues to operate with capacity for life under all circumstances. Impersonal love is *civilized* separation, in contrast to the boorish, arrogant behavior of those Christians who call attention to themselves by self-righteously "taking a stand" against the world.

DIVINE LOVE AS THE PATTERN FOR HUMAN LOVE

THE INTEGRITY OF GOD

In designing the power system that would sustain Christ's humanity on earth, God patterned the love complex after His own divine attribute of love.

God is love. (1 John 4:8*b*)

God is much more than love. He is a Person; His essence consists of many attributes, all of which exist together in complete consistency and integrity. The function of one attribute never compromises any other. God's love is perfect, but His love is also perfect in its relationship with His sovereignty, righteousness, justice, eternity, omniscience, omnipotence, omnipresence, immutability, veracity, and all other characteristics of His essence.[23]

A case in point: God never blesses us on the basis of His love. God's love *motivates* Him to prosper us, but any divine blessing given to imperfect man must be compatible with God's justice.

Justice and righteousness are the two divine attributes that directly influence all God's blessings to us. Together these two attributes have been traditionally

23. See Thieme, *Integrity of God,* app. A, "The Doctrine of Divine Essence," pp. 231-56.

designated the *holiness* of God (Isa. 6:3), but holiness has become an obscure term. *Integrity* is a more definitive and meaningful word. Righteousness is the *principle* of divine integrity; justice is the *function* of divine integrity.

God's justice is not an arbitrary or precipitous attribute but invariably operates according to the absolute standard of His perfect righteousness. What righteousness demands, justice executes: if righteousness disapproves, justice condemns; if righteousness approves, justice blesses. Hence, grace involves far more than "unmerited favor," as grace is commonly defined. Grace is the policy of the justice of God for blessing mankind.

Since our sinful status at birth violates God's standards, He cannot treat us on the basis of His personal love. Instead, every action that God takes toward sinful man must be endorsed by His justice to avoid compromising His righteousness. Because justice is the guardian of the essence of God, divine justice, not divine love, is man's point of contact with God. Justice, not love, is the source of all divine blessings. Toward us, divine justice takes precedence over divine love.

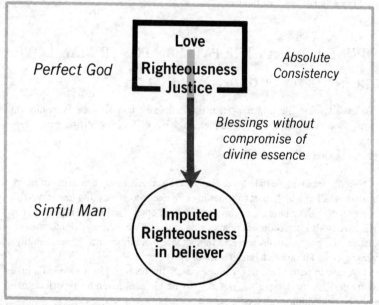

GRACE AS DIVINE JUSTICE BLESSING MAN

Under grace the justice of God has accomplished everything necessary to make us acceptable to His righteousness. This is the doctrine of propitiation

(Rom. 3:25; 1 John 2:2, 4:10) as the foundation for the doctrine of justification (Rom. 3:28; 2 Cor. 5:21). Propitiation means that on the Cross Jesus Christ satisfied the righteousness of God the Father on our behalf. Justification is the doctrine that, at the moment we first believed in Christ, God credited to us His own absolute righteousness and declared us to be totally acceptable to His integrity.

By imputing divine righteousness to us, God has made our position so absolutely, eternally secure that He blesses us on the principle of His impartial fairness. Divine righteousness, resident in us, *deserves* blessing. The approval to bless us has come from the most exalted authority, the supreme court of heaven. Nothing can overturn that decision. Divine righteousness in the essence of God gives approval for justice to bless divine righteousness in us. This judicial verdict is executed by God's absolute justice, which gives us the right blessings at the right time.

Timing is essential. Even when we are spiritually mature, timing must be right. God has a plan for each believer's life and knows each individual's capacity; too much prosperity at the wrong time can destroy a person more quickly than intense adversity (1 Cor. 10:13). Only through doctrine can we keep pace with God's timing. In grace, therefore, God gives us every blessing that we have the capacity to receive and appreciate. He has already given us the means for developing capacity: the divine dynasphere. If grace were based on love instead of justice, God's plan would be reduced to favoritism, maudlin sentimentality, and competition for divine approbation; the divine dynasphere would become a hollow shell of superficiality.

LOVE BASED ON INTEGRITY

When we understand God's policy of grace, we are confident that when He prospers us His entire essence is involved, not just His love. Divine love does not and cannot function independently of His integrity. But the connection between God's love and God's integrity has escaped most Christians today. Tragically, believers have created God in their own image, ascribing to Him their own superficial, emotional love. The Bible tells us that God is love, but that does not imply that He is sentimental about us. He does not bless or reward us for our human good works or sincerity in wanting to please Him. These are man's illusions, not God's plan. God blesses us only according to His own game plan, and He disciplines us when we depart from His plan. God never changes: only man changes. Blessing or discipline from God perfectly reflects changes in man while the justice of God remains consistent. God is completely impartial; His standards are absolute; His love comes to us only by way of His integrity.

God's love, therefore, possesses all the strength of His integrity. Likewise, in the divine dynasphere our personal love for a few derives its strength from *our* integrity, and our integrity is demonstrated in our impersonal love for all. Human integrity fulfills divine integrity.

> Beloved [members of the royal family], let us love each
> other [impersonal love in the divine dynasphere], because
> love is from God. (1 John 4:7*a*)

Love is from God because He is the source of the love complex and because His love is the pattern for all genuine human love. As John continues to explain Christian love, he specifies "everyone who loves," referring to believers only, those to whom the epistle is written. Unbelievers are never addressed as "beloved."

> Furthermore, everyone who loves [the believer's imper-
> sonal love] has been born from the source of God [initial en-
> try into the divine dynasphere at the moment of salvation]
> and has come to know God [impersonal love is *visible*
> evidence of the believer's knowledge of Bible doctrine, ac-
> quired at gate four of the *invisible* love complex]. When
> anyone does not love [with impersonal love], he has not
> come to know God [malfunction of gate four], because God
> is love. (1 John 4:7*b*, 8)

Genuine love between members of the human race originates from God because He invented the love complex and through the love complex has provided Bible doctrine. Capacity for human love involves thought, emotion, and physical and spiritual expression from doctrine in the soul. Knowledge of doctrine builds our integrity, which *is* our capacity for love, and orients us to the reality of God's essence. In God's essence His attribute of love is the pattern for human love. God's attribute of love shows us in terms of absolute, ultimate reality the difference between impersonal and personal love and the true superiority of impersonal love. These distinctions are clarified by understanding the three categories of God's love. His love is classified according to its objects: divine love directed toward God, toward man, and toward policy.

GOD'S LOVE FOR GOD

PERFECT SELF-SUFFICIENCY

God's love for His own essence explains 1 John 4:8, "God is love." Only God is said to *be* love. We may love someone or something or may be *in* love, but we never *are* love. Human love is always related to an object. "God is love" means not only that His love is an attribute of His essence, an integral part of who and what He is, and that divine love is the quintessence of love, but also that His love does not require an object.

The Bible declares that God loves the world, but the world did not always exist. Nor have angels always existed. Before God created the universe, He loved just as He loves today and will love forever. God is immutable and eternal, and as an attribute of His perfect divine essence, His love always existed, even when nothing and no one existed but God Himself, when there was no possible object of love.

We may or may not have capacity to love, depending on our integrity. Our love for another person can grow or disappear. We can fall in or out of love, but God does not. Our love fluctuates; His does not. God's love remains eternal and changeless because He is eternal and changeless. Changes in us do not create changes in God's love. His love does not depend on us or any other object.

God's integrity supports and guarantees His love, but His love also is directed *toward* His own integrity. This tremendous inner affinity within the attributes of God is expressed in the statement that God is love. He loves who and what He is. God perfectly fulfills His own uncompromising standards; therefore, He loves His own righteousness and justice (Ps. 11:7a; 33:5a; 37:28a).

In man, total self-love is arrogance because we are imperfect and sinful; in God, total self-love is legitimate because He is absolutely worthy. God would compromise His integrity if He loved anything less than perfection, but He would also be compromised if He failed to love what is perfect, His own essence. If God did not love Himself, there would be no reason for us to love Him, but when we share His thinking through Bible doctrine, we come to share His own respect and love for Himself.

> Remember the former things long past,
> For I am God and there is no other;
> I am God, and there is no one like Me,
> Declaring the end from the beginning
> And from ancient times things which have not been done,
> Saying, "My purpose will be established,
> And I will accomplish all My good pleasure."
> (Isa. 46:9, 10; NASV)

God knows Himself to be beyond comparison with any other being, and in the interest of absolute truth He claims all glory for Himself. The purpose of God's game plan is His own glorification through blessing us. Indeed, only omnipotent God is capable of glorifying Himself as He deserves, which explains why human good is unacceptable to God. Our residence and function inside His power system enables God to demonstrate the utter superiority of His character and to be glorified to the maximum in our lives.

SUBJECTIVE AND OBJECTIVE DIVINE LOVE

God exists in three separate and distinct personalities, each having identical divine attributes from eternity past: the Father (1 Cor. 8:6; Eph. 1:3), the Son (John 10:30; 14:9; Col. 2:9), and the Holy Spirit (Isa. 11:2; Ex. 31:3; Isa. 6:8,9; cf. Acts 28:25; Jer. 31:31–34; cf. Heb 10:15–17). The Godhead is one in essence, three in personality. When the essence of God is in view, God is said to be one; when the individual Members of the Godhead are in view, God is said to be three. The doctrine of the Trinity introduces a distinction in describing God's love: God's love for God is both subjective and objective.

God's *subjective* love is the love of each Member of the Trinity for His own integrity. God's *objective* love is each Person's love for the equal integrity of the other two Members of the Trinity. This means that God the Father subjectively loves His own righteousness and justice with maximum love, but since God the Son and God the Holy Spirit possess identical righteousness and justice, He also loves them with maximum objective love. Likewise, the Son loves His own integrity as a matter of subjective love and loves the integrity of the Father and the Holy Spirit with objective love. So also, the Spirit loves Himself subjectively and loves the Father and the Son objectively.

Subjectivity is different in God than in man. The attributes of God's essence guarantee that God's subjective thinking is perfect, just as His objective thinking is perfect. In human beings subjectivity is a breeding ground for evil. A subjective person, whether believer or unbeliever, is preoccupied with himself. Subjectivity cuts him off from God's game plan. Therefore, the self-occupied person is arrogantly divorced from reality and in opposition to the truth. God is the author of reality, the designer of the divine dynasphere, which is patterned after His essence. God *is* truth (John 14:6; 1 John 5:6*a*).

We can learn truth and think truth, but God *is* truth. We comprehend truth in three categories: the divine laws of establishment, the Gospel, and Bible doctrine. Every category of truth is an aspect of God's perfect purpose and design. The divine decrees, through which God established the existence of every detail of reality,[24] are based on all the attributes of who and what He is, which He has objectively revealed in the written canon of Scripture. God's veracity guarantees His absolute freedom from compromise, contradiction, or falsehood

---

24. See Thieme, *Integrity of God,* app. B, ''The Doctrine of Divine Decrees,'' pp. 257-81.

in all He thinks, says, or does (Deut. 32:4). His omniscience knows all things from eternity past, throughout history, and forever. His knowledge is not restricted, nor is His span of concentration limited, as is ours. Concentration is a human virtue, but God never needs to exclude one subject in order to focus on another. He is constantly occupied with all things at once; He cannot be distracted, lose His perspective, or become divorced from reality. Since He is a Person, God is conscious of Himself, and when He thinks about Himself, as He always does, He is thinking the truth. God's subjectivity is legitimate, necessary, and perfect, just as His self-love is legitimate, necessary, and perfect.

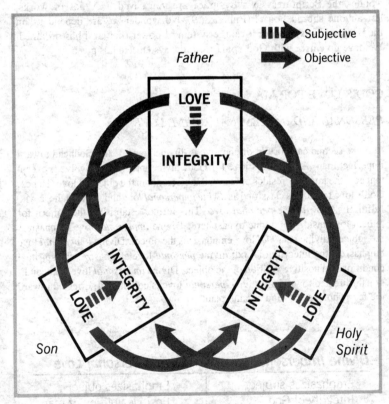

DIVINE SUBJECTIVE AND OBJECTIVE LOVE FOR GOD

God's love for God is subjectively *internal* within the essence of each Member of the Godhead and objectively *external* between the Members of the Godhead. This establishes the pattern of love as a transitive verb with a subject and an object. At the absolute source of love, both the subject and the object are equal. Both are God.

This love relationship between the three Members of the Trinity is the most exclusive relationship in the universe. The entry requirements are infinite, absolute, and perfect—impossible for sinful man to meet. As fallen mankind we simply do not qualify for the same love that the Members of the Trinity merit. Our beggarly human good, by which we attempt to impress God, is not only a blasphemous insult to His superior standards but is an arrogant attempt to intrude on God's love and God's plan. No wonder the Scriptures say, "By grace are you saved . . . not of works, lest anyone should boast" (Eph. 2:8, 9). No wonder we are dependent on the interlocking system of love, the system of power that God has ordained. We have no entree with God apart from the system He has given us.

GOD'S LOVE FOR MAN

PERSONAL AND IMPERSONAL DIVINE LOVE

The second category of divine love is directed outside the Godhead toward imperfect man. As in God's love for God, divine integrity is involved, except that now the integrity resides only in the subject, not in the object of love. Hence, God's love for man is classified as *divine impersonal love* and, toward those who fulfill His plan, *divine personal love*. This further establishes the pattern for human love inside the divine dynasphere. Divine *impersonal* love emphasizes the subject; divine *personal* love emphasizes the object. Divine *impersonal* love emphasizes the integrity of God; divine *personal* love emphasizes the spiritual condition and positive volition of the object. Divine *impersonal* love is unconditional, directed toward all; divine *personal* love is conditional, directed toward the few who execute God's game plan.

Divine Impersonal Love	Divine Personal Love
Emphasizes subject	Emphasizes object
Integrity of God	Positive volition of man
Unconditional	Conditional
Toward all men	Toward few men

GOD'S IMPERSONAL AND PERSONAL LOVE FOR MAN

The criterion for God's love, both impersonal and personal, is always His own absolute integrity: He loves only what His righteousness approves. Each Person of the Godhead loves absolute divine righteousness, but how can God direct that same love toward imperfect human beings whom His perfect righteousness rejects and His justice has condemned?

God cannot compromise any divine standard without destroying His integrity. If His integrity is destroyed, so is His love. This is a critical issue for man to understand. God cannot be God if He loves the unworthy, yet He is said to love all mankind (John 3:16), whom He condemns at birth (Rom. 5:19). The solution is found in divine impersonal love, which depends exclusively on the absolute character of God.

Perfect God can create only that which is perfect. When He created Adam and the woman, the human race was a fitting object for divine personal love. As perfect humanity Adam was not equal with God, but neither did he violate God's integrity. No conflict with divine righteousness and justice existed with man in the perfection of the Garden, with the result that divine love was God's point of contact with man. Adam and the woman were blessed from God's love rather than from His justice. Grace is the policy of God's justice in blessing *sinful* man, but man had not yet sinned. There was no need for grace until the Fall of man.

When Adam chose to sin, God condemned him. Divine justice, the executor of divine righteousness, became God's point of contact with man in place of divine love. The emphasis in God's relationship with Adam shifted from the object, man, to the subject, God, whose righteousness and justice are absolute, immutable, and eternally worthy of divine love. At the Fall of man, God switched from divine personal love to divine impersonal love. Divine impersonal love never relies on the merit of its object. Instead, the integrity of the subject established grace as an entirely new divine policy, under which the justice of God initiated a plan to save fallen man.

> For God did not send the Son into the world to judge the
> world; but that the world should be saved through Him.
> (John 3:17, NASV)

> Believe in the Lord Jesus and you shall be saved. (Acts
> 16:31*b*, NASV)

THE EXTENT OF GOD'S IMPERSONAL LOVE

Can perfect God love imperfect, condemned, depraved, unregenerate man? Yes, but only with impersonal love. We are born spiritually dead because of Adam's Fall (Rom. 5:12), but from the moment of physical birth every human being is the beneficiary of the integrity of God. Our lack of merit does not prevent God from designing and executing a plan to save us without violating His own standards. Under the principle of grace before judgment, God delays final judgment to permit us the opportunity to believe in Christ and receive eternal life.

> Or do you disparage [by maliciously judging each other] the riches of His generosity [God's impersonal love, His "kindness" to man based solely on His own integrity] and clemency [delay in judgment] and patience [His consistency regardless of our recalcitrance], not knowing that the kindness of God [His impersonal love] brings you to conversion. (Rom. 2:4)

God delayed mankind's final judgment so that He could extend to us His kindness, His impersonal love. An impassable barrier stood between man and God.[25] God cannot tolerate sin (Rom. 3:23; Jer. 17:9; Isa. 64:6b); He cannot cancel the penalty of sin (Rom. 6:23a); nor can He ignore the problem of our physical birth and spiritual death (Eph. 2:1). Our position in Adam, which makes us objects of divine condemnation, cannot suddenly become pleasing to God (1 Cor. 15:22a). God's absolute righteousness can never accept our relative righteousness (Isa. 64:6a; Rom. 9:30–33), nor can any attribute of God's character be compromised (Isa. 46:9; Rom. 8:8; 1 Tim. 6:16). This barrier was removed by the work of Christ on the Cross so that only the Cross now stands between man and God. Only one issue remains: our volition. God cannot coerce our free will without compromising His integrity; He cannot arbitrarily save us. We must freely believe in Christ to be saved and avoid the Last Judgment (Rom. 8:1).

If God preempted our volition in salvation, He would destroy His own plan. He would cancel the very purpose of salvation: that each individual might choose to have a personal relationship with Him. Therefore, in impersonal love God does everything except make the decision for us. Positive volition is the only missing link, the only factor needed to complete our reconciliation with God. We are born totally abhorrent to God, but a single decision of nonmeritorious faith in Christ closes the gap and establishes us as God's beloved sons forever. The mechanics of salvation demonstrate the tremendous scope of God's impersonal love, the absolute "riches of His generosity." Without violating His integrity or relying on the unworthy objects of His impersonal love, God marshaled all His

25. See Thieme, *The Barrier* (1977).

infinite genius and power for our advantage, "not willing that any should perish, but that all should come to repentance," to a change of mind concerning Christ (2 Pet. 3:9).[26]

THE ALL AND THE FEW IN EACH PHASE OF GOD'S PLAN

God has provided everything for the eternal salvation of every unbeliever and the maximum prosperity of every believer in both time and eternity. If an unbeliever rejects God's saving grace, he remains the object of only divine impersonal love until he dies, when the delay in judgment runs out (Heb. 10:27). When the unbeliever accepts the work of Christ, he becomes the object of divine personal love just as Adam was the object of God's personal love in the Garden. But God's plan for the royal family gives us a higher position after salvation than Adam enjoyed before the Fall. God's game plan is to make us like His Son (Heb. 2:10, 11). This is the doctrine of sanctification.

Sanctification is a technical, theological term that refers only to the royal family of the Church Age (1 Cor. 1:2, 30; Heb. 10:19, 20). We are set apart as sacred or consecrated to God; we belong to God under a unique, eternal contract. Faith in Christ affixes our signature to a royal contract under which we share the sanctification of Jesus Christ, the "Holy One from God" (Luke 4:34; John 6:69). The death, burial, resurrection, ascension, and session of Christ fulfilled and therefore abrogated the old contract or old testament of the Mosaic Law (Rom. 10:4; Gal. 4:4, 5). We live under a new grace contract, the new testament, which we fulfill inside the divine dynasphere (Gal. 5:14, 18, 23b).

Sanctification is accomplished in three phases: positional, experiential, and ultimate. At the moment of faith in Christ, the Church Age believer is placed into union with Christ—positional sanctification (1 Thess. 5:23; Rom. 6:3, 8). As the believer functions in Christ's power sphere and acquires the Mind of Christ, Bible doctrine, he reaches spiritual maturity—experiential sanctification (John 17:17). And in heaven the believer receives a body like Christ's resurrection body—ultimate sanctification (Gal. 6:8; 1 Pet 5:10; 1 Cor. 15:53, 54).

This plan is based on God's integrity and the work of Christ, not on any merit in the human race. We are the beneficiaries of *God's* plan. God loves us because of who and what *He* is, because of the provisions *He* has made, because on the Cross *His* justice fulfilled the demands of *His* righteousness. This is grace. After salvation the justice of God remains the source of all our blessings. We were saved by grace; we are always under grace, whether objects of God's impersonal love or objects of His personal love.

---

26. In *The Integrity of God,* I define God's impersonal love strictly in terms of His justice, not His love. Divine impersonal love *is* the justice of God, the subject, taking action to bless man, the unworthy object of love.

In each phase of God's plan—phase one, salvation; phase two, the believer in time; or phase three, the believer in eternity—a different category of people is specified. *All* members of each category receive divine impersonal love; a *few* in each group qualify for divine personal love by obeying God's will. The term "few" is used not in the numerical but in the logical sense. A few is any percentage less than 100 percent of the designated category. A few may be as small as one percent or as great as 99 percent.

	God's Impersonal Love for the All	God's Personal Love for the Few
PHASE ONE Salvation	**ENTIRE HUMAN RACE** *Unlimited Atonement*	**BELIEVERS IN CHRIST** *Imputed Righteousness*
PHASE TWO Believer on Earth	**ALL BELIEVERS** *Logistical Grace*	**MATURE BELIEVERS** *Supergrace*
PHASE THREE Believer in Heaven	**ALL BELIEVERS** *Resurrection Body*	**MATURE BELIEVERS** *Eternal Rewards*

OBJECTS OF GOD'S IMPERSONAL AND PERSONAL LOVE

In phase one God offers salvation to *all* mankind from His impersonal love, but only the *few* accept Christ as Savior and come under God's personal love. In phase two *all* believers on earth are sustained and protected by God's logistical grace from His impersonal love, but only the *few* utilize logistical grace, advance to maturity, and become recipients of supergrace blessings motivated by His personal love. In phase three *all* believers in heaven possess the resurrection body, but only the *few* receive special rewards, decorations, and honors as the most eminent eternal aristocrats.

DIVINE LOVE IN SALVATION

The category in view in phase one of God's plan is the entire human race. The doctrine of unlimited atonement declares that Christ died for all mankind (Rom. 5:6; 2 Cor. 5:15; 1 Tim. 2:6; 4:10; Titus 2:11; Heb. 2:9).

> And He [Jesus Christ] is the propitiation [He satisfied God the Father] for our sins, and not ours only, but also for the entire world. (1 John 2:2)

> For God so loved the world [with divine impersonal love] that He gave His uniquely-born Son, that whoever believes in Him should not perish but have eternal life. (John 3:16)

God manifests impersonal love toward everyone. He imputed human life to evil men, like Stalin and Hitler, and presented them with repeated occasions to be saved (Rom. 11:32; 2 Pet. 3:9). The Cross is unconditional. In contrast, God reserves His personal love for only those few who believe in Christ and thus fulfill the conditions of the Gospel. In each generation a different proportion of all living people will trust in Christ, but those few, whatever their number, are the objects of divine personal love with reference to phase one.

The work of salvation exacted a terrible price, the spiritual death of Christ on the Cross.[27] No unbeliever has ever earned or deserved salvation, but if God has accomplished the most for those He loves impersonally, He can do only much more than the most for those special few He loves personally. God imputed all man's sins to Christ on the Cross in behalf of the entire human race, but God goes much farther for those who believe in Christ: to them He imputes divine righteousness.

The most remarkable of all Bible doctrines is that God credits His own righteousness to every believer. We possess forever the very principle and standard of God's integrity, the quality that God has respected, honored, and loved throughout all His eternal existence. We could receive no more valuable or significant blessing. Now the same phenomenal love that has always existed between the Members of the Trinity is directed toward us. God loves His own righteousness; He has given us His righteousness; therefore, He loves us.

> He [God the Father] made Him [Christ] who knew no sin [impeccable in the divine dynasphere] to be sin on our behalf [the judgment of all human sins in Christ], that we might become the righteousness of God in Him. (2 Cor. 5:21, NASV)

> For by one man's disobedience [Adam's original sin] many [the entire human race] were made sinners, so by the obedience of one [Christ submitting to the death of the Cross] shall many be made righteous [imputed righteousness at salvation]. (Rom. 5:19)

---

27. See Thieme, *Blood of Christ*, pp. 10-13.

> And he [Abraham] had believed in the Lord, and He [the Lord] counted it to him for righteousness [Abraham received God's righteousness at the moment of salvation]. (Gen. 15:6)

> So I stand convinced that neither death nor life, neither angels nor rulers of angels, neither present things nor future things, neither powers, neither height [nothing in heaven] nor depth [nothing in hell] nor any other created thing shall be able to separate us from the love of God which is in Christ Jesus our Lord [in union with Christ we share His righteousness]. (Rom. 8:38, 39)

As spiritual royalty each Church Age believer possesses a double portion of divine righteousness. The righteousness of God the Father is imputed to us at salvation, as it is to every believer of all other dispensations (Gen. 15:6). But we also share the righteousness of God the Son through our royal position in union with Christ (2 Cor. 5:21). We are included in the dynamics of "God is love," not because of who and what we are, but because of who and what God is, because of His integrity.

DIVINE LOVE FOR THE BELIEVER IN TIME

THE GRACE PIPELINE

After salvation the imputed righteousness of God becomes the home or target for divine blessings that exceed salvation itself. This principle does not diminish God's matchless grace in saving us but reveals His infinite capacity for prospering those He personally loves. God's capacity never changes, but He can do far more for His sons than for His enemies (Rom. 5:10). Imputed righteousness creates in us a potential for blessings that never exists in the unbeliever. As a result divine blessings after salvation can be greater than salvation itself because they are easier for God to give.[28]

This is the doctrine that motivates the advancing believer to persist in learning God's Word inside the divine dynasphere. As he makes the transition from ignorance to cognizance of doctrine, the believer creates in his soul capacity for blessings. The believer's capability to receive and appreciate divine grace enables God to prosper him without distracting him and halting his spiritual momentum. Capacity from Bible doctrine in the soul is the missing link that con-

---

28. See Thieme, *Integrity of God*, pp. 80-95.

verts potential for blessings into reality. The growing believer anchors his hope or confidence in the knowledge that, far more than his first entrance into the divine dynasphere at salvation, his life in gate eight will glorify Christ and result in maximum blessing. The principle of greater grace after salvation (James 4:6) is expressed by Paul in the words "much more" and "surplus of grace."

> For if by the transgression of one [Adam's original sin],
> the death [spiritual death] ruled through that one [and
> it did; we are all condemned at birth for Adam's sin],
> much more they [mature believers] who receive in life
> the surplus of grace [supergrace blessings in phase two
> from the justice of God] and the gift of righteousness
> [imputed righteousness as the home in us for supergrace
> blessings] shall rule through the One, Jesus Christ [the
> blessings in phase three for the mature believer are greater
> yet than the surplus in phase two]. (Rom. 5:17)

By imputing to us divine righteousness, God has constructed a grace pipeline down which, in His perfect timing, He can pour all the blessings we have the capacity to receive (Job 1:21). With divine justice as the source and imputed divine righteousness as the terminus, the grace pipeline is perfectly insulated or encapsulated by the integrity of God.

The encapsulated pipeline seals out all human merit because man's relative righteousness falls short of God's absolute righteousness and would create a weak link in the plan of God. Human good does not bring us to God (Isa. 64:6). He never blesses us because of our sincerity, personality, talent, intelligence, personal sacrifice, diligence, social action, tithing, or emotionalism. Genetically acquired advantages are ultimately a gift from God, and the opportunities to exploit advantages or overcome disadvantages are also a divine gift. We cannot take credit for grace and demand that God prosper us for what He Himself has accomplished. Nor does legitimate Christian service, prayer, witnessing, or giving qualify us for divine blessings. Honorable Christian activities are in themselves blessings and privileges, not the cause but a result of spiritual growth; they are divinely afforded opportunities to express our love for God, which itself is a result of growth.

Even morality is excluded from the grace pipeline. Genuine morality must exist between members of the human race, but no human action, not even the most meritorious, has any credit with God. Divine justice can bless only divine righteousness. The encapsulated grace pipeline precludes all possibility of compromise to the essence of God while excluding all human self-righteousness. God is never impressed with what we do; only we are impressed with what we do.

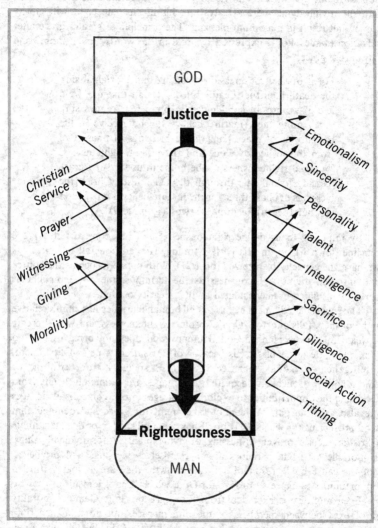

BLESSINGS IMPUTED THROUGH THE ENCAPSULATED GRACE PIPELINE

God pours blessings through the grace pipeline to *every* believer in phase two of His plan, but, as in phase one, a distinction exists between objects of divine impersonal and personal love. Phase two includes all believers alive on earth. *All* members of this category experience divine impersonal love through His ceaseless logistical support, but only the *few* who persist in the divine dynasphere become objects of divine personal love with capacity for supergrace prosperity.

Divine personal love remains constant toward imputed righteousness in all believers, but in the Christian life, God's integrity continually evaluates believers for blessing or cursing. Volition remains an issue. Even while He disciplines the reversionistic believer, God faithfully supplies all the necessities of life, just as He unfailingly supports the mature believer—while also enriching him with supergrace. Certain basic blessings are poured out to all believers; special additional blessings are reserved for the few.

LOGISTICAL GRACE

Logistical grace, imputed by the justice of God to the righteousness of God in each believer, includes four interrelated categories of blessings.

1. *Life support* keeps the believer alive until the moment God has decided to call him home (Ps. 68:19, 20).

2. *Temporal supply* furnishes such necessities as air, food, shelter, clothing, and transportation (Matt. 6:11, 25–34).

3. *Security provisions* protect the believer amid the hazards of the devil's world (Heb. 1:14; Rom. 13:4).

4. *Spiritual provisions* enable every believer to learn Bible doctrine and grow to spiritual maturity regardless of human IQ, background, or environment (Matt. 4:4; John 17:17).

No matter how you fail or succeed, God will never abandon you. Wherever you go, whatever you do, as a believer in the Lord Jesus Christ you will always be supported by the power and impersonal love of God, for "underneath are the everlasting arms" (Deut. 33:27). When the need is greatest, the Lord is nearest (Phil. 4:5*b*, 19).

The Lord is the One shepherding me. I cannot lack for anything. (Ps. 23:1)

This I recall to mind [remembering Bible doctrine]; therefore, I have hope [confidence concerning phase two]: the Lord's grace functions never cease [logistical grace], for His compassions [divine impersonal love] never fail; they are renewed every morning. Great is Your faithfulness [divine integrity]. The Lord is my portion, says my soul; therefore, I have hope in Him. The Lord is good [supergrace blessings in phase two] to those who wait on Him, to the soul who seeks Him [positive volition toward doctrine]. (Lam. 3:21–25)

In the Sermon on the Mount, Jesus illustrated God's generosity toward even the most undeserving believer by showing that every common sparrow and lily of the field receives the equivalent of logistical grace.

Look at the birds of the air, that they do not sow, neither do they reap, nor gather into barns; and yet your heavenly Father feeds them. Are you not worth much more than they? (Matt. 6:26, NASV)

Logistical grace is supplied to all believers in sufficient, though unequal, quantities to enable them to advance to gate eight of the divine dynasphere. Equality is never the issue; neither envy of those with more, nor haughtiness toward those with less, has any place in God's game plan. What matters is how you use the grace God has given you. The divine dynasphere itself is the epitome of logistical grace. All receive the love complex; few utilize its power.

Every believer in phase two has resolved the issue of salvation and constantly receives logistical grace, but many Christians fail to progress beyond salvation. If a believer rejects the doctrine of eternal security, he may repeatedly rededicate himself or reaffirm his faith, but anxiety over the accomplished fact of salvation is ludicrous. God permanently holds each believer in His omnipotent hands (John 10:28; Rom. 8:38, 39). Only a colossally arrogant believer would presume that his sins or failures are greater than the work of Christ on the Cross or that he could cancel what God has accomplished. This subjective preoccupation with salvation not only blasphemes against God but squanders the grace that God provides for our spiritual growth. Leaving behind the settled issue of salvation, we must progress in the plan of God.

But grow by means of grace [logistical grace] and by means of the knowledge of the Lord Jesus Christ [logistical grace supplies Bible doctrine for the believer's spiritual momentum]. (2 Pet. 3:18)

SUPERGRACE

Divine justice is impartial; God's game plan succeeds for anyone who executes its mandates. God imputes the "much more" surplus of grace (Rom. 5:17), or *supergrace* (James 4:6), to any believer who exploits divine logistics. In any generation relatively few believers take advantage of their spiritual royalty, "grow by means of grace," and live as true spiritual aristocrats. Only a few establish the correct scale of values with Bible doctrine as first priority, refuse to be distracted from the divine dynasphere, and maintain their momentum to gate eight. But these few believers become the objects of God's personal love.

Only Christ has ever remained perpetually inside the divine dynasphere, but those Christians who grow until they spend the majority of their time in the divine power system become the objects of divine personal love. Thousands of decisions are required: to rebound whenever necessary, to persist daily in learning the Word of God, to apply doctrine as opportunities develop. Perception of doctrine is constant, a daily habit; application varies with circumstances. The mature believer has not attained sinless perfection, but by his consistent good decisions he has established a trend of relying on God's power and wisdom.

Supergrace consists of six categories of special blessings for the mature believer.[29]

1. *Spiritual blessings* are the inherent reward of virtue directed toward God. The virtues of confidence, worship, and personal love toward God give the believer strength and happiness, while motivating the virtues of courage, morality,and impersonal love toward man.

2. *Temporal blessings* are designed uniquely for each mature believer. God gives the right blessings at the right time, which may include wealth, success, promotion, mental and cultural enrichment, leadership dynamics, improved health, stimulating social life, and romantic love (1 Pet. 5:6, 7).

29. See Thieme, *Integrity of God*, pp. 126-47.

3. *Blessing by association* overflow to family, friends, and associates as God prospers the supergrace believer through blessing those in his periphery.

4. *Historical impact* is blessing by association extended to the believer's community, state, and nation. Jesus Christ controls history for the purpose of protecting and blessing those who love Him (Lev. 26:3-13).

5. *Undeserved suffering* demands intensified application of Bible doctrine, accelerating spiritual growth and increasing the believer's appreciation of the Lord (Rom. 8:17b, 18).

6. *Dying grace* is the mature believer's final, glorious experience of divine grace on earth (Ps. 116:15). With supernatural tranquility and eager anticipation, the "friend of God" (John 15:14) crosses the high golden bridge from the blessings of time to greater blessings in eternity.

Spiritual blessings give capacity for all the others. Spiritual blessings include sharing the happiness of God, capacity for life and love, a total appreciation for grace, the ability to handle disaster, the ability to interpret contemporary history, freedom from slavery to the details of life, adaptability to change, and a sense of security from knowing the plan of God for your life. Based on these spiritual blessings at gate eight of the love complex, God can then give the five additional categories of blessings.

DIVINE LOVE FOR THE BELIEVER IN ETERNITY

In phase three of God's plan, every believer resides in heaven forever. In this category of mankind, the objects of divine impersonal love are again distinguished from objects of divine personal love. All believers in heaven receive a resurrection body (1 Cor. 15:43, 53; 2 Thess. 2:14; 1 John 3:2), but only the few receive special rewards. In heaven as on earth, divine impersonal love is unconditional; every believer receives ultimate sanctification. But divine personal love is conditional, depending on how you utilized God's grace provisions on earth.

At the Judgment Seat of Christ, our Lord as judge will recognize those who attained spiritual maturity on earth (John 5:22, 27; 1 Cor. 3:11-14). Their positive volition will have permitted God to glorify Christ by imputing supergrace to them in the devil's world. The perfect, just pronouncement of the Lord Jesus Christ will be to parlay those wonderful blessings into still greater rewards in heaven (Rom. 5:17). These surpassing grace rewards will glorify the Lord to the maximum throughout all eternity.

Believers will be rewarded in eternity in proportion to their divine blessings in time. There is no equality in time; there will be no equality in eternity. God designed man to be free, not equal, and each believer will be rewarded according to the sum total of his freewill decisions for or against the divine dynasphere. There are now on earth and always will be in heaven degrees of divine personal love according to the individual's execution of God's game plan. There are no degrees of divine impersonal love because God's impersonal love for man depends only on the unchangeable integrity of God.

GOD'S LOVE AS POLICY

God loves God; God loves man; God loves as a matter of policy. This third category of divine love has been developed in *The Integrity of God* and is not pertinent to our present study.[30] Actually this category is not divine love at all but a system of communication designed to explain divine policies to man. For this purpose the Scriptures ascribe *human* love to God, called an anthropopathism. Derived from the Greek *anthropos,* "man," and *pathos,* "an inner function of the soul with overt manifestations," an anthropopathism is language of accommodation through which infinite God reveals Himself to the finite mind of man.

The Bible declares that God hates (Rom. 9:13), harbors jealousy (Ex. 20:5a; 34:14; Deut. 4:24; 6:15a); changes His mind (Gen. 6:6); and vents a violent anger (Jer. 4:8; 12:13; 25:37; 51:45; Ezek. 5:15). These qualities are incompatible with God's essence, but such statements are descriptive and gain the attention of the hearer.

When an unbeliever first hears the Gospel, he cannot comprehend all the coordinated functions of the essence of God that guarantee salvation. Knowledge of God develops later, after he becomes a believer and learns Bible doctrine over an extended period of time. But the unbeliever can understand the Gospel message if God's motivation is described in familiar, human terms.

A classic illustration of an anthropopathism is quoted by Paul from the Old Testament (Mal. 1:2, 3) to demonstrate the contrast between God's treatment of believers and unbelievers.

I love that Jacob, but I hate that Esau. (Rom. 9:13)

---

30. Pp. 1-18.

God does not hate anyone. Personal hatred is a sin, strictly a human aberration. Since human characteristics are being contrasted in Romans 9:13, the love expressed for Jacob is also human, not divine. God did not hold a deep personal love for Jacob, who was a self-serving scoundrel (Gen. 27:19–24). When Jacob finally grew up spiritually and became the object of divine personal love, God changed his name to Israel, "Prince of God" (Gen. 32:28; 35:10). The love and hatred juxtaposed by Paul are simply two anthropopathisms, which illustrate the function of divine justice toward a man who possessed imputed righteousness and toward his twin brother who did not.

IV
Gate Three, Teachability

HUMILITY DEFINED

Strength of character and resultant happiness are constructed upon a foundation of humility. Humility is freedom—freedom from subjectivity—allowing you to comprehend objective reality, the essence and plan of God. Humility is the basic human virtue of teachability.

> Good and honorable is the Lord.
> Therefore, He instructs sinners in the way.
> In justice [divine integrity] He guides the humble.
> Consequently, He teaches the humble His way.
> (Ps. 25:8, 9)

Self-centeredness is arrogance, delusion, foolishness. You are not the center of your life; you belong to a far greater plan centered in God. He "has blessed [you] with every spiritual blessing in the heavenly places in Christ" (Eph. 1:3); your proud self-sufficiency is a myth that complicates your life, blinding you to the fascinating, gracious Person of God, separating you from your "most important love" (Rev. 2:4).

Humility seeks reality; humility desires and accepts truth. The marvelous reality of God's personality and plan gives your life its meaning, purpose, and definition, furnishing the perspective—divine viewpoint—for solving your problems. But the humility needed to learn "God's way" achieves far more than just the solutions to your problems; Bible doctrine in your soul creates Christian integrity, which is your capacity for life, blessing, and happiness. Humility is the initial virtue or strength of character that leads to all the Christian virtues in the remaining gates of the divine dynasphere.

Humility is both a system of thinking and a way of life. As a system of thinking, humility is freedom from arrogance; as a way of life, humility is submission to legitimate authority. Humility responds to establishment truth by submitting to temporal authority and responds to Bible doctrine by living in the divine dynasphere. Humility is a state of honor and integrity.

> The fear [respect] of the Lord is the instruction for wisdom, and before honor comes humility. (Prov. 15:33)

> When arrogance comes, then comes dishonor, but with the humble is wisdom. (Prov. 11:2)

> A person's arrogance will bring him low, but a spirit of humility will attain honor. (Prov. 29:23)

Humility is a system of thinking under pressure. Courage and poise are the clothing that covers such thinking with glory.

> The curse of the Lord is on the house of evil [the family living under Satan's influence], but He blesses the home of righteousness [the family whose members live in God's system]. He makes war against the arrogant, but He gives grace to the humble. The wise person [humility is teachability] will inherit honor, but fools [those who are unteachable] carry away dishonor. (Prov. 3:33–35)

> But He gives greater grace [blessings after salvation], that is why the Scripture says, "God makes war against the arrogant but gives grace to the humble." (James 4:6)

God blesses all believers with logistical grace as He keeps us alive for the purpose of advancing to spiritual maturity within His system. He gives supergrace blessings only to those who possess capacity for blessings, and humility is essential for capacity.

> In the same way, comparative novices [in the Christian life], be under the command authority of the pastors [elders]. All of you [in the congregation], fasten yourselves to each other with grace thinking [impersonal love], because God makes war against the arrogant, but He gives grace to the humble.

> Therefore, become grace-oriented under [the authority of] the ruling hand of God, that He may promote you at the proper time. (1 Pet. 5:5, 6)

If God does not promote you, you are not promoted. Humility precludes inordinate competition, self-advancement, and the arrogance of achievement. Achievement belongs to God; happiness belongs to the believer. This principle is fulfilled only in the life of the believer who resides and functions inside the divine power system.

> For everyone who exalts self shall be humbled, and he who humbles himself [living in God's system] shall be exalted. (Luke 14:11)

ORIENTATION TO REALITY, AUTHORITY, AND TRUTH

Both humility and arrogance are patterns of thought, but a humble person is oriented to reality whereas an arrogant person is divorced from reality. A genuinely humble man acknowledges his weaknesses and depends on a strength greater than his own, the power of the divine dynasphere. Since he recognizes and submits to truth, he thinks and acts from a position of strength. Paradoxically, an arrogant person places himself in a position of weakness by overestimating his strengths. He lives in a house of cards built on illusions of self-importance. He can neither think rationally nor make wise decisions, but succumbs to flattery or subjectivity, allowing his soul to be dominated by the old sin nature. Nearly every sin that man can commit expresses some form of arrogance, whereas the relaxed mental attitude of basic impersonal love demonstrates humility. Gates two and three of the divine dynasphere interlock: no one can build the virtue of impersonal love except on the foundational virtue of humility.

> Stop thinking of yourselves in terms of arrogance beyond what you ought to think, but think in terms of sanity [the divine viewpoint] for the purpose of being rational without illusion as God has assigned to each one a standard of thinking from doctrine. (Rom. 12:3)

No sane person considers himself perfect, nor is any man an island. People who live in close proximity to each other or who belong to any organization that seeks to accomplish an objective must submit to authority. Authority is the primary issue that humility faces. Submission to legitimate authority is humility; rebellion is arrogance.

There is nothing demeaning or degrading in obedience to authority. Humility is not humiliation. True humility must never be confused with self-effacement or asceticism. Nearly every self-abnegating person held up as a model of humility lives for the approbation of others and cultivates their pity or sentimentality as a means of controlling them. False humility is a virulent strain of arrogance.

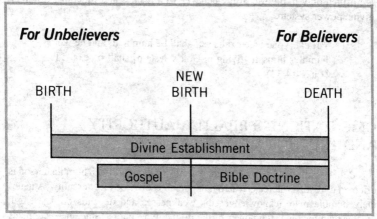

CATEGORIES OF TRUTH

Humility is always related to truth, and the source of all truth is the character of God. The Bible delineates three categories of truth: the divine laws of establishment, the Gospel, and the spiritual truth of Bible doctrine. The laws of establishment are designed by God for the survival, orderly function, and prosperity of the human race; these laws pertain to believer and unbeliever alike (Rom. 13:1-6; Matt. 22:21). The Gospel of salvation is addressed to unbelievers only, since believers are already eternally saved (John 10:28; Heb. 7:25a). And Bible doctrine is the province of believers only, because unbelievers cannot comprehend spiritual truth (1 Cor. 2:9-16). Orientation to any category of truth requires humility. Humility provides teachability.

THE UNBELIEVER WITHIN GOD'S SYSTEM

The third gate of the love complex allows the *un*believer to enter God's power sphere. *All* human virtue is developed only inside the love complex, and God's attribute of love is the pattern for *all* genuine love in the human race. Virtue and love among unbelievers, although limited, manifest God's design just as do virtue and love among believers. The believer has full access to the divine dynasphere through the filling of the Holy Spirit and Bible doctrine; the unbeliever has limited access through genuine humility in obedience to the laws of establishment.

Under the laws of establishment, the unbeliever can function in two gates of the divine dynasphere, entering through gate three and interlocking with certain aspects of gate two. Although he lacks the spiritual dynamics of gates one, four, five, six, seven, and eight, the unbeliever in the divine dynasphere can enjoy a happier life than the believer who never resides in God's system. In gate three the unbeliever can display greater common sense, objectivity, intellectual receptivity, and capacity for life than the believer outside the love complex. In portions of gate two, the unbeliever can create stronger personal integrity and as a result can sustain a better marriage, achieve greater professional success, and develop richer, more lasting friendships than can his reversionistic Christian neighbors.

> Enjoy life with the woman you love all the days of your life
> of vanity [the unbeliever's life on earth] which He [God] has
> given to you under the sun; for this [marriage as a divine in-
> stitution for believers and unbelievers alike] is your reward
> in life, and in your toil [profession] in which you have
> labored under the sun. (Eccl. 9:9, NASV)

The honorable unbeliever may be oblivious to the divine origin of his personal principles and will spend eternity in hell, but in the few gates available to him, he can experience a marvelous life on earth. God's power system never depends on man but is effective for anyone, including the unbeliever, who will reside under its influence.

If the spiritually dead unbeliever can discover happiness in a limited portion of the love complex, how much more the believer can anticipate blessings in the complete, interlocking system. The believer outside the divine dynasphere cannot be distinguished from the unbeliever outside the divine dynasphere, except that divine discipline compounds the believer's self-induced misery (Heb. 12:5, 6). The believer who rejects God's game plan still belongs to the royal family and will live forever in heaven, but his own negative decisions make his life on earth inferior to the life of the genuinely humble unbeliever.

THE HERITAGE OF FREEDOM

The laws of establishment declare that freedom is man's most valuable possession. Human freedom is the heritage of human birth, the extension of the volition of the soul as the uncaused cause of man's thought and action. Freedom is self-determination, the function of free will uncoerced by threat or violence and not determined by environment, society, or genetics.

As a true man with human volition, Jesus Christ was free to accept or reject God's plan for His first advent, and, contrary to personal desire (Matt. 26:39), Christ agreed to be "obedient to the point of death, even the death of the Cross" (Phil. 2:8). In the prototype divine dynasphere our Lord established the precedent of voluntary obedience to divine authority (Heb. 5:9); in the sphere of freedom, He freed us to receive salvation and to advance in the divine dynasphere (Gal. 3:13; 5:1). Thus freedom also becomes the heritage of the new birth or regeneration, which gives the believer access to the complete love complex, the realm of spiritual freedom. With reference to gate one: "where the Spirit of the Lord is, there is freedom" (2 Cor. 3:17), and regarding gate four: "you shall know the truth and the truth shall make you free" (John 8:32). Bible doctrine is called the "law of freedom" because doctrine defines the believer's freedom to glorify God (James 1:25; 2:12). Positive volition toward the Word of God is the basis for freedom, as the Jewish prisoners of 586 B. C. dramatically proved while marching in chains to Babylon.

> For I will walk in freedom because I seek Your doctrine.
> (Ps. 119:45)

Not even the cruelest tyranny can remove your freedom to think doctrine, nor can any extenuation relieve you of your responsibility for "redeeming the time" inside the divine dynasphere (Eph. 5:15, 16; Col. 4:5).

Freedom as our human heritage and spiritual heritage also has become our national heritage. The Founding Fathers rose to the challenge of "Give me liberty or give me death" and prefaced the Constitution with their determination to "secure the blessings of liberty." The existence and perpetuation of national liberty demands respect for legitimately established authority and depends on the cumulative personal integrity of all citizens, believers and unbelievers. Ultimately, national freedom is maintained by military victory (2 Chron. 20:27–30; Neh. 4:14).[31]

FREE WILL AND THE ANGELIC CONFLICT

God invented human volition to resolve the angelic conflict, the prehistoric warfare between God and Satan. As one of the most powerful angels, Satan abused his freedom by revolting against God (Isa. 14:13, 14; Ezek. 28:14–16)

---

31. See Thieme, *Divine Establishment* (1973).

and then accused God of injustice in sentencing him to the Lake of Fire (Matt. 25:14). God created the human race in answer to Satan's false charge. God made man lower than the angels, established him on one planet in the universe, and endowed him with free will. The human race is a demonstration of God's perfect essence in relation to free individuals. Volition is the one characteristic that man has in common with angels. Thus, through mankind Satan and his demons are shown that they are responsible for their own condemnation.

In order to strip Satan of all defenses, God demonstrates His integrity to man under every possible variation of historical, personal, and spiritual circumstances. Some people live in the ideal environment of Eden or the Millennium; others amid the terror of the Tribulation. Some are born into nobility and wealth; others into relative obscurity or poverty. Some have advanced under the spiritual heritage of Israel; others under the divine dynasphere of the Church. Each life is a unique demonstration of human volition and divine grace in the angelic conflict.

Men were never designed to be equal. We are born unequal, and human free will insures further inequality. The more decisions people make, the more unequal they become. Some people make wise decisions that create future options for greater decisions; others make wrong decisions that close down future options. No two people are equal, but in every case man in his own strength is too weak to resist the craft and power of Satan. We acquire strength only by relying on the power of God.

In all dispensations the Lord Jesus Christ is the key to history; Jesus Christ controls history and personally entered history to defeat Satan at the Cross (Eph. 6:11–13; Heb. 2:9, 14; 1 Pet. 3:19, 22). The glorification of Christ is the purpose of man's existence, and in bringing all things into conformity with the divine objective, God treats each person on an individual basis.

God had you personally in mind when He designed the universe. He decreed a plan for your life that gives you a unique combination of limitations and opportunities within which to exercise your free will. As you freely choose to obey or disobey God's mandates, you create your own integrity or dishonor, success or failure, happiness or misery, reward or retribution from the justice of God. But whether or not you succeed in the Christian life, God continues to treat you as a person, not as a failure or a success, not as attractive or unattractive. In impersonal love He continues to faithfully provide logistical grace. Likewise, we must learn to treat others as individuals, not as rich or poor, smart or stupid, black, white, or brown, someone who can advance us or someone who might hinder us. In impersonal love from our own integrity, we must offer toleration, thoughtfulness, and kindness to all. Each human life plays an essential role in revealing to Satan and all the angels the absolute integrity of God (1 Cor. 4:9*b*; Eph. 3:10; 1 Pet. 1:12).

In perfect justice God permits Satan the freedom to prove his boast that he is equal with God (Isa. 14:14), but Satan continually fails. He usurped the rulership of the earth from Adam but has never been able to control his ill-gotten kingdom. Like a roaring lion, Satan is angered and frustrated (1 Pet. 5:8) because the counterfeit Millennium he seeks to establish is marred by arrogance, evil, suffering, and disaster, while God's plan of grace extends the blessings of divine impersonal love to all mankind. God's perfect character is demonstrated in every human life; divine impersonal love reveals the integrity of the subject, never the merit of the object. With us or without us, through us or in spite of us, God will win the angelic conflict. Christ purchased the salvation of every human being (1 John 2:2), and God desires that all believe in Christ (2 Pet. 3:9); but even those who emulate Satan's arrogance and reject the riches of God's generosity inadvertently reveal God's justice. Like Satan, the unbeliever rejects the fabulous potential that God has given him; then after maximum grace before judgment (Gen. 6:3; 15:16), eternal condemnation expresses God's uncompromising integrity.

> For the wrath of man [maladjustment to God] will praise
> You [God]. (Ps. 76:10a)

In the negative volition of every unbeliever, Satan witnesses his own culpability and God's patience, kindness, and fairness, but the justice of God is revealed to the maximum in the mature believer. The doctrine of the angelic conflict explains the importance of human volition: our free decisions to reside and function in the divine dynasphere enable God to glorify Himself by blessing us. The angelic conflict also explains why increasingly marvelous blessings on earth become the criteria for eternal rewards in heaven (Luke 19:26; Rom. 8:14–18, 21). The positive volition that glorified Christ in the devil's world will much more glorify Him in eternity.

THE LINK BETWEEN FREEDOM AND AUTHORITY

As the author of deceit, violence, and tyranny, Satan is the enemy of human freedom, which must be protected in the devil's world. When God fashioned human freedom, he also designed multiple systems of authority to protect that freedom. Authority and freedom are not antithetical concepts, as presumed by arrogant, undisciplined people who consider themselves free spirits. Freedom cannot exist without authority, nor can authority exist without freedom. There must be a balance. Freedom without authority becomes anarchy, in which no one is free; but authority without freedom is tyranny, which ceases to be legitimate authority. No tyrant can remain in power without the consent and cooperation of his victims. Freedom and authority are two sides of the same coin, and the divine laws of establishment delineate the ideal systems of authority to sustain human freedom. Divine establishment is God's organization of the human race.

This first category of truth—divine establishment—defines the proper balance between freedom and authority. But humility is the link, the human virtue of voluntary obedience to authority, that ties freedom and authority together. Whereas impersonal love is the supreme *Christian* virtue, humility is the basic *human* virtue: for believer or unbeliever humility is orientation to life. Humility is also the foundation for all other categories of virtue. The believer can have neither the motivational virtue of personal love for God nor the functional virtue of impersonal love for the human race unless first he possesses humility. Without humility he is unteachable. Humility is the virtue directed toward authority.

Just as God's attribute of love is the pattern for *all* true human love, so also divine sovereignty is the ultimate basis for *all* genuine humility in the human race. God is absolute authority (Ps. 145:14; Matt. 20:15; 1 Tim. 6:15). Nothing exists that is not subject to Him. All reality is based ultimately on His divine essence. Satan remains free to operate only by God's permission (Job 1:6–12); evil and human good continue only under the principle of delay in divine judgment by which God allows the angelic conflict to run its course. We exist by God's sovereign decree and cannot challenge Him: either we adjust to His justice or we are ultimately destroyed by His justice.

God's authority is not a separate attribute of His divine essence but is derived from all His attributes functioning together in perfect harmony. He renders account to no one; He consults no one; He needs no counsel or encouragement. God holds authority over us because He is the creator and owner of all things (Ps. 50:10), because He is the Redeemer of mankind (Isa. 47:4; Eph. 1:7; Col. 1:14; 1 Pet. 1:18), and because He is the source of all truth (John 14:6; Prov. 8:1, 22–30). From His sovereignty God has delegated authority to positions of responsibility in the human race so that those who hold them may sufficiently control and protect the freedom of mankind. Delegated authority "is a minister of God to you for good," furnishing the environment for human prosperity (Rom. 13:1–6).

AUTHORITY IN HUMAN GOVERNMENT

The laws of establishment recognize four divine institutions in the human race: volition, marriage, family, and nation.[32] For each divine institution God created a system of authority. The authority in volition is each person's self-

---

32. See Thieme, *Divine Establishment*, pp. 5-12.

discipline, in marriage the husband, in the family the parents, and in the national entity the government in whatever form it is established.

Authority in a nation may be vested in one person, a small group, or a large segment of the nation's population. Any of these governmental systems can be good or evil, depending on the integrity or arrogance of those in authority. Monarchy, aristocracy, and republic are positive forms of government; tyranny, oligarchy, and democracy are negative forms. Arrogance converts any legitimate governmental organization into a system of evil. Under the distortions of arrogance, monarchy, which is the rule of one man for the common good, is transformed into tyranny, the rule of one man for his own benefit. Through arrogance aristocracy, which is the rule of a small elite for the common good, becomes an oligarchy, the rule of a small group for its own benefit. And through arrogance a republic, which is rule by the best of the population for the common good, degenerates into a democracy, rule by the worst of the population for their own benefit.[33]

	Good FOR THE BENEFIT OF THE GOVERNED	*Bad* FOR THE BENEFIT OF SELF
One Man Rules	**Monarchy**	**Tyranny**
Small Group Rules	**Aristocracy**	**Oligarchy**
Large Group Rules	**Republic**	**Democracy**

GOOD AND BAD SYSTEMS OF GOVERNMENTAL AUTHORITY

When the king is honorable and astute, monarchy is the most effective form of government. Jesus Christ will return as the King of Kings and Lord of Lords and as the absolute monarch of the earth will establish perfect government dur-

---

33.   See Erik von Kuehnelt-Leddin, *Leftism* (New Rochelle: Arlington House, 1974), p. 28.

ing the Millennium (Rev. 19:15, 16; 20:6). The worst form of government is democracy, which is a thin veneer over anarchy devoid of virtue and integrity.

The United States Constitution established our nation as a republic, guaranteeing maximum personal freedom to every citizen. With freedom comes responsibility, and, more than any other form of government, a republic stands on the personal integrity of its people.[34] In the Founding Fathers' original concept only the most qualified citizens could vote and participate in government, but when the franchise is extended to nearly all, a republic degenerates into a democracy in which the right to vote means little. When every irresponsible Jacobin has a voice in government, candidates for public office need not appeal to honorable, lucid people but campaign with slick public relations and mudslinging emotionalism. Policies are often established on expediency and fear, catering to the greed of anyone who can organize a crusade and gain national publicity. A democracy fosters dishonor; a burgeoning bureaucracy expands to appease the selfishness of arrogant people and encroach on private enterprise. Republic and rampant bureaucracy cannot coexist; one destroys the other. The purpose of governmental authority is to protect citizens from criminals and foreign aggressors so that each individual might express his volition in an environment as free as possible from violence and coercion.

HUMILITY IN THE HOME

ORGANIZATIONAL, ENFORCED, AND GENUINE HUMILITY

Authority precedes freedom. The divine pattern for nurturing and protecting freedom involves three categories of humility: organizational humility, enforced humility, and genuine humility. This pattern is repeated in the family, in the soul, in the local church, and, unique to the Lord Jesus Christ, in the plan of God for the Incarnation.

Humility begins when the fetus becomes a living human being at the moment of physical birth.[35] We entered the human race as helpless infants. God could have created each of us as an adult, as He formed Adam and the woman, but after the Fall of man, we require immediately an environment of authority if we are to have any hope of happiness in life. The old sin nature must be restrained. Parents must control the sin nature in their children through discipline and training so that the children can eventually assume responsibility for themselves. The family is *organizational humility,* God's initial defense of each person's freedom in the devil's world.

---

34. See below, p. 166.
35. See Thieme, *Integrity of God*, pp. 55-57.

	Child	Adult	Christian	Christ
Organizational Humility	Home and Family	Soul	Local Church	Plan of God for Incarnation
Enforced Humility	Parental Authority	Authority of Volition	Pastor's Authority	Sovereignty of God the Father
Genuine Humility	Positive Response to Parents	Self-discipline	Positive Volition to Bible Doctrine	Obedience to the Plan of God

CATEGORIES OF HUMILITY

In the home authority resides with the parents. This is *enforced humility*. Whether a child is reared by both parents, only one, or another adult as a surrogate parent, the parents possess the authority and responsibility to train their children, to designate policy, and to require that their children comply with that policy. As long as a child resides under his parents' roof or receives their financial support, he is subject to their jurisdiction.

> Train up a child in the way he should go,
> Even when he is old he will not depart from it. (Prov. 22:6, NASV)

> Children, obey your parents in the Lord, for this is right. Honor your father and mother (which is the first commandment with a promise), that it may be well with you [in adulthood], and that you may live long on the earth. (Eph. 6:1–3, NASV)

> Children, be obedient to your parents in all things for this is well pleasing to the Lord. (Col. 3:20, NASV)

Hopefully, parents are more discerning, prudent, and disciplined than their minor children, but this head start quickly disappears as the child approaches adulthood. In the child's early, formative years, the father and mother must exploit these advantages to establish an environment of authority in which their children can grow and mature. Certainly love is not excluded from the training process, but parents properly express their love and instill a true sense of adventure, self-esteem, and personal destiny in their children only when the family organization establishes, enforces, and maintains high standards of thought and action. Within this structure of stability and discipline, the parents treat the child as a person, not as an achiever who must constantly prove himself, earn his parents' love and approbation, and uphold the family name. When excessive pressure to justify himself is removed, the child has maximum opportunity to live his own life and develop capacity for happiness and freedom as an adult.

Authority demands responsibility, but no parent is perfect; all make mistakes from time to time. God's system of enforced humility in the home does not require perfection. Certainly every responsible parent strives to be as fair as possible (Eph. 6:4a), but most important is a consistent system of authority (Col. 3:20). The objectivity of enforced humility, implemented by his parents, gives the child a stable, external support on which to grow and learn. The child himself is unstable enough without having to contend with weakness, permissiveness, vacillation, and continual inconsistency from his parents.

When a child responds positively to parental discipline and respects authority in the home, he becomes teachable. This *genuine humility* gives him the capacity to learn from his parents; he is receptive to being inculcated with truth. All parents are responsible for teaching their children to be thoughtful, courteous, and respectful of the privacy, property, and authority of others, as demanded by the laws of establishment. Christian parents are entrusted with the additional responsibility of presenting the Gospel to their children and educating them in Bible doctrine (Eph. 6:4b). Genuine humility in the home is the child's self-motivated obedience to parental authority and instruction.

IMMATURE ADULTS

The objective of rearing a child is to prepare him to eventually leave home with an adult soul to match his adult body. This transition from authority in the home to freedom in life is one of the most difficult of all transitions. Many people never make the changeover. Enslaved by ignorance and arrogance, they remain mentally childish long after they become physical adults.

Such people never acquire the true independence of human maturity, which is self-restraint in accepting responsibility for one's own life. They would rather be slaves than free. Slaves are restrained by others and are responsible for nothing; juvenile "adults" shrink from controlling themselves or accepting the liability for their own thoughts, decisions, or actions. They avoid the most basic freedom, the freedom within one's own soul to think, decide, and feel. Their unwillingness to be free manifests itself in incessant complaining. They blame their past or other people for all their failures, insecurity, and frustration; they are preoccupied with themselves.

An immature person has no capacity for impersonal or personal love. Like a cocked pistol with a hair trigger, his arrogance waits to take offense at the slightest snub or inattention. And anyone hypersensitive about himself is always insensitive to others. His subjectivity precludes alertness to anyone else's feelings; the thoughtfulness of impersonal love cannot exist when a person concentrates only on an exaggerated image of himself.

Instead of operating from a position of strength in the divine dynasphere, the childish person depends on others for his happiness. In weakness and selfishness he demands the impossible: unconditional personal love, such as an infant receives from its parents. He demands unmerited love and attention from other people, and if such approbation is not forthcoming he conspires to make them as miserable as he is. This is the demand syndrome, in which a weak person seeks to control everyone in his periphery.

The courtesy and generosity of a truly noble individual may render him vulnerable to such unscrupulous manipulation. By exploiting the strengths of honorable people, the weak control the strong. Eventually the man of integrity must discern that he is being victimized and separate himself mentally or physically from the petty tyrant in his midst. The arrogant believer in the demand syndrome has never learned that his happiness depends on his own free will exercised in the divine dynasphere, not on what others must think of him or do for him. Inordinately possessive, perpetually jealous, and in love with himself, he never acquires the capacity to admire or love anyone else.

HUMILITY IN THE SOUL

HUMAN INEQUALITY

When a young person leaves home, the new organization for humility is his own soul. He must face the reality of who and what he is; he must assume responsibility for all his thoughts and actions and for the development of his own integrity. He must learn his limitations, abilities, and strengths and live within them without frustration, without fighting them, without demanding equality with anyone else.

Freedom and equality can never coexist. God's protection of freedom guarantees that inequality will be a perpetual historical trend. Never in the history of mankind can equality be achieved: first, because Satan gives preferential treatment to his servants (Rev. 6:15; 13:4) and, second, because God has designated human volition to be the key issue in the angelic conflict. Both Satan's injustice and God's perfect justice insure human inequality in all dispensations.

We are born unequal, but the very fact that God perpetuates our lives after birth means that we are also born with opportunity. Each individual is given the chance to succeed or fail, but even in success or failure inequality still exists. No two people succeed to the same degree, and no two equally fail. In periods of general prosperity, some people prosper more than others; in hard times some still prosper more than others. In an environment of freedom, as in the United States, good inequality exists; under tyranny, as in the Soviet Union, bad inequality exists. But whatever the economic, social, or political conditions, inequality remains an inescapable fact of life.

One person may be less intelligent than another, yet he may surpass the intellectual in common sense, practicality, integrity, physical attractiveness, or athletic ability. Everyone possesses some trait in which he stands above other people and other traits in which he is inferior. No equality exists in any category, but that should not be a cause of frustration. There is nothing wrong because someone is better than you are in some field. A humble person eschews jealousy and appreciates excellence wherever it is found.

Inequality is not detrimental in itself. Inequality is distorted into a problem by the arrogance of resenting inequality or by the self-pity of refusing to face reality and exploit the opportunities of one's own capacity in a particular realm.

Beginning with the woman in the Garden, who desired to be equal with God (Gen. 3:5, 6), mankind continually seeks to solve the problem of inequality, but alleged solutions merely create new inequalities. "Liberty, equality, fraternity" became the motivation of the French Revolution, but in deposing the crown and declassing the aristocracy, the conspirators elevated themselves. They did not want equality; they lusted for power, vengeance, and superiority. Robespierre climbed to power proclaiming equality but inaugurated the Reign of Terror, in which the guillotine claimed 40,000 lives, in order to control his fellow citizens and prevent his rivals from resolving their inequality with him. Victor Hugo later wrote that equality is merely the political translation of the word envy.

Violence or revolution never solves any personal, social, economic, or political problem, but inequality is not even a problem. The solution to people's problems is not equality but happiness and the "pursuit of happiness," as expressed in our Constitution.

INEQUALITY AND HAPPINESS

Happiness can and does exist in every category of society (Phil. 4:11–13). Some poor people are happy; some rich people are happy. Some who would be considered failures are happy; some successful people are happy. The dissatisfied office boy who assumes he would be happy as the president of the company is deluded. He would only take his old unhappiness with him into his new situation.

A dramatic historical example of a man who maintained his capacity for life under diverse circumstances is Joseph (Gen. 38–50). As a youth in Canaan, he was happy while superior to his elder brothers. During his adventures in Egypt he was happy as a slave, as the overseer of Potiphar's estates, as a forgotten prisoner, and as prime minister of the Egyptian empire. Although Joseph was stripped of his insignia of rank—the coat of many colors—by his jealous brothers, he retained his leadership ability. They could not remove his mental attitude. His integrity and happiness remained. Joseph was a leader under any circumstances and was as industrious at the bottom of the social scale as he was at the top. Slavery and prison tested and strengthened Joseph; God included inequality tests in his education, grooming this man of genuine humility to become the greatest man of his generation. Joseph remained faithful to the Lord, and his abilities were recognized, although he remained a slave. He was promoted within the system of slavery (Gen. 39:1–5) and within the system of prison administration (Gen. 39:21–23). Rather than complain or conspire to gain his physical freedom, Joseph exercised the freedom in his soul. He oriented to his circumstances while exploiting the opportunities that God provided.

Joseph illustrates the principle that there is nothing demeaning in inequality. Overt status symbols and success standards are not the issue. The true issue is: Are you adjusted to life where you are? Are you grateful for what you have? Are you happy where you are? If you make yourself miserable there, you will never be happy anywhere else. Nor is there any excuse for unhappiness, because God has provided the logistical grace for every believer's spiritual momentum in the divine dynasphere. The believer's happiness depends on his attitude toward learning and applying Bible doctrine. Only you can make yourself happy; only you can make yourself unhappy.

By the time a person leaves home, he must understand that the most significant issue in his life is his own volition. Each individual life is determined by volition, not by environment, genetics, or any other factor that psychology or sociology might hypothesize. Decision creates environment, not environment decision. Man is designed to be formed and shaped by his volition. The proper use of volition makes freedom a reality; the ignoble or irresolute use of volition enslaves him to the details of life. Despite any limitations in circumstances, talent, mentality, health, or appearance, each person has a soul— organizational humility—and the realization of his life's potentialities comes from his free will. Within the organizational humility of the soul, volition carries the authority.

ENFORCED AND GENUINE HUMILITY IN THE SOUL

When a person uses his volition to obey legitimate authority, he has enforced humility. In his job or profession he submits with enforced humility to the authority of his boss. In athletics he willingly respects the authority of the coach and officials. In school he respects the teachers and administrators and adheres to their policies. In every contact with other people, his enforced humility causes him to respect their personal freedom, rights, privacy, and property. Even good manners manifest gate three of the divine dynasphere.

If a child fails to learn humility in the home, he must eventually learn it the hard way from the police officer, the judge, a demanding coach, an exacting employer. In this regard universal military training is vital to any nation. Military training contributes to national defense and, whether or not required by law, represents each man's obligation to his nation's freedom. Military service also sets up a buffer zone in which young men can acquire the discipline they lacked at home—only now under the more stringent demands of a tough drill sergeant.

Still, the best conditions for developing humility are in the home. Few people who establish a pattern of rebellion against their parents ever develop capacity for life, love, or happiness. The young person immersed in unrestrained recalcitrance closes down his future options. Bad decisions become cumulative; each abuse of freedom further reduces his chances of exploiting what God has provided.

Every person lives within the overlapping jurisdictions of different systems of authority, each of which predetermines certain decisions by its policies. If he obeys the rules and contributes to the purpose of those systems of authority that pertain to him, he possesses enforced humility. Orientation to authority is orientation to objective reality.

Genuine humility in an adult soul is a system of thinking and a way of life. As a system of thinking, humility is freedom from arrogance and human viewpoint; as a way of life, humility is grace orientation and capacity for life, thriving under legitimate authority. A believer with genuine humility has the self-discipline necessary to fulfill his objectives in life beyond what anyone requires, forces, or influences him to do. He possesses a personal sense of destiny in that he eagerly submits to the plan of God. He understands the eternal significance of the glorification of the Lord Jesus Christ, so that he positively controls his life, redeems his time, and keeps his priorities straight. He knows that God's plan is greater than he is; he keeps his eye on the goal.

> I have fought that honorable fight. I have finished the course. I have guarded the doctrine [resident in my soul]. In the future a wreath of righteousness [one of many eternal rewards] is reserved for me, which the Lord, the righteous judge [evaluator], will award to me on that day [the Judgment Seat of Christ], and not only to me but also to all those [mature believers] who love His appearance [the Rapture].
> (2 Tim. 4:7, 8)

The believer with genuine humility knows the doctrines of supergrace and eternal rewards, lives in the light of eternity, and enjoys life to the maximum.

HUMILITY IN THE LOCAL CHURCH

God has established a third category of organizational humility, besides the home and the soul, for believers in the Lord Jesus Christ. In addition to the divine institutions for believer and unbeliever, the autonomous local church is a Christian institution, a provision of logistical grace.

Like all effective organizations the local church has purpose, policy, and authority. Its purpose is the communication and inculcation of Bible doctrine. Local church policy is derived from the doctrine taught by the pastor, and all policy and enforcement of policy must support objective Bible teaching. The pastor insists on good manners and restricts activities that would distract serious students from concentrating on the Word of God (2 Tim. 2:14–17). The pastor holds the highest authority in the local church (Heb. 13:7, 17). He oversees a system of administration which, under his overall authority, is staffed by various church officers and deacons to insure the efficient, responsible operation of the church. The pastor's authoritative teaching and his system of delegated authority constitute enforced humility for the royal family.

Within this system of enforced humility, genuine humility is the believer's positive volition toward Bible doctrine. Humility, both enforced and genuine, provides teachability. If you are subjective, if you are continually proving yourself to others, if you relate everything in life to yourself, you are arrogant and unreceptive to all categories of truth. As does any unbeliever, the believer requires genuine humility to adjust to life in general, but he also needs genuine humility to faithfully learn and apply doctrine in the divine dynasphere. The believer's humility is positive volition toward the truth of Bible doctrine as well as the truth of divine establishment.

An arrogant believer may listen to Bible teaching every day, but he is unteachable. He may go through all the proper motions; he may be considered a pillar of the church; but he remains preoccupied with himself. He is too subjective to accept the doctrines that expose his frailties and foibles. A hypocritical eclectic, he chooses to believe only what he wishes to hear and refuses to submit to the whole realm of doctrine. As a result he never grows spiritually despite his continual exposure to doctrine. The humble believer attends Bible teaching to *learn* God's system, not to agree or disagree with the pastor. When a person does not know what God's plan is, his agreement or disagreement means nothing. His pompous pronouncements are the braying of a fool. The humble believer grows because he is receptive to the truth rather than protective of his inflated opinion of himself.

A person who becomes a believer in adulthood has an advantage in the Christian life if he was authority-oriented as an unbeliever. When he accepts Christ, he already resides in gate three, the teachability gate of the love complex. That gives him an edge; he will have little difficulty respecting the authority of the Bible and the pastor. He had something wonderful going as an unbeliever; now he has something better. New gates are available to him. Instead of gate three alone interlocking with basic impersonal love in gate two, now both gate three and gate one, the filling of the Spirit, will interlock with gate two. He has access to new power in gate one, to new truth in gate four, and if he persists his momentum will carry him to the marvelous advantages of maturity in gate eight. The genuinely humble unbeliever who accepts Christ already possesses an affinity for the divine dynasphere. He has a foundation for virtue. As he learns the doctrine of the love complex, he recognizes this system to be the accelerator of his freedom rather than a confining maze of mandates, commandments, and prohibitions, as seen by a believer who resists authority.

A person who has grown up a rebel will have a difficult time as a Christian, just as he will in any endeavor in life. He brings with him into Christianity the prejudices and reactions from his past, all of which he must overcome. But while there is life there is hope; God supplies him with the logistical grace to grow up spiritually. His environment or background is no excuse for failure to advance in the plan of God. He can develop respect for authority and truth, but he must enter gate three the hard way. Under strict academic discipline and enforced humility he must persevere under the authority and doctrinal teaching of his pastor. He must interlock gates one and three with gate two, avoiding mental attitude sins when he is tempted to malign the pastor, resent his message, or criticize other believers in the congregation. He must remain constantly alert and rebound quickly when he sins.

For any believer the transition from ignorance of doctrine at salvation to cognizance at maturity is as difficult as the transition from authority in the home to freedom in adulthood. Few believers succeed. Most lack the tenacity day after day, year after year, to make the many right decisions to learn and apply Bible doctrine, to keep residing and functioning in the divine dynasphere.

THE HUMILITY OF CHRIST

SUBMISSION TO ESTABLISHMENT AUTHORITY

The divine laws of establishment embrace all mankind. Since our Lord Jesus Christ was true humanity, He too was subject to these laws. Born into the organizational humility of a family, He grew up under the enforced humility of His parents. In genuine humility He was always obedient to His parents until He reached maturity (Luke 2:40, 51).

Christ as an adult was subject to the same system of humility that for us replaces the authority of the home. Our Lord's human soul was His organizational humility, and His positive volition in resisting every temptation to sin was

His enforced humility. He was always obedient to the truth. By His own self-discipline He perpetually resided inside the divine dynasphere and developed maximum capacity for life. His enforced humility merged into genuine humility.

Since our Lord lived during the Age of Israel, the local church was not yet established, but Jesus fulfilled the principle of learning doctrine under authority (Luke 2:46). So diligent was He in His studies that at age twelve He surpassed the theologians in His understanding of Old Testament Scriptures (Luke 2:46, 47).

SUBMISSION TO A UNIQUE DESTINY

The prototype divine dynasphere was designed to sustain the humanity of Christ in accomplishing His unique mission, His destiny on earth. God's plan for the First Advent called for Christ to enter Satan's domain as a man, to remain impeccable and thus acceptable to divine righteousness, and to voluntarily go to the Cross as our substitute in payment for the sins of mankind. Christ lived under this additional system of humility to which we do not and cannot adhere.

The plan of God was organizational humility for Christ. The will of God—the sovereignty of the Father, the author of the divine plan—was enforced humility. And Christ's obedience to the Father's plan by going to the Cross was genuine humility. Shortly before He was betrayed, Jesus expressed in prayer His genuine humility under divine authority.

> Saying, "Father, if Thou art willing [God's sovereignty over the humanity of Christ], remove this cup [the Cross] from Me; yet not My will, but Thine be done [Christ's genuine humility]." (Luke 22:42, NASV)

Although the prospect of bearing our sins was abhorrent to Christ, He humbly submitted to divine judgment in our place.

> Keep on thinking this within yourself [gate four of the divine dynasphere], which was also resident in Christ Jesus, who though He existed eternally in the essence of God [Christ is God], did not think equality with God a profit to be seized and held [unlike Satan, Jesus was not arrogant], but He deprived Himself [of the proper function of deity, voluntarily limiting Himself in order to execute God's plan] when He had received the form of a slave, when He was born in the likeness of mankind [perfect man, like Adam before the Fall]. In fact, although He was discovered in the outward appearance as a man [without a sin nature], He humbled

Himself [genuine humility] by becoming obedient to the
point of death, that is, the death of the Cross. (Phil. 2:5–8)[36]

Christ's attitude sets the example: equality was unimportant to Him.
Although coequal with the Father and Holy Spirit, "He did not think equality
with God a profit to be seized and held." Our Lord the Creator submitted to the
utter humility of becoming a creature, a man who was ignored, rejected, mis-
represented, ridiculed, and ultimately crucified. Despite abuse and injustice
from people and the ignominy of exposing Himself to presumptuous, arrogant
attacks from Satan, whom He had created, Christ never succumbed to approbation lust or inordinate ambition. He was motivated by His personal love for God;
genuine humility gave Jesus capacity to appreciate God's faithful support (John
11:41). Far from being discouraged or bitter, our Lord's attitude was one of constant thanksgiving, which is the essence of true worship. Yet without humility
gratitude cannot exist.

NO SELF-GLORIFICATION, NO SELF-DEPRECATION

Jesus Christ had nothing to prove. He came to pay for man's sins, not to
trumpet His own cause. Our Lord did not exalt Himself (John 8:50); the Father
exalted Him (Ps. 110:1). The mission of glorifying Christ on earth was assigned
to the Holy Spirit (John 16:14). The Holy Spirit empowered the apostles to
spread the Gospel of Christ and to record Church Age doctrine in the New Testament; the Spirit also empowers us to glorify Christ inside the divine dynasphere.

God the Father loved the humanity of Christ with conditional, personal
love, which hinged on our Lord's obedience to the Father's plan (John 10:17,
18). Christ succeeded in every respect (John 15:10). He relied on the Father's
power system and was sustained by the Holy Spirit throughout His life, never
once utilizing His own divine power to act independently of the Father's plan or
to benefit Himself (Matt. 4:3–11).[37] Christ's submission to the plan of God
resulted in *judgment*; our submission results in *blessing*. This complete reversal
of the purpose of the divine dynasphere reveals the efficacy of Christ's finished
work and the scope of God's impersonal love for mankind.

Knowledge of Bible doctrine fuels in us the same mental dynamics that
Christ possessed. But our genuine humility orients us to blessing, not cursing,
from the justice of God. Humility generates gratitude, which results in true worship and love of God. In blind arrogance some Christians falsely claim to be
humble in that they follow Christ in His sufferings, failing to recognize that

---

36. Philippians 2:5-8 is further analyzed below, p. 199.
37. See below, pp. 196-99.

Christ's sufferings were unique. There is no spiritual significance or merit in our pain; only the work of Christ on the Cross was efficacious for our salvation. We add nothing to His finished work. There is no objectivity in the round-shouldered, self-deprecating manner affected by some Christians as a supposed sign of spirituality. This is not what the Bible means by humility. Christianity is not a religion that glorifies believers for their legalism, sacrifice, and self-denial; Christianity is a life of multifaceted prosperity that glorifies the Lord Jesus Christ. Humility is orientation to principle, to truth, to the reality of God's grace. False modesty is a subtle form of arrogance.

V
Gate Four, Spiritual Momentum

THE MOST IMPORTANT GATE

The fourth gate of the divine dynasphere is a double gate—perception and application of Bible doctrine—that opens upon the richest treasure in the universe. Bible doctrine is the thinking of God. The Bible is designated as the Word of God (Heb. 4:12), the Mind of Christ (1 Cor. 2:16), and the Voice of the Holy Spirit (Heb. 3:7). Doctrine is our door to the reality of God and His marvelous plan. His Word is more reliable than anything we see, hear, smell, taste, or feel; more real than empirical knowledge (2 Pet. 1:12–21).

Bible doctrine preexisted the human race (Prov. 8), so that through the generosity of logistical grace, God makes available to us the wisdom of the ages. During the Church Age God reveals His essence and plan only through His written Word, the completed, inerrant canon of Scripture. Our attitude toward doctrine *is* our attitude toward God. If we pursue doctrine, we love God; if we listen to Bible teaching only at our convenience or when we are in trouble, then we ignore and insult God, despite our pious pretenses. The one form of worship that gives meaning to all other expressions of worship is the perception and application of doctrine. Without a thorough, growing knowledge of doctrine, any alleged worship of God becomes ritual without reality (Heb. 10:1–4).

> I myself will worship toward the temple of Your holiness.
> (Ps. 138:2*a*)

When David wrote Psalm 138, the earthly temple did not yet exist. He was reflecting on the doctrine in his soul, which revealed God in the true Holy of

Holies located in heaven.[38] In the next generation David's son, Solomon, would construct the temple in Jerusalem to exacting divine specifications. As a place of worship, the temple itself was designed to communicate doctrine by its very structure and furnishings.

> And [I will] celebrate Your Person because of Your grace
> and because of Your truth [doctrine]. (Ps. 138:2*b*)

God's grace enabled David to learn doctrine, which gave him capacity to appreciate and delight in the essence of God. God's Person is who and what He is, His divine essence, the perfect coalescence of all His attributes. God *has* attributes, but God *is* a Person. Now David makes one of the most dramatic statements in all of Scripture.

> Because You have magnified Your Word [doctrinal
> teaching] over Your reputation. (Ps. 138:2*c*)

God Himself elevates Bible doctrine above all else, above even His own name. In no other way can we approach Him, understand Him, or fulfill His plan for our lives. Bible doctrine is more important than the food we eat or the air we breathe. Divine blessings in both time and eternity are distributed according to the believer's understanding of doctrine (Isa. 53:12). Nations rise or fall because of doctrine (Micah 4:1-6). Jesus Christ controls history in reverence for the doctrine in the souls of believers. As we grow in knowledge of doctrine, we become personally familiar with the Lord Jesus Christ.

Perception and application of Bible doctrine constitute the central gate of the divine dynasphere. The gates that precede gate four support its function; those that follow result from its function. Perception and application of God's Word generate spiritual momentum in the Christian's life.

MANDATES TO LEARN AND APPLY DOCTRINE

The Scriptures repeatedly mandate the intake and use of doctrine, as expressed by John in relation to several young people in his congregation in Ephesus (2 John 1-6). They were children of Lady Nympha, a noblewoman who opened her home in Laodicea to one of John's six nonresident congregations (Col. 4:15, 16; Rev. 2, 3). John recognized Nympha's magnificent work in rearing her children. Evidently she had accomplished this alone, as a widow, inculcating into them the respect of enforced humility. Several of her children

---

38. See Thieme, *Blood of Christ,* pp. 26-29; idem, *Levitical Offerings* (1973), p. 70.

had developed genuine humility and were positive toward Bible doctrine. They had moved from Laodicea to Ephesus in order to learn doctrine from John face to face, while their mother continued to hear his written sermons, or epistles, which were read to the congregation in her home.

> I was very pleased because I discovered that some of your children continued their momentum by means of doctrine, even as we have received mandate from the Father. (2 John 4)

John explains that this divine command for "continued...momentum by means of doctrine" is obeyed only inside the divine dynasphere.

> And now, great lady, I make a request of you, not as writing to you a new mandate but a command which you have heard from the beginning [of the Church Age], that we might love one another [with impersonal love], and the love [love complex] is this, that we should keep walking in compliance with His commands [learning doctrine depends on the other gates of the system]. And this is the mandate just as you heard from the beginning, that you should keep walking in it [residence and function in the love complex]. (2 John 5, 6)

The divine mandate to learn and apply doctrine is implied in Paul's dissertation on the pastor's professional objectives.

> And He [glorified Christ, the initial giver of spiritual gifts] gave some [certain members of the royal family]...[to be] pastor-teachers for the purpose of training and equipping the saints for spiritual combat, for the purpose of the occupation of the ministry [each pastor's congregation will include future pastors], for the purpose of the edification [the edification complex of the soul, completed upon reaching gate eight of the divine dynasphere] of the body of Christ [the royal family on earth], because of the consistency of doctrinal teaching and the full knowledge of the Son of God, to a mature status, to the standard of maturity that belongs to the fullness of Christ [in the prototype divine dynasphere]. (Eph. 4:11-13)

Spiritual maturity comes through knowledge and application of the Mind of Christ, which results in emulating the integrity and capacity for life He acquired in the original love complex. "Full knowledge" or *epignosis* in the Greek (pronounced eppy-*no*-sis) is doctrine that the Christian understands and believes, doctrine available in his soul for immediate, accurate application to life.[39] The development of *epignosis* in those who listen to his teaching, in contrast to *gnosis*, which is purely academic knowledge, is the professional objective of the pastor.

Paul continues with the pastor's job description. The pastor must study and teach doctrine in the power of the Holy Spirit inside the love complex.

> In order that we no longer be immature, but by the teaching
> of doctrine in the sphere of love [the love complex], you
> [pastors] might cause them [believers in the congregation] to
> grow up by the all things [of Bible doctrine] with respect to
> Him who is the absolute, even Christ. (Eph. 4:14, 15)

Writing to the Thessalonians, Paul reiterates the divine mandate, but this time the command is related to the congregation. Those who listen to the pastor must also reside in the love complex in order to benefit from the spiritual truth they hear.

> But we request you, brethren [members of the royal family],
> that you appreciate those [pastors] who diligently labor
> among you and have charge over you [enforced humility]
> and give you instruction [doctrinal teaching], that you
> esteem them very highly in the sphere of love [the love com-
> plex] because of their work. (1. Thess. 5:12, 13*a*).

A pastor should be respected for his sound knowledge and conscientiousness in teaching. His "diligent labor" consists of long hours every day in disciplined, concentrated study, complemented by an appropriately full teaching schedule. He *is* an authority on doctrine; he *has* authority in the local church. Members of the congregation demonstrate their appreciation for the pastor by submitting to his authority and concentrating on his teaching—gates three and four of the divine dynasphere.

Believers appreciate their pastor by allowing his work to produce its intended result in their lives. Any other expression of gratitude comes in a distant second place. The honest, humble pastor considers himself a voice, a spokesman who communicates God's Word (Matt. 3:3). He does not promote himself. He is impressed with God's wisdom, not his own. He is most gratified by those who receive his doctrinal teaching as from the Lord and use that doctrine in their own lives as they advance to maturity.

---

39. See below, pp. 98-100. See also Thieme, *Grace Apparatus Perception* (1974).

DOCTRINE AND LOVE AS A WAY OF LIFE

All virtue, love, and genuine humility, for believer or unbeliever, are found only inside the divine dynasphere. Now gate four represents the principle that all truth is found only in the divine dynasphere. In gate three the unbeliever can comprehend the truth of divine establishment, but the believer alone has access to the doctrines of the Word of God. In gate four he advances beyond any strength, integrity, humility, wisdom, or happiness that the unbeliever can achieve.

Love cannot exist without truth. Truth makes love possible, because genuine love is rational, never absurd, always dependent on thought, never strictly emotional. As the pattern for the love complex, divine love is rational because it is always linked with God's absolutely consistent integrity. Consistency of thought *is* rationality, and by virtue of His immutability, omniscience, and veracity, God is perfectly rational, totally logical. God is truth, and God is love; these two attributes are inseparable.

Nor can truth and love be separated in the believer. The Christian's capacity for impersonal and personal love is increased by his consistent function in gate four. Understanding of doctrine creates capacity for love. At gate four the believer fulfills the ultimate purpose of the divine dynasphere: God's objective for us is that we understand and live by His Word. God reveals Himself in the Scriptures, and a believer's daily attitude toward Bible doctrine is the index of his love for God.

Learning Bible doctrine requires academic discipline, but God's Word surpasses any subject that he might be taught in a school or college classroom. Doctrine is supernatural information. God's revelation extends beyond the range of human intellect or concentration and beyond man's empirical powers to observe his environment. More than mastering and reciting an academic subject, learning and applying doctrine constitute a way of life, the Christian way of life in the divine dynasphere.

> But He [Christ] answered and said, "It is written, 'Man shall not live on bread alone, but on every word that proceeds out of the mouth of God.'" (Matt. 4:4, NASV)

The Christian life both depends on doctrine and supports the intake of doctrine. Learning God's Word is not an isolated activity; it is part of the complete, interlocking system. The first three gates of the divine game plan operate in concert to motivate faithfulness to doctrine, which in turn strengthens all the gates.

THE INTERLOCK OF THE FIRST THREE GATES

POWER AND OBJECTIVITY

Spiritual momentum from gate four of the divine dynasphere depends on the first three gates. Gates one, two, and three furnish the power, objectivity, teachability, and motivation needed to transfer doctrine from the written pages of Scripture into the believer's soul and then out again as application to life.

We possess no capacity to assimilate doctrine apart from the unseen power of the Holy Spirit.

> I [Jesus Christ, speaking to His disciples prior to the Church Age] have many more things to teach you, but you cannot carry them [in your minds] now. But when He, the Spirit of Truth, comes [when the divine dynasphere is given], He [the Holy Spirit] will guide you into all doctrine....He shall glorify Me, for He shall take of Mine [Bible doctrine is the Mind of Christ], and He shall communicate it to you. (John 16:12, 14)

We are able to understand spiritual truth only when filled with the Spirit. As doctrine accumulates in our souls, the Holy Spirit uses that doctrine to increase our capacity to understand more doctrine. The more you learn, the more you can learn. Doctrine builds on doctrine.

You must be objective to avoid misinterpreting or misapplying doctrine. This objectivity derives primarily from gate two. In gate two reliance on divine promises and the exercise of impersonal love secure freedom from mental attitude sins, eliminating the subjectivity of arrogance, jealousy, self-pity, bitterness, or a guilt complex. By exercising basic impersonal love, and rebounding when necessary, you maintain your orientation to the essentials of life, even when people or circumstances challenge you to lose your perspective and turn your eyes on self. The two primary techniques for applying doctrine in gate four are extensions of gate two: claiming promises and implementing basic impersonal love. Stage one of the faith-rest drill, claiming promises, establishes the relaxed mental attitude needed to rationally *think* doctrine, and the switch from personal love or hatred to impersonal love maintains objectivity.

Gate three of the divine dynasphere also contributes to objectivity. Humility is obedience to authority, and authority-orientation is orientation to reality. Reality is objective, not subjective. The genuinely humble believer understands his significance in the overall scheme of God's plan and human history; he recognizes that he is dependent on doctrine for his integrity and that the source of his happiness is the divine dynasphere. The humble believer possesses a personal sense of destiny as he witnesses the glorification of Jesus Christ in his life. Objectivity in gate three makes him receptive and teachable; he is motivated to learn the truth rather than prove how much he knows or how superior he is. The more doctrine he learns in gate four, the stronger becomes his objectivity in gates two and three, which, barring the intrusion of arrogance, motivates him to learn and apply still more doctrine.

MOTIVATION

OBEDIENCE AND MOTIVATIONAL VIRTUE

Motivation is a major issue in the Christian life. When we study virtue, we will discover that motivational virtues exist inside the divine dynasphere. A motivational virtue is the invisible counterpart for each visible, functional virtue. For example, the virtue of confidence toward God motivates the functional virtue of courage toward man and circumstances.[40] All functional virtues stem from motivational virtues, and all motivational virtues originate from your free-will decisions to obey God's mandates.

God's power system is perfect in that it not only leads to spiritual maturity but also motivates its own momentum (Phil. 2:13). Motivation for the perception and application of doctrine is created by obedience to the mandates related to gates one, two, and three. But even in God's complete, self-energized system, human volition remains the key. You can choose to reside in the divine dynasphere or reject God's plan and live in one of Satan's counterfeit systems.

No one can reach into another person's soul and switch on motivation like a light in the dark. Nor can God force you to have the correct motivation toward His plan. He will never coerce your free will. Although God's game plan is designed for your maximum benefit and His eternal glory, you are free to ignore His mandates. If you assume that your own plans are better than God's design, you oppose yourself and Him, create your own misery, and incur divine discipline. But fear of punishment is not the proper motive for adhering to divine policy. If you are objective, you obey initially out of respect for God and eventually from personal love for God as you come to know and appreciate Him through His Word. This motivation—this positive volition—must emanate from your own soul, not from any external source.

---

40. See below, pp. 114-15, 117-20.

ESTABLISHING PRIORITIES, ORGANIZING A ROUTINE

Among believers or unbelievers the most admirable and successful people are self-motivated. In the conscience of the soul, where the norms and standards and scale of values reside, these individuals have established true priorities, and they make decisions consistent with those priorities. The self-motivated believer has identified his primary objective in life: spiritual maturity, which glorifies Christ. This objective becomes the criterion for interpreting any situation that may arise. Every decision and every course of action supports this chosen objective; Bible doctrine takes first priority. This lucid self-motivation places him in a position of strength. He understands what is most valuable, and he will not be deceived or cajoled into opposing himself. Good decisions can be made only from a position of strength, inside the divine dynasphere. Only bad decisions can be made from a position of weakness, outside the divine dynasphere.

A self-motivated believer operating from a position of strength builds his life on the principle of virtue first, doctrine first. He establishes a routine: for each day he decides what he wishes to accomplish that day. He sets aside time for doctrine, time for work, time for family, time for eating and sleeping, time for entertainment and social life. Routine must be built on priorities, ranked according to importance. Routine organizes a person's life each day so that he accomplishes his objectives, fulfills his own principles. A routine is not a negative concept for dull, humorless people. Only through a routine can anyone harness his own time and energy and achieve anything in life either spiritually or temporally. Organization is good routine. Routine should be broken only by unusual events, like disasters or celebrations, not by illegitimate distractions. Routine and organization are professionalism in every area of life. A disorganized person is a loser.

Some noble person may positively influence you to learn God's Word, but that external impetus will not carry you. There is no substitute for self-motivation. *You* must give doctrine first priority, make your own decisions, establish and maintain your own integrity. We all face distractions, opposition, and influences that would prevent us from consistently learning and applying Bible doctrine. We must be motivated from within if we hope to fulfill God's game plan over the course of our lives. Self-motivation is a synonym for one's own positive volition. Even the best influence, the wisest advice, the most positive encouragement cannot keep you in the divine dynasphere and sustain your spiritual momentum.

IMMATURE AND MATURE MOTIVES

Self-motivation, like teachability, is an offshoot of humility. A humble person is receptive to truth and motivated to learn. Self-motivation can be developed by believer or unbeliever under the laws of divine establishment in gate three. When a young person becomes an adult, he assumes responsibility for his own motivation, his own thoughts, decisions, and actions. From genuine humility he begins to make his own decisions rather than depend on his parents, although humility does not exclude seeking good advice when necessary.

Unlike the youth who eventually leaves behind parental authority, a believer never outgrows his need for Bible teaching and the authority of his pastor. But, as in the home, the believer's motivation does change as he grows up spiritually. A new believer is not motivated by love for God. He may have a new lease on life, knowing that his sins are forgiven; he may be grateful for the Cross; he may inordinately fear divine retribution; he may be caught up in emotional zeal; he may be currying divine favor or striving to please the person who presented the Gospel to him. Some of his motives may be legitimate, others not, but even the best salvation motivation will not carry him far. The realization that he is forgiven and going to heaven is a feeble flame. The divine mandates connected with gate four of God's power system demand that he take up the challenge of the Christian life, to grow in the full knowledge of God.

Initially you must execute God's game plan from enforced humility. God commands perception of doctrine; you simply obey. As you learn doctrine, you realize that God has a purpose for your life. You discover that you possess God's righteousness, that He supports you with logistical grace, that rebound is instantly available, that God has adopted you as spiritual royalty forever. You learn that you already possess tremendous blessings for which to be grateful, with greater blessings yet to come, and you begin to appreciate the source. You begin to love the Lord Jesus Christ. Within your soul your motivation changes from enforced humility to genuine humility, to love for God, to occupation with Christ. Doctrine becomes supremely important to you. Although you are never impervious to distractions, you are not as vulnerable as when a new believer. You have learned to maintain your own priorities. You have learned to say no to people and decline "opportunities" when necessary. You have learned to center your life on the treasure of highest value, the Word of God.

Most believers never parlay their initial motivation into the daily self-motivation that can carry them through many years to spiritual maturity. They lack the humility to accept a doctrinal pastor's authority, or they lack the will and discipline to master doctrines that are difficult or seemingly irrelevant. They never make a habit of learning doctrine. Instead of seeking the truth, they search for a pastor who will flatter and fawn over them. They do not desire truth or a mature relationship with God; they want the approbation of a scintillating personality who will visit them, counsel them, entertain their questions, and stimulate their emotions—everything but teach orthodox Bible doctrine. Believers who gravitate to such a pastor appease their own arrogance and accommodate themselves in weakness. A believer consolidates a position of strength only through his personal initiative in submitting to gate four.

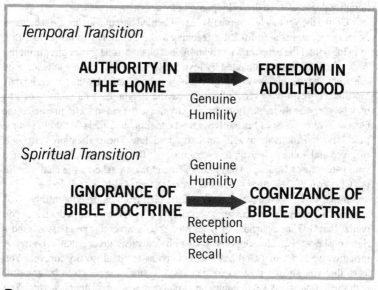

Temporal Transition

AUTHORITY IN THE HOME   →   **FREEDOM IN ADULTHOOD**

Genuine Humility

Spiritual Transition

Genuine Humility

IGNORANCE OF BIBLE DOCTRINE   →   **COGNIZANCE OF BIBLE DOCTRINE**

Reception
Retention
Recall

THE TWO MOST DIFFICULT TRANSITIONS IN LIFE

The two most difficult transitions in life overlap at gate four of the love complex. At physical birth we begin life under parental authority and protection; we must become worthy of adult freedom. We make this transition through teachability under the virtue of genuine humility. At spiritual birth we begin spiritual life ignorant of God and His plan and must become cognizant of His purpose for our lives. Again, we make this transition through enforced and genuine humility. Consistent intake and application of Bible doctrine over an extended period of time accomplishes this second difficult transition, the requisite momentum being sustained by self-motivation. The believer's self-motivation manifests itself as academic discipline under his pastor's Bible teaching in the local church.

> Therefore, humble yourselves ["humble": achieve genuine humility; "yourselves": from self-motivation] under the mighty hand of God [the Father, the inventor of the divine

dynasphere] that He may promote you [with supergrace blessings] at the proper time [after you reach maturity]. (1 Peter 5:6)

CONCENTRATION

All true love requires concentration. In impersonal love the subject concentrates on his own priorities; he declines to besmirch his integrity by succumbing to hatred, envy, bitterness, self-righteousness, or disillusionment toward the object. In personal love the subject concentrates on the object, on that person's attractiveness, character, thoughts, and feelings. Concentration is essential to genuine sensitivity toward others. Without concentration there can be no capacity for life, no success in any endeavor, and most detrimental, without concentration no one can learn or use doctrine in the divine dynasphere.

In addition to divine power, objectivity, and the teachability that accompanies self-motivation, the ability to concentrate is another prerequisite for the function of gate four. This requirement is also fulfilled by the first three gates of the love complex.

At gate one God the Holy Spirit enhances the believer's concentration. This is the teaching ministry of the *Parakletos,* the Energizer or Helper, who enables man's finite mind to comprehend the infinite wisdom of God in Bible doctrine.

At gate two, divine promises and basic impersonal love set aside distractions that would disturb concentration. Concentration is the opposite of distraction; it is focusing your attention on a single object to the exclusion of all others. If you cannot sustain mental focus, you are unstable. You lack the attention span required to pursue any thought to its conclusion. You vacillate from one subject to another. The relaxed mental attitude of gate two enables you to operate from your own mental integrity rather than swerve indiscriminately from topic to topic.

In gate three teachability makes you a good listener. As you learn doctrine under enforced humility in Bible class, you simultaneously develop your ability to concentrate. When first you listen to Bible teaching, you may be able to concentrate for only five minutes before you become bored and restless. You may have to fall back on stoic poise and plain good manners toward others in the congregation to get you through to the benediction. But if you keep returning to Bible class, obedient under enforced humility (Heb. 10:25), your span of attention will gradually increase until you can easily follow the entire message, even when the topic is technical or unappealing to your usual interests.

As a by-product of gate four, this increased ability to sustain your concentration will carry over into everything you do. You are able to devote more concentrated energy to your business or profession. History and literature become fascinating. Your capacity for love improves. Life becomes richer.

PERCEPTION AND APPLICATION RELATED TO TWO ROYAL WARRANTS

PRIESTS AND AMBASSADORS

At the moment of salvation, when we first enter the divine dynasphere as believers, we receive two commissions from God related to the perception and application of Bible doctrine. I call these commissions "warrants," since God has given them to us in the content of His Word.

A warrant is a written document that conveys certain powers and authorizes the performance of certain duties and responsibilities. A warrant officer in the army, for example, has received a document from the President entrusting him with the authority to carry out his assigned duties. Even a warrant for arrest illustrates the principle, since such a legal warrant is a document issued by a judge authorizing a police officer to carry out the duty of taking someone into custody.

As members of the royal family of God, we have received two warrants from God, which authorize us to carry out certain spiritual responsibilities. We have been appointed *royal priests* and *royal ambassadors*. These two appointments define our function in the divine dynasphere and explain the invisible and visible aspects of the Christian life.

> And He [Jesus Christ] has provided for us a royal power [the divine dynasphere] [to function as] priests to God, even His Father. (Rev. 1:6)

> But you [members of the royal family] are an elect race [chosen for privilege, regardless of human ancestry], a royal priesthood, a holy nation [the spiritual pivot of God's client nation], a people for God's own possession [purchased at the Cross and dependent on God's power system, you are not your own], that you may proclaim [through the production of virtue] the virtues of Him [Jesus Christ in the prototype divine dynasphere] who has called you [selected you for the privileges of royalty because you believed in Christ during the Church Age] out of darkness [satanic influence] into His marvelous light [the divine dynasphere) (1 Pet. 2:9)

> Therefore, we are ambassadors for Christ, as though God
> were making His appeal through us. (2 Cor. 5:20*a*)

A divine warrant is never to be treated frivolously. These warrants from God appoint us to the two highest offices anyone can hold in this life. In *The Integrity of God,* the doctrines of our priesthood and ambassadorship are developed in detail.[41] We need only summarize these principles.

THE ROYAL PRIESTHOOD

During the previous dispensation, a specialized priesthood existed in Israel.[42] The priests were members of the tribe of Levi; they carried out the detailed responsibilities connected with animal sacrifices and holy days, which taught Bible doctrine by means of ritual training aids. The Levitical priests proclaimed written doctrine and represented the people before God.

Now that the Jewish Age has been interrupted and the Church Age inserted in its place, a universal priesthood exists. Jesus Christ is our High Priest (Heb. 6:17–20). Since every member of the royal family is in union with Him, we all share His priesthood. Unlike the Levitical priesthood, the office of the royal priesthood is not hereditary, but perpetual; not based on physical birth, but regeneration. You are a priest; I am a priest. Whether young, old, male, female, mature, immature, in the divine dynasphere, or in Satan's system, all Church Age believers are permanent members of our Lord's *royal order of priesthood* (Heb. 7:1–3).

That does not mean, however, that we are equal. A few priests are pastors (one in charge of each congregation); most priests are members of the congregation. After many years of academic preparation, the priest who is also a pastor can grow spiritually through his own full-time study of the Word, whereas the priests in the congregation grow only under the pastor's authoritative teaching. Spiritual growth is always a function of the priesthood; the privacy of the priesthood is designed for maximum perception of doctrine. Likewise, spiritual blessings from God are always given to us under our priesthood. Whether in the pulpit or in the pew, the priesthood is our invisible, personal relationship with God.

As believer-priests we represent ourselves before God. We do not need to confess our sins to a member of the clergy; we confess them immediately, silently, privately, directly to God (1 John 1:9). Nor do we need anyone to pray on our behalf. We are commanded to come boldly before the throne of grace (Heb. 4:16). And we do not require a special category of priests to perform rituals for

---

41. Pp. 95–100.

42. See Thieme, *Levitical Offerings.*

us. The rituals of the Levitical priesthood were fulfilled by Christ at the Cross and have been superseded as teaching aids by the completion of the canon of Scripture. The Church Age is the age of thought, not ritual. The only ritual mandated for the royal family is the Eucharist or Communion, in which every believer is commanded to participate (1 Cor. 11:23–26).[43]

The divine warrant that appoints us priests to God authorizes us to represent ourselves before Him. Our responsibility as priests is to grow spiritually through the perception of doctrine at gate four of the love complex. Our priesthood is the invisible side of the Christian life.

THE ROYAL AMBASSADORSHIP

Christ was a priest during the First Advent, but He was also an ambassador. In hypostatic union—undiminished deity and true humanity united in one Person forever—Christ represented God to man in the devil's world (Heb. 1:2). In union with Christ, every member of the royal family shares His ambassadorship.

Christ has been absent from the earth since His ascension, and we now represent Him, the King of Kings glorified at the right hand of the Father (Heb. 1:3–9; Rev. 19:16). Our ambassadorial instructions are in written form, the completed canon of Scripture, which is the Mind of Christ (1 Cor. 2:16). By word and by life, we represent *His* policies, not our own. We are citizens of heaven, not of Satan's kingdom, and as God's emissaries we are supported and protected by Him in the enemy kingdom of the devil.

Every believer is in full-time Christian service. We may not wear Prince Albert coats, striped pants, and top hats and mix with foreign nobility, but we are *ambassadors* nonetheless. Whatever we do, wherever we are, we are Christ's representatives (Rom. 12:11).

In contrast to our priesthood, our ambassadorship is our overt, visible relationship with people and circumstances. As royal ambassadors we proclaim Christ in the love complex.

> That [we] may proclaim the virtues of Him who called [us]
> out of darkness into His marvelous light. (1 Pet. 2:9*b*)

We are responsible to present the Gospel to unbelievers (2 Cor. 5:20; Eph. 6:20), but our ambassadorship goes farther than that. Witnessing, giving testimonies, serving in the local church, working in evangelistic meetings, in foreign missions, or in Christian service organizations—all this, if properly motivated, can be part of the spiritual ambassador's function. The believer's royal ambassa-

---

43. See Thieme, *Blood of Christ*, pp. 31–34.

dorship encompasses all the visible virtues produced by the application of doctrine. Hence, our ambassadorship, like our priesthood, is related to gate four of the divine dynasphere.

Gate four of the love complex is the key to the Christian life. All the gates that precede gate four are support gates, and all those that follow are result gates. All spiritual advance and momentum come from the dual functions of the fourth gate of the divine dynasphere. The *perception* of doctrine is the primary responsibility of the royal priest; the *application* of doctrine is the primary responsibility of the royal ambassador.

Royal Priest	Royal Ambassador
Represent self before God	Represent God before man
Directed toward God	Directed toward man
Invisible	Visible
Relationship with God	Relationships with man
Produce motivational virtues Worship Confidence Personal love	Produce functional virtues Virtue-Morality Courage Impersonal love
Perception of doctrine	Application of doctrine
Powered by the divine dynasphere	Powered by the divine dynasphere
Blessings from God	Blessings to man

CHURCH AGE WARRANTS AS PRIEST AND AMBASSADOR

As priests we represent ourselves before God; as ambassadors we represent God before man. Our priesthood is directed toward God; our ambassadorship, toward man. Furthermore, our warrants explain the invisible and visible parts of the Christian life. Our priesthood is our invisible private relationship with God in which we produce the motivational virtues; our ambassadorship is our visible public relationship with people and circumstances.

The ambassadorship depends on the priesthood; the visible depends on the invisible. And the power in both the perception and application of doctrine, toward both God and man, is the power of the divine dynasphere. No matter what we may do or how spiritual we may appear to others, we have no Christian impact without the concurrent execution of our priesthood and our ambassadorship in all of the pertinent gates of God's game plan. As priest and ambassador, each member of the royal family of God lives his own life before the Lord and makes his own decisions based on the truth resident in his soul.

FAITH-PERCEPTION

Never do we earn or deserve any credit in the divine dynasphere. God's game plan for the royal family is animated by grace, not human achievement. In gate four of the love complex, as in every gate, God does all the work and we reap the benefits.

Man possesses three basic means of perception: rationalism, empiricism, and faith. In rationalism man engages his intellect, deducing a logical system to explain reality. In empiricism man hones his powers of observation for discovering answers in the world and the universe around him. Man has explored and exploited many combinations of rationalism and empiricism throughout history, but in every philosophical or scientific system, man's abilities and efforts receive the credit. If God's plan relied at any point on our merits, that would become the weak link that would destroy the chain. Imperfect man can have no meritorious role in God's perfect plan.

I believe in	Christ
Subject	Object
Accomplishes no work for salvation	Accomplished all the work for salvation
No merit	All the merit
Receives no glory	Receives all the glory

FAITH AS NONMERITORIOUS PERCEPTION

Man's third system of perception is nonmeritorious. In faith the credit does not belong to the subject but to the object, not to the one who believes but to what is believed. This explains why faith is the only means of appropriating salvation. When sinful man believes in Christ, the subject has no merit. The object, Jesus Christ, has all the merit. Only Christ satisfies the absolute standards of God's integrity. In this manner fallen man enters the plan of God without compromising God's character or corrupting His plan.

After salvation the believer is commanded to reside and function in the divine dynasphere, but God does not suddenly reverse His policy. We are saved by grace; we must live by grace. Grace continues to exclude all human merit. Faith remains the only means of perceiving and applying Bible doctrine.

God has supplied us with every prerequisite for learning His Word: the canon of Scripture, a pastor-teacher, the local church, the filling of the Holy Spirit, rebound, the human soul, the human spirit, physical life, and protection in the devil's world. These grace provisions are part of the grace apparatus for perception, or GAP, which is the subject of a separate book.[44]

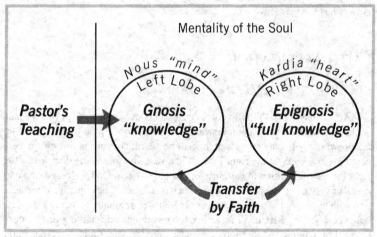

FAITH-PERCEPTION IN LEARNING BIBLE DOCTRINE

To summarize GAP: the believer filled with the Spirit concentrates on the pastor's message, resulting in *gnosis,* "knowledge," in the mentality of the soul. The mentality has two parts: the *nous,* translated "mind," and the *kardia,*

---

44. Thieme, *Grace Apparatus Perception.*

"heart." I call the *nous* the left lobe and the *kardia* the right lobe.[45] The left lobe is the home of *gnosis;* the right lobe is the repository of *epignosis,* "full knowledge."

Gnosis in the left lobe is receptive comprehension, academic knowledge that is not usable for application to life. A believer may be able to quote many verses or talk at length about many Biblical subjects, but if his knowledge is only *gnosis,* it is not edifying. Academic arrogance can exist in theology as easily as in any other field of learning (1 Cor. 1:17—2:16; 3:19; 8:1). The application of *gnosis* doctrine is *mis*application, and true doctrines misapplied generate legalism, inflexibility, insensitivity, and intolerance, compounding arrogance.

At the *gnosis* stage of GAP, the believer clearly perceives a point of doctrine and now faces the issue of faith: does he or does he not believe what he has learned? If he believes, that doctrine is transferred to the right lobe and becomes *epignosis.* By means of faith, temporary comprehension becomes genuine understanding of divine truth. Only *epignosis* can be applied as wisdom and spiritual common sense. *Epignosis* is also the building material for the edification complex of the soul.[46] The process of transferring doctrine from the left to the right lobe, of converting *gnosis* to *epignosis,* is faith-perception. Doctrine always has the merit; we who believe do not.

FAITH-APPLICATION

RECEPTION, RETENTION, RECALL

According to his ability to concentrate, a believer may hear or *receive* half of the doctrinal message communicated by his pastor. By faith-perception, he may *retain* only twenty percent of the half he heard, converting this twenty percent into *epignosis* in his right lobe. When required to use the doctrine in his right lobe as application toward man or worship toward God, he may be able to *recall* only one percent of the *epignosis* he has retained. The objective is inculcation with the truth, but usable doctrine accumulates gradually in increments. The believer develops a frame of reference for receiving and retaining further doctrine. Truth builds upon truth. He must persist in learning "precept upon precept, . . . line upon line" (Isa. 28:10). This explains why the believer must be faithful in listening to Bible teaching as a daily routine and emphasizes the value of repetition by the pastor. Bible doctrine cannot be absorbed on a spurt of inspiration.

---

45.   These are not the physical lobes of the brain but refer to the immaterial soul and illustrate the function of mentality.

46.   See below, pp. 183-88.

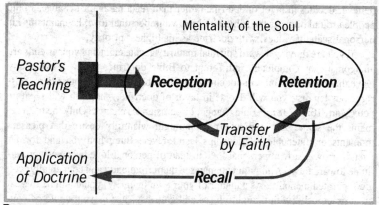

RECEPTION, RETENTION, RECALL

Spiritual maturity belongs to the pluggers, to those who perpetuate momentum in the divine dynasphere undeterred over the years. Your personal intake and application of doctrine constitute their own reward as you benefit from living the truth. But learning and using God's Word also represent an extended, lifelong display of your positive volition. Nonmeritorious positive volition resolves the angelic conflict: the angels watch mankind and observe man's positive volition, which glorifies the Lord Jesus Christ (Luke 15:7, 10; 1 Cor. 4:9; 6:3; Eph. 3:10; 1 Tim. 3:16; 5:21; 1 Pet. 1:12). As in perception, so also in application, human merit is excluded from God's perfect plan. Both retaining and recalling the Bible doctrine that you receive are accomplished by faith.

In faith-application the believer draws upon his inner resources of doctrine to maintain his own integrity, cope with his own problems, and take control of his own life. With *epignosis* doctrine in his soul, he becomes spiritually self-sustaining. He is mentally well-organized so that he can face life with courage. By faith he employs both of the two basic techniques for applying doctrine: impersonal love and the faith-rest drill.

EMPHASIZING IMPERSONAL LOVE

The first technique in the faith-application of doctrine is the utilization of *impersonal love* in place of personal love. In the prototype divine dynasphere Christ applied this principle most dramatically on the Cross. Separation is always directed *toward,* never *away from,* so that when tested, the advancing believer decides in favor of doctrine rather than reacting against changes in the people around him. As the subject of his own impersonal love, he maintains his personal scale of values, with doctrine as his highest priority.

If you are moving toward spiritual maturity at gate eight and your friends are antagonistic or completely indifferent to Bible doctrine, you will eventually leave them behind. You will not choose against them, becoming a strident, self-righteous legalist; you will decide in favor of doctrine. The truth will separate you (Matt. 10:34–38). People change; circumstances change. Only the truth remains the same. An immature person might wishfully desire that pleasant moments or untenable relationships last forever. But when you and former friends grow apart, impersonal love instead of personal love becomes your attitude toward them. Although you may see them frequently and congenially, you are separated mentally. As a matter of your own integrity, you continue to treat them graciously, with thoughtfulness and courtesy, just as you would be considerate of anyone else in your periphery.

The most demanding tests involving people are not tests that require a gradual shift from personal to impersonal love but those that demand an immediate application of impersonal love. When a friend or loved one offends you in some way, you are not justified in lowering yourself to the level of hatred, self-pity, or retaliation. Resentment or hostility would only complicate the matter, and two wrongs never make a right. Instead, you fall back on your own integrity. You remember the character of the subject rather than the imperfections of the object. No one is perfect. Everyone has weaknesses. From time to time we all require toleration from the integrity of those we love. Impersonal love covers a multitude of flaws and permits personal love to flourish between imperfect, changing people.

THE FAITH-REST DRILL

CONQUERING FEAR WITH PROMISES

The second technique for applying doctrine is the *faith-rest drill,* a versatile technique for overcoming any difficulty, problem, or disaster in life. By *faith* the believer applies doctrine logically while *resting* in God's promises. In the three steps of the faith-rest drill, the believer first establishes the relaxed mental attitude of gate two. He then concentrates on pertinent doctrines in a logical rationale, restoring divine-viewpoint thinking. Finally, he reaches doctrinal conclusions and takes control of the situation.

Since concentration on doctrine requires a relaxed mental attitude, the believer's mental attitude becomes a prime target of satanic opposition against the power of God's Word. Mental attitude sins and lucid, doctrinal thought cannot coexist. Everyone is susceptible to different combinations of events, circumstances, or people that ignite arrogance, jealousy, bitterness, depression, or anger, obliterating divine viewpoint. But perhaps the most potent enemy is fear. Fear is the mental attitude sin that shuts down thought and makes doctrinal application impossible. No matter how much doctrine resides in your right lobe, none of it can benefit you if your mind is immobilized in a state of panic. The difference between a brave man and a coward is that the brave man *thinks* under pressure whereas the coward does not. Satan knows that fear eliminates thought, and he has formulated a strategy to induce fear in believers (Rom. 8:15).

Stage One	*Claim a Biblical Promise*
Stage Two	*Apply a Doctrinal Rationale*
Stage Three	*Reach Doctrinal Conclusions* *Take Control of the Situation*

THE FAITH-REST DRILL

Fear is antithetical to the believer's confidence and courage inside the love complex.

> Fear does not exist in love [in the love complex], but mature love [virtue-love][47] drives out this fear, for this fear causes punishment [self-induced misery]. In fact, he who is afraid has not been matured in the love [has not developed virtue in the love complex, lack of momentum from gate four]. (1 John 4:18)

Everyone is susceptible to fear, even the mature believer. When fear catches you off-guard, you must quickly recover your mental poise, your ability to think and apply the doctrine in your soul. Rebound is the first requirement, for fear is a sin. But rebound alone will not conquer the source of fear. You need a technique that will interlock gate one with gate two and then, with the function of the love complex restored, will enable you to apply doctrine in gate four. The relaxed mental attitude of gate two is recovered by claiming promises found throughout the Bible.

---

47. See below, pp. 120-23.

> Do not fear for I am with you;
> Do not anxiously look about you, for I am your God.
> I will strengthen you, surely I will help you,
> Surely I will uphold you with My righteous right hand.
> (Isa. 41:10, NASV)

The classic delineation of the faith-rest drill is presented by Paul in Romans 8:28–32. There verse 28 is a divine promise intended to dispel worry or fear.

> We know in fact that, to those who love God [mature or growing believers], He works all things together for the good [the final objective of God's plan, eternal rewards], to those who are the called ones ["elected to privilege," the royal family; mature Church Age believers fulfilling their spiritual potential] according to a predetermined plan [God's system for spiritual advance, executed in the love complex]. (Rom. 8:28)

Stage One | *Claim a Biblical Promise*
| **"God works all things together for good"**

THE FAITH-REST DRILL IN ROMANS 8:28

A promise is a divine guarantee, a capsule statement of doctrine, a solid rock on which to anchor your mental attitude. Promises express the essence of God, provide instantaneous perspective, and reduce complicated situations to utmost simplicity. When you lay hold of the fact that God is working all things together for good, fear is brought under control. Where panic reigned, peace is now restored. But the inner peace of the relaxed mental attitude is only the beginning of the faith-rest drill. Claiming promises is never an end in itself; divine promises alone can neither sustain the relaxed mental attitude nor solve complex problems. Promises set the stage for the most important aspect of faith-rest: thought.

REVERSE CONCENTRATION

The application of doctrine calls for *reverse concentration*. Concentration during Bible teaching brings doctrine into the soul; now concentration moves doctrine out to meet the demands of the moment. On the strength of Romans 8:28, verses 29 and 30 present a logical rationale extracted from *epignosis* doctrine stored in the right lobe. This series of five basic doctrines restores divine-viewpoint thinking.

Stage Two | *Apply a Doctrinal Rationale*

A. Foreknowledge
God thought about you in eternity past

B. Predestination
God designed a plan for you in eternity past

C. Election
God chose you for the privileged part of His plan

D. Justification
God can bless you now because you possess His righteousness

E. Glorification
God can bless you forever in heaven

THE FAITH-REST DRILL IN ROMANS 8:29,30

A rationale is a "reasoned exposition of principles, an explanation or statement of reasons, a set of reasoned rules or directions."[48] By mentally tracing out a rationale in a crisis, you are reexplaining to yourself basic concepts of doctrine that pertain to your relationship with God. This is necessary because fear and emotion have revolted against thought, and you must take conscious, deliberate steps to reinstate the rightful authority in your soul.

---

48. *Oxford English Dictionary*, s. v. "rationale."

> For [we know that] whom He foreknew He also predestined
> to be conformed to the image of His Son, that He [Christ]
> might be the firstborn among many brethren. (Rom. 8:29)

Divine foreknowledge is God's awareness of all the advantages He has prepared for each believer. "Foreknowledge" is a technical, theological term, referring to a category of God's knowledge different than "omniscience." Omniscience encompasses all divine knowledge of the universe and angelic and human history, including all the alternatives and possibilities that *could* exist but *will not*. Foreknowledge is one portion of omniscience, a subcategory focusing on what will actually occur in the believer's life. Foreknowledge is a positive concept that implies divine care and support.

Foreknowledge assures us that God thought about us in eternity past; *predestination* means that He designed a plan for us in eternity past. That plan calls for our sanctification,[49] which culminates in eternity future, when we are completely "conformed to the image of His Son" in our resurrection bodies.

> And whom He predestined, these same ones He also elected
> to privilege, and whom He elected to privilege, these same
> ones He also justified [declared righteous], and whom He
> justified, these same ones He also glorified. (Rom. 8:30)

In God's entire plan for human history, the Church Age stands out as the era of unique privilege. God chose or *elected* each Church Age believer to be spiritual royalty, just as in the previous dispensation He selected Israel to be His client nation, chose the line of David to bring forth the Messiah, and elected Christ to be the Redeemer of mankind. Divine election bestows special privilege, the honor of having an impact on history. Until Jesus Christ, the Messiah, restores Israel to client nation status at His second advent, God's purpose is for each Church Age believer to influence history as part of the spiritual pivot of a Gentile client nation. The believer fulfills his election by advancing to maturity in the divine dynasphere.

Believers of other dispensations were not *elected* to the high privilege we enjoy, but all believers of every dispensation are *justified* or declared righteous. God imputes divine righteousness to everyone in any era of history who believes in Christ as Savior, and with imputed righteousness God creates the grace pipeline, the potential for fabulous blessings on earth. Believers who exploit this potential and attain supergrace status will be rewarded or *glorified* in heaven. Supergrace believers participate forever in the eternal glorification of the Lord Jesus Christ, who receives all the credit for any privilege or blessing we possess.

---

49. See above, p. 49.

In two verses, Romans 8:29, 30, Paul has outlined the plan of God. In their logical order the five doctrines of foreknowledge, predestination, election, justification, and glorification encapsulate God's design, beginning in eternity past and concluding with the mature believer's rewards in eternity future.[50] By utilizing this systematic reverse concentration on doctrines previously learned, the believer can immediately recall his place in the overall picture of God's grace. By this faith-application of Bible doctrine, he stabilizes his objectivity.

DOCTRINAL CONCLUSIONS

After the plan-of-God rationale in verses 29 and 30, Romans 8:31, 32 reach doctrinal conclusions.

> To what conclusion are we forced face to face with these things? If God [is] for us, who [can be] against us? Who [God the Father] did not even spare His own unique Son, but delivered Him over in behalf of all of us, how shall He not with Him graciously give to us the all things? (Rom. 8:31, 32)

Stage Three	*Reach Doctrinal Conclusions* *Take Control of the Situation*
	A. "If God is for us, who can be against us?"
	B. "If God gave us His Son, He will also give us all things."

THE FAITH-REST DRILL IN ROMANS 8:31,32

These conclusions, which are stated as rhetorical questions, enable you to take control of the situation that ignited fear and anxiety only a few moments before. With objectivity and confidence restored, you can evaluate your circumstances and make the decision or take the action your good judgment and common sense dictate as a solution to the problem. If the problem is hopeless,

---

50. The five basic doctrines are taught in greater detail in Thieme, *Integrity of God*, pp. 184-89, 212-24, 257-81.

entirely beyond your ability to resolve, you can cope with the situation by intelligently trusting the Lord for a solution, as the Jews should have done at the Red Sea.

> But Moses said to the people, "Do not fear! Stand by [do nothing] and see the deliverance of the Lord, which He will accomplish for you today." (Ex. 14:13*a*)

Romans 8:28–32 occurs in a context that explains undeserved suffering. The mature believer employs the faith-rest drill to transform this maximum pressure into blessing. In dramatic contrast to your adverse circumstances, God demonstrates His power through your application of His Word. If Bible doctrine in your soul gives you mastery over the most difficult, frightening, and shocking situations in life, certainly doctrine can sustain and bless you under more tranquil circumstances.[51] The faith-rest drill maintains your ability to think and to appreciate the grace of God.

THE FLEXIBILITY OF FAITH-REST

Various promises can be used in stage one of the faith-rest drill, and other rationales are available for stage two. Besides the plan-of-God rationale, the more advanced essence-of-God rationale can be adroitly applied by mature believers, or the more basic logistical-grace rationale can comfort and strengthen even new believers. We previously noted the rebound rationale. The imputations rationale is developed in *The Integrity of God.*[52] Any doctrine you have stored as *epignosis* in your right lobe can be developed into a rationale to meet a test or crisis in your life. At one time or another you will need every doctrine you have had the opportunity to learn. If ever you lack inner resources, you have failed to arm yourself in advance. God provided the opportunity; the fault is your own (Matt. 24:25).

The three stages of the faith-rest drill are flexible and adaptable to the needs of the moment. You may claim a Biblical promise in stage one, only to succumb to fear again. You simply return to stage one and start over. Or you may leap from stage one directly to doctrinal conclusions in stage three and then recall the logical rationale that bridged the gap. The faith-rest drill is active thinking; it is not a mechanical step one, step two, step three regimen that you switch on like an automatic pilot. Certainly there are those rare, shocking disasters that so upset your concentration that you can recover your mental poise only by strict ad-

---

51. See Thieme, *Integrity of God,* pp. 137-42.

52. Chapters 2 and 3.

herence to the step-by-step discipline of the drill. The point is that the Christian way of life demands *thought*.

The divine dynasphere is fueled by true thinking. Christianity is not a religion of zombies or automatons. Nor is Christianity a cult of unreined emotion. You must learn Bible doctrine on a daily basis as your first priority in life. When difficulties arise, you must switch from personal to impersonal love or claim one of the promises that you maintain on twenty-four-hour standby in your soul. From your stabilized soul you rationally call to mind pertinent doctrines that you have retained as *epignosis*. Sustained by your doctrinal conclusions you can proceed to use common sense in dealing with the specific problem at hand. Knowledge of doctrine is the environment for thought.

Gate four of the divine dynasphere opens to the most rewarding activity in life: in gate four you explore the thinking of God and employ His eternal wisdom as your guide and counsel. This vital endeavor gives life its meaning, purpose, and definition. Standing as the main portal of the divine dynasphere, your perception and application of doctrine represent your personal destiny, your calling, your true vocation in life.

CHRIST'S RELIANCE ON BIBLE DOCTRINE

The humanity of Jesus Christ depended continuously on Bible doctrine in the prototype divine dynasphere, setting the precedent for our function in the operational divine dynasphere.

In the Person of Christ are two natures—divine and human—inseparably united without mixture or loss of separate identity, without loss or transfer of properties or attributes. Designated in theology as the *hypostatic union*, the union of God and man in the Lord Jesus Christ is personal and eternal. That is, as the God-Man, He is one Person, and He will exist forever as both undiminished deity and true humanity. As of the virgin birth, our Lord is the unique Person of the universe, permanently different from God in that He is man, and permanently different from man in that He is God (John 1:1–14; Rom. 1:2–5; Phil. 2:5–11; 1 Tim. 3:16; Heb. 2:14).[53]

In His deity, Christ possesses all the attributes of divine essence, coequal with the Father and the Holy Spirit. Our Lord is omniscient; He never needs to learn anything because He has always known all things. Bible doctrine is His mind revealed to man (1 Cor. 2:16). But in His humanity, Jesus was born as a helpless infant who needed to learn doctrine under authority just as we do (Luke 2:46-52).

---

53. See below, pp. 193-96.

Jesus received the divine dynasphere at birth. This power system was the first Christmas present, from the Father to the humanity of Christ. We have noted Christ's genuine humility at gate three as He submitted to the authority of His parents and teachers. Empowered by the filling of the Spirit at gate one, Jesus functioned at gate four for the perception of doctrine. In that same power He also applied Bible doctrine inside the love complex.

In the application of doctrine, Christ continually switched from personal to impersonal love. God the Father incorporated impersonal love into His blueprint for the divine dynasphere knowing that Jesus would be surrounded by vacillating, unreliable people (John 6:60-66; 13:38; cf. 18:17, 25-27). Our Lord also applied doctrine by means of the faith-rest drill. Perpetually inside the love complex, He never committed a mental attitude sin; stage one of the faith-rest drill did not apply to Him. He was never afraid. He maintained a perfectly stabilized mental attitude. However, stages two and three were in constant use.

Christ was always rational and logical because truth is rational and logical. He thought rationally and reached true doctrinal conclusions upon which His every action was founded. Even in the most dreadful ordeal ever suffered by a human being, the judgment of our sins in Him on the Cross, Christ was sustained by the Bible doctrine in His soul.

> Be concentrating on Jesus Christ, our Prince-Ruler [the example for the royal family], even the One who brings us to the attainment [of the objective, gate eight] by means of doctrine ["faith" in the objective sense: "what is believed"], who [Jesus] instead of His present happiness endured the Cross, having disregarded the shame [of bearing our sins and being judged by the Father], and has sat down at the right hand of the throne of God [the place of supreme honor]. For begin thinking about such a Person as Jesus Christ, having endured such opposition by sinners against Himself, in order that you do not become fatigued [by perpetual residence outside the divine dynasphere], fainting in your souls. (Heb. 12:2, 3)

Deity cannot bear the sins of mankind or be judged for them. God had to become man to purchase our salvation. The humanity of Christ "was made sin for us . . . that we might be made the righteousness of God in Him"(2 Cor. 5:21). On the Cross, Jesus suffered alone, rejected by man (Isa. 53:3), hidden in utter darkness (Matt. 27:45), judged by the Father (Isa. 53:4, 5), forsaken by the Father and the Holy Spirit (Matt. 27:46). His agony was excruciating, but the Bible doctrine in His right lobe sustained Him and kept Him true to His purpose until the last sin of the last individual in human history had been paid for in full.

Our Lord's final words on the Cross were His testimony to the supreme importance of Bible doctrine. Both Matthew and Mark record the fact that He made a final statement before He physically died. They do not record the content of Christ's statement but emphasize what impressed them most, His phenomenal strength and breath control after His horrible, debilitating ordeal (Matt. 27:50; Mark 15:37). Luke, too, remarks about the strength with which Jesus spoke, but he also records part of what Christ said.

> And when Jesus had shouted with a loud voice, He said, "Father, into your hands I deposit My spirit," and having said this, He let out His breath. (Luke 23:46)

Jesus quoted from His *epignosis* knowledge of the Old Testament Scriptures; Luke recorded the Scripture reference. Luke did not copy down the complete statement but pointed to the place where we can find it. We must go to the Psalms for the text of Christ's powerful last statement.

> Into Your hands I commit My spirit; You have delivered Me, O Jehovah, God of doctrine. (Ps. 31:5)

The last word our Savior spoke on earth prior to His resurrection was "truth" or "doctrine." The Lord Jesus Christ left us a legacy of utilizing doctrine within God's system. The perception and application of doctrine in the divine dynasphere sustained Christ under circumstances far worse than we can imagine. Certainly doctrine can sustain us.

VI
Gates Five and Six, Motivational and Functional Virtue

VIRTUE DEFINED

God loves you because He has integrity; with Christian integrity you can love Him in return.[54] You acquire virtue, honor, and integrity not to impress God but to gain capacity to appreciate Him and enjoy His blessings. There can be no lasting happiness apart from virtue. Indeed, virtue or strength of character is itself a divine blessing. God has given you the power system that produces virtue in you when you faithfully obey His mandates.

The most ancient definition of virtue connotes *power,* the *ability* that produces certain sublime effects. Our English word is derived from the Latin noun *virtus,* based on the root word *vir,* "heroic man." *Virtus* originally referred to "the qualities of a man": strength, bravery, courage, capability, worthiness, manliness, excellence in physical, mental, and moral standards. Virtue implies the fulfillment of moral duties, conformity to moral law. Virtue refers to man as he *should* be, as God designed him to be.

This inherent power is generated by God, the inventor of virtue. Virtue or honor or integrity is His monopoly, and since we are inherently weak, we can acquire virtue only inside His sphere of power.

> By this the love of God [divine impersonal love] has been
> manifested in our case, because God has sent His unique Son

---

54. See above, pp. 39-42.

into the world in order that we might live by means of Him.
(1 John 4:9)

"That we might live by means of Him" refers to more than eternal life. God the Father sent His Son to provide eternal salvation *and* to provide the environment in which we can produce virtue in this life. The environment of virtue is the divine dynasphere.

In his second epistle, Peter uses the Greek noun *arete,* "virtue," describing virtue as those qualities produced by the believer in the divine system.

> Grace and prosperity [the blessings of maturity] be multiplied to you [through spiritual momentum] in the knowledge of God and of Jesus our Lord. Seeing that His divine power [the divine dynasphere] has given to us everything pertaining to life [logistical grace] and godliness [blessings of spiritual maturity] through the true knowledge of Him [Christ] who called us to His own glory [the prototype divine dynasphere] and virtue [*arete,* manufactured in the divine dynasphere], through which things [both the divine dynasphere and virtue manufactured in it] He has given to us His precious and magnificent promises, that by them [Bible doctrines learned and applied] you might become partakers of the divine nature, having escaped the corruption that is in the world [Satan's counterfeit system] by lust. (2 Pet. 1:2–4)

We "partake of the divine nature," fulfilling our design "in the image of God" (Gen. 1:27), by following the precedent of our Lord Jesus Christ. Throughout the First Advent He resided continuously in the prototype divine dynasphere. He perfected all the virtues commanded of us and shared the happiness of God at gate eight. Man needs a power greater than himself in order to generate virtue; he needs the same power that sustained the humanity of our Lord, the system that conquers the devil's kingdom.

Paul uses the word *arete* when he issues a mandate to concentrate on the qualities that develop virtue.

> Therefore, brethren [royal family], everything that is true [doctrinal], everything that is honorable [having integrity, which comes from doctrine], everything that is righteous, everything that is pure, everything that is capacity for love, everything that is commendable; if there is any virtue [*arete*—and there is] and anything worthy of praise [and there is], concentrate on these things. (Phil. 4:8)

You "concentrate on virtue" by concentrating on Bible doctrine; doctrine reveals Jesus Christ, the perfect example of virtue. Christian virtue is not superficial adherence to religious tradition or self-righteous avoidance of taboos; virtue is strength of character based on objective reality—based on the essence of God revealed in the Person of Christ. The Mind of Christ, Bible doctrine, in your soul forms the character of Christ in your life. Thought precedes action; motivation precedes function.

MOTIVATION TOWARD GOD, FUNCTION TOWARD MAN

Anyone who consistently resides in the first four gates of the divine dynasphere develops Christian integrity, first toward God, then toward man and circumstances. Among the virtues of the Christian life—humility, worship, morality, confidence, courage, love—humility is unique. Humility is directed toward legitimate authority, both divine and human. Standing alone as the foundation for all other virtues, gate three makes the believer receptive to Bible teaching and the unbeliever receptive to establishment principles. The resultant virtues for the believer are divided into two categories in gates five and six: *motivational* virtues and *functional* virtues. These two categories are inseparable and must be studied as one doctrine. Gates five and six stand or fall together. Like two sides of the same coin, one cannot exist without the other.

All virtue has direction. The motivational virtues are directed toward God; the functional virtues, toward man and circumstances. Each motivational virtue sustains a functional virtue; each functional virtue depends on its counterpart motivational virtue.

There are three outstanding pairs of counterpart virtues in the Christian life. The motivational virtue of *worship* toward God generates the functional virtue of *morality* toward man. The motivational virtue of *confidence* in God supports the functional virtue of *courage* toward man. And the motivational virtue of *personal love* for God sustains the functional virtue of *impersonal love* toward man.

These virtues correspond to your two areas of responsibility as a Christian. You hold two divine warrants: you are a royal priest and a royal ambassador.[55] Your priesthood is invisible and private, directed toward God. Your ambassadorship is visible and public, directed toward mankind. As a priest you are responsible to represent yourself before God as a growing believer; as an ambassador you are responsible to "proclaim the virtues of Christ" before man (1 Pet. 2:9). The motivational virtues belong to your relationship with God; the functional virtues enrich your relationships with other people. Motivation precedes

---

55. See above, pp. 94-98.

function; the priesthood sustains the ambassadorship; your relationship with God strengthens you in your relationships with people.

Motivational and functional virtues are explained by defining their characteristics and by describing how these virtues become absurdities when aimed in the wrong direction.

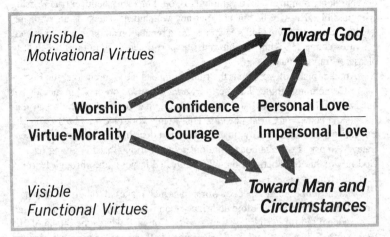

THE DIRECTION OF COUNTERPART VIRTUES

MISDIRECTED VIRTUE

WORSHIP AND MORALITY

The strength of virtue is distorted into weakness when a virtue is directed toward the wrong object. *Worship* is a virtue directed toward God, which motivates *morality* as a virtue directed toward man. To worship man, however, becomes arrogance, and to direct morality toward God becomes legalism and self-righteousness.

True worship is a priestly function. Assembling in the local church (Heb. 10:25a), singing hymns (Eph. 5:19; Col. 3:16), offering prayer (Eph. 6:18; 1 Thess. 5:17), giving money (2 Cor. 9:7)—these are all aspects of worship. Worship always involves giving back to God something we possess from Him.

We can learn to worship from descriptions of high ranking elect angels who "give glory, honor, and thanksgiving" to the Lord (Rev. 4:9–11). We cannot yet fully join these angels in giving glory to God, because we will be glorified only in heaven (Rom. 8:30); we cannot give in worship what we do not possess. We will acquire glory when we receive resurrection bodies and eternal rewards.

We *can* give honor to the Lord in this life, but only when we have acquired honor, virtue, integrity. If we lack Christian integrity from residence and function in the divine dynasphere, we cannot offer integrity or honor to God.

Likewise, we can give God thanksgiving only if we have gratitude to give. Any believer who does not understand from knowledge of Bible doctrine what God has done for him cannot be grateful to God. For such a believer true worship is impossible. He may be sincere, but any worship he affects is an arrogant, legalistic attempt to win God's favor or gain a reputation among men. Any overt activities connected with worship must be performed as unto the Lord, not to please or impress man.

Another phase of worship is the ritual unique to the Church Age, the Eucharist or Communion Table. This periodic *auld lang syne* observed in memory of our Lord and Savior calls upon the doctrine in your right lobe. The bread represents the Person of Christ; the cup, His saving work (1 Cor. 11:23–26). The Eucharist tests your maturity, understanding of doctrine, and ability to concentrate. Memory is reverse concentration; remembering Christ is giving back to God in worship the doctrinal thought inculcated in your soul through learning Bible doctrine.

The most important aspect of worship, which makes all other worship possible, is the perception of Bible doctrine. God gives us time, one day at a time; we "redeem the time" by devoting a portion of each day to the intake of His Word (Eph. 5:16). Concentration in learning the Word of God in gate four of the divine dynasphere is the highest form of worship directed toward God (1 Tim. 4:12, 15, 16). When you elevate yourself or any other person above Bible doctrine on your scale of values, you have misdirected your worship (Ps. 138:2). The virtue in worship is nullified; you live in subjective reality. Worship by those outside the divine dynasphere becomes religion, the enemy of Christianity.

A strong *social life with God* is *occupation with Christ* in gate five of the love complex. These are synonyms for worship, motivating *morality* toward men. Morality is a function of the ambassador. Morality is not the narrow, priggish self-righteousness practiced by so many fundamentalist denominations. For many Christians the word "morality" means no more than abstinence from illicit sex. Most certainly that is part of morality, but in its wider sense morality extends to all facets of life. Virtue-morality is honorably motivated adherence to the divine laws of establishment and is required of the entire human race, believers and unbelievers alike. What the unbeliever can produce cannot be the Christian way of life, but residence and function in the few gates available to him can contribute to the stability of his nation and his own happiness in this life. Christianity *includes* morality but *exceeds* morality through the combined operation of all the Christian virtues.

A believer misdirects and distorts morality when he assumes that he is pleasing God by being good. He believes that if he is nice to people, has a sweet disposition, helps the poor, avoids certain taboos, and follows certain traditional Christian practices, then God must approve of him and bless him. This is utterly false. Blessings from God are related to the priesthood, not the ambassadorship; they belong to the believer's relationship with God, not his relationship with the human race.

Supergrace prosperity comes from God's justice, down the grace pipeline to imputed divine righteousness in us when we develop the capacity to appreciate and enjoy that prosperity (Isa. 30:18). We never earn or deserve blessing from God; God's own perfect righteousness is at the receiving end of the pipeline. He has done all the work. If we think we can merit God's favor by our works, we are legalists (Eph. 2:8, 9). The legalist may look impressive on the surface and may be involved in many legitimate activities, but, again, a misdirected virtue has been robbed of its impact. Many believers appear to be extremely moral, but they do not reside in the divine dynasphere. The believer who confuses his priesthood with his ambassadorship has placed himself under Satan's influence.

CONFIDENCE AND COURAGE

The second pair of counterpart virtues is also distorted if virtue is misdirected. *Confidence* is a priestly virtue directed toward God; *courage* is a virtue of the ambassador directed toward man. Confidence toward God is the invisible strength behind the believer's visible courage toward other people or adverse circumstances. But if the objects are reversed, the virtues are destroyed: courage toward God is blasphemous; complete confidence in man is naive at best and evil at worst (Jer. 17:5).

We are justified in placing total confidence in God because He is infinite, absolute, eternal; He never has and never can fail anyone who trusts in Him. He is totally worthy of our complete trust. Confidence is a function of the priesthood and is related to learning doctrine. The more doctrine we know, the greater is our confidence in God.

Eternal security creates confidence in God.

> For I am convinced that neither death, nor life, nor angels,
> nor principalities, nor things present, nor things to come,
> nor powers, nor height, nor depth, nor any other created
> thing, shall separate us from the love of God, which is in
> Christ Jesus our Lord. (Rom. 8:38, 39; NASV)

Prayer is an expression of confidence in God.

> Beloved, if our heart [right lobe] does not condemn us
> [rebound not demanded because we reside in the divine

> dynasphere], we keep on having confidence before God
> [face to face with God]. Furthermore, whatever we have
> asked we receive from Him because we continue to keep
> [execute] His mandates [residence and function inside the
> divine dynasphere]. (1 John 3:21, 22)

We can repose our complete trust in perfect God, but we cannot place unqualified confidence in any member of the human race. Everyone fails from time to time (1 John 1:8, 10). We all possess the old sin nature as the inner distorter of life (Rom. 6:6; 7:5), and Satan's influence is too powerful for us to resist in our own strength (John 17:8–23; 1 Pet. 5:8, 9). A man may have strength of character and may have honorable friends, but still he cannot afford to invest complete confidence in himself or anyone else. There are too many variables, too many unknown factors.

An employer must be able to rely on his employees to do their jobs; husbands and wives must trust each other; there is trust involved in friendship. However, trust in another person can extend only so far before it becomes naïveté. Total confidence in man is sheer idiocy. Confidence in man is never virtuous in itself but is virtue-dependent; your confidence in God gives you a sense of proportion toward man.

Jesus Christ in the prototype divine dynasphere did not consider confidence in mankind to be a virtue.

> Now when He was in Jerusalem at the Passover, during the
> feast, many believed in His name, beholding His signs
> which He was doing. But Jesus, on His part, was not en-
> trusting Himself to them, for He knew all men, and because
> He did not need anyone to bear witness concerning man for
> He Himself knew what was in man. (John 2:23-25, NASV)

Confidence without cognizance is not true confidence and is ultimately self-destructive. This is the problem when you place someone on a pedestal of perfection and then react with disillusionment when you discover his feet of clay. Likewise, false confidence in the alleged goodness and nobility of mankind is the root of political liberalism. When you are so arrogant as to place your confidence in man, you are under the control of Satan's deceit.

> Thus says the Lord, Cursed is the man who trusts in man-
> kind and makes flesh [old sin nature] his strength, and
> whose heart turns away from the Lord [rejection of Bible
> doctrine]. (Jer. 17:5, NASV)

Confidence in man is not a virtue, but courage toward man and circumstances is a functional virtue of the royal ambassador.

> Fear not, for I am with thee. Be not dismayed, for I am thy God [courage is motivated by confidence in God]. I will strengthen thee, yea, I will help thee, yea, I will uphold thee with the right hand of my righteousness. (Isa. 41:10, AV)

Courage is an ambassadorial virtue. The believer overcomes fear with the faith-rest drill, by which he applies doctrine at gate four of the divine dynasphere. Courage is thinking under pressure; cowardice is failure to think under pressure. The royal ambassador uses stage two of the faith-rest drill—reverse concentration in a logical rationale—to establish and sustain his courage. Failure to do so is failure to properly represent Christ. Every act of moral or physical cowardice is a malfunction of the royal ambassadorship. And since fear is a mental attitude sin, cowardice removes the believer from the environment of virtue, the divine dynasphere.

> Fear does not exist in the love complex. (1 John 4:18a)

Cowardice is never legitimate, but courage, too, can be impertinent if misdirected. Courage toward God is presumptuous blasphemy. God's objective is to bless not destroy you. When you use His logistical grace and execute His game plan, you have nothing to fear from God; courage is unnecessary and completely out of order. You may need courage to face life but never to face God. He has already blessed you beyond measure and is waiting to give you greater grace. He is always near to help in time of need. The blasphemy of misdirected courage is illustrated in the improper use of rebound.

When you exit the divine dynasphere and commit a sin, you must acknowledge that sin privately to God to be restored to fellowship. When you follow God's policy, you do so as a royal priest from your confidence in God's ability to forgive you. The more you understand about rebound, the greater is your confidence in God: you know with absolute certitude that at the Cross He has already judged the sin in question.

The believer who abuses rebound, however, attempts to distort this simple grace procedure of the royal priest into a function of the ambassador. He faces his sinfulness with great courage, standing before God and promising to do better next time. He performs some overt penance for all to see; he makes a great show of his remorse so God will be convinced of his sincerity. But a virtue that is misdirected ceases to be a virtue. Bravery in making promises to God, which cannot be kept, boils down to sheer presumption and arrogance. God does not want our human good; He has already done all the work necessary to restore us to residence in the divine dynasphere. When substituted for the matchless work of Christ on the Cross, misdirected courage becomes an insult to the character of God.

PERSONAL AND IMPERSONAL LOVE

The quintessence of motivational and functional virtue is virtue-love: *personal love for God* and *impersonal love for mankind*. At gate five of the divine dynasphere, personal love for God is a function of the royal priest developed through the persistent intake of doctrine. At gate six impersonal love for all mankind is the integrity of the royal ambassador displayed in the application of doctrine. This is *the* structure of the Christian way of life.

Hatred of one's fellow believer is a malfunction of the ambassadorship. The lack of impersonal love as a functional virtue, which can be seen, indicates the lack of personal love for God as a priestly, motivational virtue, which cannot be seen. Malfunction in the visible indicates malfunction in the invisible. Any believer who lacks the integrity of impersonal love toward others and yet claims to love God lives a lie (1 John 4:20).

The objects of personal and impersonal love cannot be switched without destroying the virtue of love. When misdirected toward God, impersonal love becomes the arrogance of assuming that God must be tolerated or that we as sinners have greater integrity than God. It is the impertinence of presuming we know how to run our lives better than He does and, therefore, that we can dispense with His mandates.

On the other hand, personal love misdirected toward man becomes weakness. Obviously any attempt to love the entire human race with personal love is ludicrous and doomed to failure, but even legitimate personal love for the worthy few creates vulnerability. We tend to make exceptions for those we love; we are susceptible to making emotional instead of rational decisions; and we are often wrongly influenced by our desire to please the one we love. Personal love for a member of the human race can be wonderful and rewarding, but it is not a virtue.

For any believer who lacks the motivational and functional virtues, personal love becomes a dead end for his spiritual life. Personal love can destroy common sense, discernment, and good judgment. Close friends or loved ones may influence a growing believer to ignore or reject certain doctrines, to leave the right church, to quit a job where he is satisfied and doing well, to move to another geographical area, even to enter a life of crime. Every important decision a person makes will be influenced by those he has chosen to love.

> Be not deceived, evil companions corrupt good morals.
> (1 Cor. 15:33)

> He who walks with wise men will be wise, but the companion of fools will suffer evil [harm]. (Prov. 13:20)

The only category of personal love that is a virtue in itself is personal love for God in gate five of the divine dynasphere. Personal love for a man, a woman, friends, or family is not a virtue in itself but is virtue-dependent; successful personal love for people depends on the virtue of impersonal love in gate six. When based on impersonal love, personal love for a select few people can flourish. But lacking the virtue of impersonal love, personal love becomes subjective self-gratification, emphasizing self and producing arrogance, hypersensitivity, and misery.

Impersonal love is the supreme functional virtue, the dynamics of the ambassador's testimony to the human race, and the primary Christian virtue required by the royal family honor code. But the strength of impersonal love dissipates if not nurtured, sustained, and motivated by a growing personal love for God.

VIRTUE-LOVE AND OBJECTIVE REALITY

God is the paragon, the exemplar of *virtue-love*. Our standard of virtue is His divine essence, not relative systems of human ethics. For our understanding of virtue-love, we go to the source, to *objective reality,* to God's love for us.

God loves us because *He* has integrity. Love requires integrity; integrity comes first. Each divine attribute has equal importance in the essence of God, but in the logical presentation of His essence to man, God's holiness or integrity precedes His love. God is perfect; therefore, God is perfect love. Divine love is far superior to the strongest human love we will ever know, because God has absolute integrity that cannot and will not be compromised or violated. God's attribute of righteousness is the *principle* of His integrity; His justice is the *function* of His integrity. Divine righteousness and justice secure God's love for every believer.

Divine justice condemned all mankind for Adam's original sin, making salvation by grace possible.[56] Justice judged Christ as our substitute on the Cross. Justice imputed divine righteousness to us at the moment of faith in Christ. Our point of contact with God is the functional half of His integrity, divine justice.

---

56. See Thieme, *Integrity of God,* pp. 57-77.

The justice of God did not impute His love to us; justice imputed His righteousness. We have direct contact, not with His love, but with the attributes that protect and guarantee His love for us, the integrity of God.

We now possess the righteousness of God. Imputed righteousness is more valuable than anything we could imagine or desire. We *have* it; it is *there,* within us. Now and forever there is no possibility that divine integrity will be compromised as God pours out grace and blessings to believers; God can love His own righteousness in us with absolute, eternal love. In God's dealings with mankind, integrity always takes precedence over love.

Divine integrity not only gives us a point of contact with perfect God but also lays the foundation upon which we can build virtue. The principle that God's integrity exists in every believer is the basis for the system, the Christian way of life, within which we are commanded to live. In the Church Age the system that accompanies, exploits, and is demanded by imputed righteousness is the divine dynasphere. Residence and function in the divine dynasphere constructs *our* integrity upon *divine* integrity. God has given us limitless potential for producing virtue. In the divine dynasphere we imitate God as we build virtue on the divine righteousness He has imputed to us. The love complex is the sphere of Christian integrity.

> No one has fellowship with God who keeps advancing out of
> bounds and does not remain [on the playing field] through
> the doctrine of Christ. (2 John 9*a*)

Capacity to love God emanates from Christian integrity—loyalty to the truth and orientation to the reality of God's system. We advance *in bounds* inside the divine dynasphere, in which Jesus Christ lived throughout His first advent. In gates one through four, we develop integrity. As we build integrity, personal love for God and advanced impersonal love for man enter into the system at gates five and six. The essence of God establishes the pattern for the Christian life: He loves us because He has integrity; we love only when we possess integrity or virtue. The motto of the Christian way of life is *Virtue First,* and we acquire virtue, honor, and integrity only inside God's system.

Love is never stronger than honor. The English Cavalier poet Richard Lovelace expressed this truth when he wrote,

> I could not love thee Dear so much,
> Loved I not honour more.[57]

A man might tell a woman, "I love you," but if he lacks integrity, his love is false. His words manifest only arrogance, whether lust, infatuation, response

---

57. *To Lucasta, On Going to the Wars.*

to flattery, desire to control, or fear of facing life alone. No matter how sincere or emotionally smitten he may be, if he lacks virtue, honor, and integrity, he does not love. He does not love any member of the human race; he does not love God.

Subjectivity is living in a false reality which is ultimately *un*reality, a position of weakness. Virtue is strength of character, which brings happiness to the believer and glorifies the Lord.

> We have learned that the Son of God has come [the First Advent], and He has given us the faculty for perception [*dianoia,* the divine dynasphere] so that we may understand objective reality; and we are in the sphere of objective reality [the divine dynasphere] by means of His Son, Jesus Christ. This One [Christ] is the true God and eternal life. (1 John 5:20)

The Attic Greek noun *dianoia* means "the ability to think, a way of thought, a purpose, a plan," and in this verse, "faculty for perception." *Dianoia* calls attention to the divine dynasphere as the believer's God-given power to think spiritual truth, resulting in virtue (1 Cor. 1:26–2:16). The result of functioning in the divine dynasphere is expressed by the conjunction *hina* plus the verb *ginosko*: "so that we may understand." The grammatical mood of *ginosko* is called the potential indicative mood of obligation. This means that any believer's understanding of Bible doctrine is a potential, not an actuality, and that every believer is obligated to fulfill this potential through his own decisions to reside and function in the divine dynasphere. The object of the verb is *alethina,* "that which is true, correct, genuine, dependable." *Alethina* denotes objective reality. Jesus Christ gave us the divine dynasphere so that, through the perception and application of God's Word, we might understand and appreciate objective reality, so that we might know and love God.

PERSONAL LOVE FOR GOD

MANDATES TO LOVE GOD

The mandates for gate five are not unique to the Church Age. Every believer of every dispensation is commanded to love God.

> You yourself shall love the Lord your God with all your heart [your right lobe], with all your soul, and with all your power. (Deut. 6:5)

In the Church Age "all your power" takes on added significance: we have received the power of God the Holy Spirit as the Energizer of the divine dynasphere. We love God only inside the love complex.

No one loves God by being ordered to love Him, but God never issues a mandate without supplying the means of compliance. Through spiritual momentum from the perception and application of Bible doctrine, we obey the divine mandate to love God.

> Even though you do not see Him [empiricism fails to bring us to God] you love Him, and though you do not see Him now but believe in Him [faith-perception] you greatly rejoice with happiness inexpressible and full of glory. (1 Pet. 1:8)

Jesus Christ in glory at the right hand of the Father is invisible to us now; we love Him through the Word of God resident in our souls.

Paul's prayer in Ephesians 3:19 expresses his desire that we "come to know the surpassing knowledge [surpassing *gnosis*] love of Christ." *Gnosis* or academic knowledge is not sufficient; our understanding of Christ must be *epignosis*, "full knowledge," through the grace apparatus for perception. But the statement that personal love for God surpasses mere *gnosis* carries historical significance. Interpreted in light of the times in which he wrote, Paul's prayer declares that man by man's efforts neither comes to know nor loves God.

In Paul's day the philosophy of Gnosticism was an insidious adversary of Christianity. Gnosticism combined Platonic rationalism with Eastern mysticism, added Persian dualism, and expressed itself in Christian vocabulary. Advocating strict asceticism on one hand while encouraging lascivious debauchery on the other, Gnosticism offered something for everyone and appealed to many people, believers included. The Gnostics derived their name from *gnosis*, which they used as a technical term for the special quality of knowledge they sought. But neither true *gnosis* in the left lobe of the soul nor false *gnosis* glorified by human philosophy measure up to the believer's *epignosis* love for Christ. Paul's prayer is partly polemical: it refutes the Gnostics. But it is also offered to God on the true assumption that the believer's love for God through Bible doctrine is infinitely superior to any human philosophy or academic knowledge.

THE ESSENCE-OF-GOD RATIONALE

Who is God? What is His nature? The essence of God is revealed in every direct statement of Bible doctrine, in each line of Biblical poetry, in every historical or prophetical narrative recorded in the Bible. God is revealed in the God-

Man, Jesus Christ, whose thinking *is* Bible doctrine (John 14:6; 1 Cor. 2:16; Heb. 1:2, 3). Each line of Scripture is essential to God's revelation of Himself. Man and human history change; God remains the same. Different circumstances elicit different aspects of His character, so that His attributes are presented in Scripture through a wide variety of divine decisions and actions. The doctrine of divine essence becomes the common theme that unifies all other doctrines; all doctrine emanates from the essence of God.[58]

With *epignosis* knowledge of divine essence, the believer is able to see God's plan being fulfilled in the kaleidoscope of human events, but knowledge of God also causes the believer to personally love God. The essence-of-God rationale is the most advanced rationale in the faith-rest drill because *epignosis* of divine essence belongs only to advancing or mature believers. Familiarity with the essence of God develops only through extended obedience in learning and applying Bible doctrine. When the believer advances to the point that he can reverse his concentration and remember the attributes of God and how they function, he derives stability, objectivity, happiness, and motivation from his personal love for God.

The essence-of-God rationale illustrates personal love for God, which is a stabilizing factor in any situation. Imagine a personal crisis that catches many people off guard, the sudden death of a loved one. Certainly the mature believer grieves, but "not as the Gentiles [unbelievers] who have no hope [no confidence in God]" (1 Thess. 4:13*b*).

Sovereignty	*Omniscience*
Righteousness	*Omnipotence*
Justice	*Omnipresence*
Love	*Immutability*
Eternal Life	*Veracity*

THE ESSENCE OF GOD

When he is bereaved, the mature believer remembers the attributes of God. God is *sovereignty*: no one departs from this life without divine permission. God's plan calls for each person to die at precisely the right time and in the right manner. God is absolute *righteousness* and *justice*: He is always fair to every individual, both the departed and the bereaved. And if the one who has died was a believer in the Lord Jesus Christ, he possesses God's righteousness forever; he is qualified to reside in heaven in the presence of God.

---

58. See Thieme, *Integrity of God*, app. A, "The Doctrine of Divine Essence," pp. 231-56.

The believer who has lost a loved one also remembers that God is *love*: in divine impersonal love, God goes to the farthest extreme, short of compromise, to save the unbeliever and to bless the believer. The only limiting factor in anyone's spiritual status is his own volition. God is also *eternal life*: if the deceased was a believer, he possesses eternal life and is at this very moment face to face with the Lord, where there is "no more death, neither sorrow, nor crying, neither shall there be any more pain; for the former things are passed away" (Rev. 21:4*b*).

God is *omniscience,* and the advanced believer recalls that God knows all the repercussions of every event in human history, future as well as past—including the death of this person—and has chosen the most advantageous moment for him to depart from the earth. To remain a moment longer would have been less than the best. God also knew billions of years ago that those left behind would need comfort and that, often, such a personal disaster can bring someone to the point of accepting Christ as Savior.

The believer also remembers that God is *omnipotence*: He has infinite power to fulfill all His promises concerning death. Moreover, He has provided a sphere of power for the royal family. God is also *omnipresence*: He has overlooked no detail of this situation, and His comfort is as near as Bible doctrine in the soul. God is *immutable*: the situation has changed; a wonderful relationship has been severed by death, but God has not changed. God's faithfulness continues; life goes on. The believer's relationship with God continues now as before and as it will continue when the believer himself is dying and on the threshold of the Lord's presence. Finally, the believer using reverse concentration in the essence-of-God rationale remembers that God is *veracity*: He tells the truth; He is truth. The Bible doctrine that lives in the believer's soul is the revelation and expression of God's character.

In all His attributes God is totally worthy of love. The more any believer knows about God, the more he loves Him. The initial function in gate five of the love complex is gratitude for who and what God is. In every doctrine learned, the believer recognizes that the marvelous blessings of God's plan are expressions of divine essence. The believer who remembers the attributes of God has confidence, peace, and strength through all the storms of life.

> This I recall to mind, therefore, I have hope [confidence
> directed toward God]: the Lord's grace functions never
> cease, for His compassions never fail, they are new every
> morning. Great is Your faithfulness. The Lord is my portion
> says my soul, therefore I have hope in Him. The Lord is
> good to those who wait on Him [comparable to residence in
> the love complex during the Church Age], to the soul who

seeks Him [equivalent to gate four of the love complex].
(Lam. 3:21–25)

As a believer advances toward spiritual maturity, his love for God matures
as well. Love for God determines capacity for supergrace blessings. The reality
of gate eight is based on attainment in gate five.

But just as it stands written [in Isaiah 64:4; 65:17]: things
which the eye has not seen and the ear has not heard [beyond
empiricism], nor has it entered into the right lobe of man
[beyond rationalism], the things [blessings of maturity] that
God has prepared for those who love Him. (1 Cor. 2:9)

This principle is familiar from Romans 8:28. There, Paul illustrates stage
one of the faith-rest drill with a promise that is pertinent only to mature believers
or to those approaching maturity. Only the advancing believer who has momentum from Bible doctrine knows and loves God, and only the believer who loves
God has the capacity for the blessings of maturity.

For we know that for those who love God [gate five of the
divine dynasphere], He works all things together for the
good. (Rom. 8:28a)

"The good" includes all the blessings God can pour out to us in time. These
supergrace blessings will be parlayed into fabulous rewards in eternity. This glorifies Christ now and forever and is the ultimate fulfillment of God's game plan.

OCCUPATION WITH CHRIST

As a believer continues to interlock the first four gates of the divine dynasphere, he expands his capacity for love in gate five. Gate five increases from
love for God, which characterizes the growing believer, to *occupation with
Christ*, which characterizes the mature believer.[59]

Christ was the focus of Paul's life. Despite the pressure and controversy that
continually surrounded the great apostle, he was stabilized by his constant
awareness of the Lord. Better than anyone else, Paul defines occupation with
Christ: Jesus Christ was Paul's very life.

Indeed I know [Romans 8:28] that this [controversy] shall
turn out for deliverance to me through your prayers [in-

---

59. See Thieme, *Integrity of God*, pp. 172-74, 184.

tercessions] and logistical provision [monetary gift] motivated by the Spirit of Jesus Christ [the Holy Spirit in the
divine dynasphere], according to my intense concentration
[on doctrine, gate four] and resultant confidence [in God,
virtue in gate five] that in nothing shall I be disgraced [the
integrity of impersonal love when facing dishonorable
people, cf. Phil. 1:16], but with the integrity of maturity
[complete courage] even now, as always, Christ shall be
exalted in my person, whether by life [the blessings of
supergrace] or by death [the blessings of dying grace]. For
me, living is Christ [occupation with Christ]; likewise,
dying is gain [the profit or advantage of eternal rewards].
(Phil. 1:19–21)

The supergrace blessings in gate eight of the love complex fall into six categories, the first and most important of which comprises spiritual blessings.[60]
Spiritual blessings constitute your capacity for all other forms of prosperity, and
occupation with Christ is itself one of the spiritual blessings of supergrace. The
greater your momentum from gate four, the greater your capacity for loving
God. When your capacity for personal love for God has reached the point of
occupation with Christ, God can entrust you with phenomenal blessings without
distracting you from what is most important—the source, God Himself. The
fruits of spiritual momentum continually increase until you possess the capacity
of soul that allows God to bless you to the maximum.

God gives supergrace only to mature believers, because few individuals
pass the prosperity test.[61] Only the mature believer who is occupied with Christ
keeps Bible doctrine as his first priority and, whether in national or personal prosperity or national or personal adversity, passes each test with flying colors.

King David, whom the Bible recognizes as "a man after God's own heart"
(1 Sam. 13:14a; Acts 13:22b), expressed this continual desire for doctrine motivated by his mature love for God.

One thing have I desired of the Lord, that will I seek after;
that I may dwell in the house of the Lord all the days of my
life, to behold the beauty of the Lord, and to enquire in his
temple [keep learning Bible doctrine]. (Ps. 27:4, AV)

Love for God is the basis for all true worship, all motivation for Christian
production, all fulfillment of the plan of God, and all glorification of the Lord

---

60. See above, pp. 57-58.
61. See below, pp. 172-74.

Jesus Christ in our lives. The divine dynasphere empowers the royal family to love God, even as the humanity of Christ in the prototype divine dynasphere loved Him.

IMPERSONAL LOVE FOR MANKIND: THE ROYAL FAMILY HONOR CODE

The honorable Christian lives by a code of honor. Virtue First is his motto: he respects authority, loves God with personal love, and loves man with impersonal love. The honor code demands all the virtues of God's protocol system, the divine dynasphere. As the supreme functional virtue, which depends on foundational and motivational virtues, the believer's impersonal love manifests the dynamics of Christian integrity. The honorable believer represents Christ in a gracious style that reflects our Lord's eternal aristocracy.

Aristocracy is maligned as snobbery, social injustice, and tyranny, but in its true sense aristocracy connotes excellence, achievement, courage, and a sense of responsibility. Extraordinary men become outstanding by accomplishing more than their contemporaries, and when this superiority is passed down from generation to generation, the children, too, are inculcated with superior standards. Often the descendants of illustrious men do not share the energy or strength of character that distinguished their forebears. Therefore, the vigor of the nobility must be perpetuated through a code of honor. The young heir is taught the protocol of aristocracy. He is trained from birth to think and act with poise and courage, always in keeping with his own personality, yet to the manner born.

We are spiritual aristocrats. We did not earn our exalted new birth, just as no royal infant deserves to be a prince. Our royalty is the result of the accomplishments of someone else. Jesus Christ founded our royal dynasty nearly two thousand years ago as a result of His strategic victory over Satan, for which He earned the exalted title King of Kings and Lord of Lords. At spiritual birth we enter the royal family of the Lord Jesus Christ, and He has given us His code of honor by which to live.

Our royal code of conduct is taught throughout the New Testament, especially by Paul in Romans 12–16. We do not live under systems of legalism or religious tradition. We live objectively and with divinely shared happiness inside the dynasphere of the King of Kings, not under the subjective, deceptive influence of the ruler of this world. The divine dynasphere is the power system that fulfills the royal family honor code.

I have taught the principles of the honor code in *The Integrity of God*;[62] they are here capsulized as a functional list of standards.

---

62. Pp. 199-210.

1. Respect the privacy of the royal priesthood.

The Christian way of life is a life of freedom (Gal. 5:1), exceeding even the freedom of divine establishment. Privacy is essential to freedom. The principle of the honor code, then, is "live and let live" (Rom. 14:7, 8). This means abstaining from gossip, maligning, judging, character assassination, and evil speculation from rumors and hearsay evidence (Rom. 14:10–13). Respect for the privacy of the priesthood also demands toleration for the erroneous opinions of immature believers on nonessential matters (Rom. 14:2, 3). Ultimately Bible doctrine is the essential; everything else, to a greater or lesser degree, is nonessential (Rom. 14:19). As a believer grows in the Word, doctrine corrects his opinions, with no need for unsolicited interference from other Christians. Toleration permits all believers to assemble in the local congregation and approach the Word of God with objectivity. As royal priests, representing themselves before the Lord, the immature have the privacy and freedom to grow, while the mature have continued opportunities to develop strength through flexibility.

2. Love all people with impersonal love.

Impersonal love emphasizes your own integrity, which demands that you hold no grudge or resentment against anyone, especially other believers, who possess the same imputed righteousness of God that you possess (Heb. 13:1; 1 John 3:11). Impersonal love also rejects self-pity and never seeks to arouse or exploit the pity of others (John 15:12; Rom. 12:9, 10; 1 John 4:11).

3. Recognize that all believers have a common objective.

God keeps each believer alive to advance to maturity in the divine dynasphere. Under the honor code, therefore, you must persevere in the perception and application of Bible doctrine. You must submit to the authority of your pastor-teacher, but this also means that you must demonstrate courtesy, thoughtfulness, and sensitivity toward those in the congregation who may be at a different stage of spiritual growth (Rom. 15:5–7).

4. Build integrity; do not distort morality.

Integrity is the standard of the royal family, superior to morality, which belongs to believer and unbeliever alike. The believer's integrity is rooted in the filling of the Spirit and in Bible doctrine, whereas morality is the fulfillment of the divine laws of establishment. Integrity, therefore, exceeds but also includes morality. Personal integrity is the *sine qua non* of the Christian life; morality devolves into legalism when it is assumed to be the Christian way of life (Rom. 13:1, 8-10).

>   5. Never assume that production is a means of divine
>   blessing.

Your talent, personality, intelligence, sacrifice, asceticism, and ability never merit blessing from God. He blesses His own imputed righteousness in you. God recognizes only integrity, which is the standard of maturity attained through residence and function in His power system. Divine integrity is the source of all blessings to man, and God blesses *from* integrity *to* integrity, not from His integrity to human works. Production is a *result* of spiritual advance, never the cause. When momentum from Bible doctrine in the divine dynasphere is recognized as the cause of spiritual growth, integrity, and blessing, then self-righteousness is excluded from your life (Matt. 6:33).

>   6. Depend totally on the integrity of God.

In order to depend on God, you must be intimately aware of His attributes through understanding Bible doctrine. Your point of contact with God is His integrity. Hence, the entire Christian life can be summarized as Integrity First, or adjustment to the integrity of God. This total dependence on God's justice and righteousness is called "hope," the confident expectation of blessing (Rom. 15:13).[63] Such confidence motivates and sustains your spiritual momentum: you are carried to maturity by *thinking,* thinking under an honor code principle. Right thinking creates right motivation, and right motivation leads to right action (Rom. 12:1, 2).

>   7. Remember that the honor code is for all believers.

The royal family honor code is not just for brilliant or accomplished people. Simply because the royal code is superior to all other approaches to life is no excuse for arrogance. It is *God's* system, *His* code, not yours. Both the divine laws of establishment and the royal family honor code sustain your advance, blessing, and happiness. All believers, including you, rely on these two divine systems (Rom. 12:3; 13:1-8).

---

63. See Thieme, *Integrity of God,* pp. 142-45, 165-72.

8. More is demanded of the strong than the weak.

We are all royalty, yet no two believers are equal. Even among royalty some are stronger and more advanced than others by virtue of their more consistent perception and application of doctrine. The principle of *noblesse oblige* applies. *Maturity* imposes the obligation of honorable, generous, and responsible behavior that is the concomitant of high rank or noble birth (Rom. 15:1–4). The strong are obliged to tolerate the nonessential, inconsequential, and occasionally obnoxious opinions and actions of the weak (Rom. 14:1). An arrogant person might assume you are weak and might ridicule you for bending to the demands of immature believers, but there is no weakness in such flexibility. The strong believer is confident and says, "I may bend, but I will not break." He maintains a relaxed sense of humor about himself, about life, and about others. Impersonal love implements the strong believer's duty to the weak believer.

9. Orient to authority.

Arrogant people are weak, and the weak resent authority. But authority protects freedom (1 Pet. 2:13–18). Like human freedom, Christian freedom is not an isolated quality. Your freedom as a believer in the Lord Jesus Christ is an integral part of a system that includes free will, privacy, private property, and authority. Genuine humility submits to the pastor who faithfully teaches orthodox Christian truths from a systematic exegesis of the Scriptures (Heb. 13:7, 17). God has delegated His authority to pastors (Eph. 4:11) and always protects His servants (Isa. 54:17).

10. Reciprocate for the privilege of hearing doctrine taught.

Christian giving is a matter of honor under the royal family's code of conduct. God measures giving by the motivation behind the gift, not by its monetary value (Mark 12:41–44). Thus, the honor code demands a generous attitude in return for benefits received (Rom. 15:26, 27), and this mental attitude is molded only from within by the gradual buildup of Bible doctrine in the soul. No one can force any believer to be properly motivated to give. The church may make needs known but must never beg or dun the believer for money. The pastor's generosity in teaching doctrine deserves to be compensated, but if a believer is not motivated to give, impersonal love is not offended. Giving is commanded, but your giving must not be irresponsible. You must never jeopardize the health and welfare of your family or renege on your financial obligations in order to donate to the church (1 Tim. 5:8).

JOHN TEACHES VIRTUE-LOVE

VIRTUE FROM BIBLE DOCTRINE

Virtue must be learned. We begin with doctrine, not with virtue. We must obey God's mandates and make the many positive decisions necessary to submit to the *process* of learning doctrine: reception, retention, recall.

> Furthermore, we have come to know [reception of doctrine at gate four of the divine dynasphere] and have believed [retention of doctrine] this love that God keeps having toward us [toward His righteousness in us]. (1 John 4:16*a*)

Bible doctrine reveals the nature of virtue-love, which reflects the essence of God.

> God is love [He loves His own integrity, establishing the policy of Virtue First]. In fact, the one who resides in the sphere of love [the love complex] continues in the [plan of] God, and God [the Holy Spirit, the Energizer of the divine system] stands fast [resides, continues, persists] in him. By this [living in the power of the divine dynasphere] the love [virtue-love: personal toward God and impersonal toward man] has been achieved by us. (1 John 4:16*b*, 17*a*)

The Greek noun *agape,* "love," establishes a category that encompasses the entire system of practical theology. Virtue-love becomes a description of the Christian way of life (1 Cor. 13:13). God's purpose in keeping you alive is that you may develop a personal love for Him inside the love complex. Until you have achieved love for God, you have accomplished nothing as a believer. Christianity is not witnessing, prayer, giving, singing, sacrifice, emotion. Even in their proper places these are secondary. Your primary function as a believer is virtue-love as a result of residence in the divine dynasphere. Personal love for God is the motivator of all the normal, legitimate activities of the Christian way of life.

God derives pleasure from giving us the option of going through life with virtue; He has established the game plan by which we can succeed. When we possess motivating virtue, we can obey all the functional mandates found in the Word of God, including the command to love all mankind—with impersonal love.

VIRTUE-LOVE AND FEAR

Along with virtue-love comes confidence. The advancing believer has mental poise and eager anticipation regarding even the ultimate test in life, the Judgment Seat of Christ, where our lives will be evaluated for eternal reward or loss of reward. Summoned before the God-Man, Jesus Christ, the absolute judge—who will decide the gravest possible issue, the final evaluation of each believer's Christian life—the mature believer will stand in complete freedom from anxiety or trepidation. Such confidence, which we can also possess in this life, is half of another pair of counterpart virtues: confidence in God and courage toward man and circumstances. The motivational virtue of confidence in God stands behind the functional virtue of courage toward people and circumstances.

> In order that we may have confidence in the day of evaluation [the Judgment Seat of Christ], because just as He is, so also are we in this world. (1 John 4:17b)

Christ, the future judge, possessed impeccable honor and virtue in the prototype divine dynasphere. We cannot be impeccable, but constructed upon the imputed divine righteousness that we received at salvation, our honor and virtue imitates Christ as we persist in the divine dynasphere in the devil's world.

> Fear does not exist in love [in the love complex]. (1 John 4:18a)

Uncontrolled fear is the opposite of courage. Courage toward man and confidence toward God stand together as counterpart virtues, so that when the mental attitude sin of fear controls the soul, all virtue is eliminated. Fear is a destroyer of love because fear destroys virtue. The love complex is the sphere of virtue, in which fear cannot possibly persist.

Because courage toward man is the functional virtue motivated by confidence in God, the believer who is sure of God's omnipotence, faithfulness, and logistical grace remains in control of his life even under maximum stress. Courage is *thinking* under duress; fear is inability to think. The coward is not necessarily the one who runs away but the one who freezes mentally under pressure.

When a mature, virtuous believer continues to conduct himself with poise and carry out his responsibilities under tremendous strain, he makes the pressure look like no pressure and his courage look like perfect aplomb. By learning doctrine in the power of the divine dynasphere, the believer builds confidence in God, which gives him courage, poise, and freedom from anxiety in applying doctrine to life.

> But virtue-love [*teleios*-love] expels [drives out, banishes]
> this fear. (1 John 4:18*b*)

Describing love, the Greek adjective *teleios* indicates that nothing which belongs to this love is left out; nothing can be added to it as an improvement; nothing of its own excellence is lacking. Often translated "perfect," *teleios* is an adjective of excellence. Aeschylus applied *teleios* to the gods as a divine attribute: "mighty, efficacious." Plato used *teleios* interchangeably with *arete*, "virtue." *Teleios* becomes a synonym for virtue, so that what is often quoted from the King James Version as "perfect love" takes on tremendous significance when recognized to mean "virtue-love." Satan sponsors false systems of love that depend on fear. Only virtue-love, which is the monopoly of God in the divine dynasphere, expels fear.

> For this fear causes punishment. (1 John 4:18*c*)

This is not a reference to divine discipline administered by the justice of God. The believer outside the divine dynasphere produces both the fear *and* his own punishment. Fear causes self-induced misery. By remaining in a position of weakness, a believer becomes his own worst enemy. He continually makes poor decisions, dedicating himself to a life of self-punishment. He cannot blame circumstances, environment, or other people for his unhappiness. He is the product of his own decisions to disobey the divine mandates concerning rebound, to ignore God's game plan, and to refuse to live in the sphere of virtue. He has failed to achieve virtue-love.

> In fact, the one who is afraid has not been matured in the
> love [has not attained virtue in the love complex]. (1 John
> 4:18*d*)

VIRTUE-LOVE AND HATRED

In verse 19, John presents the pattern of virtue-love as found in the essence of God.

> We love because He first loved us. (1 John 4:19)

In eternity past God knew every act of sin, human good, and evil that every believer would commit, yet He loved us with divine impersonal love based on His own integrity. Integrity characterizes His every action toward us. Because of divine integrity God the Father sent His Son to be born a man. As true humanity Christ paid the penalty for sin, which was demanded by divine integrity, so that anyone who believes in Him might be reconciled to God. Christ Himself possesses double integrity: as God He has divine righteousness and justice; as a man He remained impeccable in the prototype divine dynasphere.

God the Father has always loved the Son with perfect, eternal love, but from eternity past the purpose of Christ's first advent was always that He die on the Cross. At the Cross the integrity of God took precedence over divine love as the justice of the Father imputed our sins to Christ and judged them in Him.

The integrity of God makes His love for us possible. Therefore, we love on the same principle: integrity first. The depth of our personal love for God and the stability of our impersonal love for man depend on our virtue, honor, and integrity developed inside the divine dynasphere. Indeed, impersonal love is a technical term for the integrity or virtue of the subject.

First John 4:20 presents a hypothetical case in which a believer has lost control of his life, as manifest in the malfunction of virtue-love.

> If anyone should allege, "I love God," and yet he hates his
> fellow believer, he is a liar [he lives a lie]. (1 John 4:20a)

When a believer is filled with self-righteousness, guilt, self-pity, jealousy, antagonism, bitterness, or implacability, he is not in control of his life. Mental attitude sins are a sign of having relinquished command of the soul to the old sin nature, succumbing to the devil's influence.

If a believer does not control his life, he cannot produce virtue. He has no functional virtue toward man and circumstances, and if no functional virtue, no motivational virtue toward God. Gates five and six of the love complex stand or fall together; they are coexistent or nonexistent. If one part is missing, the whole is destroyed. The Christian who hates his fellow believer has arrogantly elevated himself above others; he has obscured his personal sense of destiny, which is fulfilled through spiritual momentum inside the divine dynasphere. Having removed himself from the power sphere of God, he resides in a position of weakness from which he can make only bad decisions. Satan is "a liar and the father of lies" (John 8:44), and the believer who rejects God's system lives a lie in Satan's counterfeit system.

> For he who does not love his fellow believer [malfunction of
> virtue, lack of impersonal love], whom he has seen, is not
> able to be loving God, whom he has not seen. (1 John 4:20b)

When the virtue of impersonal love in gate six is obliterated by mental attitude sins, the virtue of personal love in gate five also fails to operate. Hatred toward anyone robs you of virtue toward everyone, including God. It is self-deception to claim that you have virtue toward invisible God if you have none toward people. Gate five is the beginning of the batter's swing; gate six is the follow-through. There is no functional virtue without honorable motivation, and no motivational virtue exists if its inevitable result—a relaxed mental attitude toward people—is absent. Gates five and six of the divine dynasphere are interdependent.

DIVINE MANDATES FOR VIRTUE-LOVE

> Furthermore, we have this mandate from Him that he who loves God should also love his fellow believers. (1 John 4:21)

This is the divine mandate for a *totality* of virtue, for the *unity* of virtue-love toward God and man. You obey this command, not by seeking to love God and man, but by acquiring virtue in the sustained, coordinated function of gates one through four of the divine dynasphere.

You cannot possess permanent virtue without a permanent source of motivation. Anyone can put on a show of loving his fellow believer, but in time, as circumstances change, the deception inevitably crumbles. Virtue must be properly motivated. In order to love all mankind with impersonal love, you need a strong personal love for God. Love for God is based on a solid foundation of Bible doctrine in the soul, applied in the power of the Holy Spirit, the objectivity of basic Christian modus operandi, and the continued teachability of genuine humility. Gates five and six of the love complex stand as one principle, but ultimately *all* the gates of God's system stand or fall together.

First John 5 continues from chapter 4 and reiterates the link between motivational virtue and functional virtue.

> Everyone who believes that Jesus is the Christ [Messiah, the Anointed One] has been born from God. Furthermore, everyone who loves the Father loves everyone who has been born from Him. (1 John 5:1)

At the moment of salvation, every believer first enters the divine dynasphere through gate one, the filling of the Holy Spirit. The system that was a birthday gift from the Father to the Son on the first Christmas becomes a birthday gift to us, not at our physical birth, but at our spiritual birth. We possess the sphere of virtue, but no one automatically loves God. Nor does anyone automatically love all mankind. As we advance in the Christian life, we acquire that capacity for love. In the interlocking gates of the divine dynasphere, motivational virtue toward God and functional virtue toward man gradually develop as one entity. As we enter gate five, we simultaneously enter gate six.

> By this [development of virtue-love] we know [have a personal sense of destiny] that we keep loving the children of God [gate six], when we simultaneously love God [gate five] and keep His mandates [gates one through four]. For this is the love for God, that we might continue executing His mandates. (1 John 5:2, 3)

No one can live the Christian way of life outside the factory that manufactures virtue, the divine dynasphere. Every stage of the manufacturing process is clearly delineated in divine instructions and commands, and the Lord's mandates are not difficult to fulfill.

> Come to Me, all who are weary and heavy-laden, and I will give you rest. Take My yoke [the prototype divine dynasphere] upon you, and learn from Me [Bible doctrine, gate four, is the Mind of Christ], for I am gentle and humble in heart [gate three, genuine humility]; and you shall find rest for your souls. For My yoke is easy, and My load is light. (Matt. 11:28-30, NASV)

We all enter the Christian life with some handicap from our lives as unbelievers or from exposure to false teaching. But every handicap and difficulty is nullified by God's system of grace. Divine logistical grace, which provides the love complex, makes the difficult easy. Only your own negative volition prevents you from living the Christian way of life and advancing in virtue. The only issue that remains to be settled is, How will your volition function?

VII
Gate Seven, Momentum Testing

ACCELERATED GROWTH UNDER PRESSURE

You will inevitably face momentum tests as a necessary part of life; obstacles lie astride the path of every believer's growth. Testing in gate seven of the divine dynasphere is not an *exception* to God's grace; testing is an *expression* of God's grace. God either permits testing or directly sends testing, but His timing is always perfect. Only doctrine can keep pace with God's timing, and you accelerate your advance only by successfully overcoming obstacles. Indeed, you must pass tests in order to obtain the prize of sharing God's happiness in gate eight of the love complex (Phil. 3:14).

When you periodically encounter challenges to your progress, you either increase or lose momentum, depending on whether you pass or fail the test. Distractions to spiritual momentum can become the Christian's nemesis or one of the greatest opportunities for scoring tactical victories in the angelic conflict. If you are right with God, you can face the wrongs of injustice, disaster, or pressure with the power of the divine dynasphere.

As a believer you sustain your spiritual momentum through daily decisions to learn and apply Bible doctrine. You manifest the truth resident in your soul through growth and application, but spiritual growth withers and faith-rest will not function outside of the divine dynasphere. Man's volition is designed to obey the mandates of God. Volition can be used to succeed or fail; grace provides only for success.

The proper function of volition is hindered by arrogance, which also neutralizes doctrine in the soul. The arrogant believer, therefore, may know doctrine, but he cannot make prudent, judicious, and correct application. He can only distort the Word of God. He follows the path of Satan in eternity past. The devil knew more doctrine than any other creature, yet arrogance precipitated his fall (Isa. 14:14-16).

In opposition to God's game plan, Satan administers his own power system—the cosmic system—to prevent, impede, and reverse your spiritual momentum.[64] Although the power of God is greater than the power of Satan, the devil can lure you into arrogance or hatred so that you never attain spiritual strength. You attain cosmic strength, which cannot sustain you. When you reside in Satan's interlocking system of arrogance, you are a loser entangled in self-centeredness; in his interlocking system of hatred you are a dupe in rebellion against the mandates of God.

Volition is basic authority in life, the guardian of the soul. Because your free will can rebuff the ingenious strategy of Satan, you must strengthen your positive volition. You do so by consistently choosing to function in God's system: concentrate to learn doctrine, then concentrate to apply doctrine. The mental exercise of making right decisions to use the *epignosis* doctrine in your soul in life's pressures builds spiritual muscle and resolves momentum testing.

TAKING EXAMS, ENJOYING THE GAME

Momentum testing has a counterpart in academic life. In school you progress from one grade to the next because you have passed a series of tests. You have demonstrated your knowledge and application of the subjects taught in the previous grade. Likewise, as you achieve each level of spiritual growth, you will be tested for knowledge and application of doctrine in that increment of your Christian development. If you have been constant in learning doctrine under your pastor in the academic environment of the local church, you must take an exam, sometimes a pop quiz. Someone you love may die unexpectedly; an old friend may malign you; a cherished possession may be lost; your wealth taken from you. When misfortune comes, you take an exam. How do you face catastrophe? You have already learned the doctrine necessary to control the situation, so you *apply* the doctrine you know. You open the bluebook and begin to write, giving back to the Lord all He has taught you through the grace apparatus for perception.

Your use or misuse of the truth you have learned determines whether or not you will grow at this particular stage in your Christian life. If you fail, you retrogress spiritually and must fall back and regroup for an opportunity to learn more and be tested again at a later time. But you have missed the chance to accelerate your capacity for life. You cannot afford to flunk too many tests if you hope to

---

64. See below, pp. 158-70.

advance all the way to maturity. God gives each believer only a finite number of days, and you must continually learn and apply the truth, "redeeming the time" (Eph. 5:16).

I learned to play football under a system called the single wing, which involved making the same moves over and over in practice, a hundred times, a thousand times, before I ever had the opportunity to execute plays in a game. There was no brush blocking; everything was precise. To be effective I had to practice each play the same way again and again. All this was accomplished under the gruelling but relatively no-pressure situation of scrimmage. After the team had mastered the system and could execute the plays perfectly on the practice field, then we were faced with real opponents. The pressure situation was the actual game. But I had to perform exactly as I did in practice: execute the play; throw a perfect block. Our opponents fell all over themselves while our team gained yardage. We were actually having fun, even under pressure, because the system worked.

The same principle applies in coping with pressure in life. You may hear a doctrine repeated many times as the pastor faithfully exegetes the Scriptures over a number of years. Repetition means inculcation; under pressure you will need the entrenched knowledge of doctrinal concepts. When a crisis comes, you will discover that Bible doctrine works. Faith-rest is designed for pressure situations; indeed, the only tranquility in Christianity is humility, borrowing God's strength inside the divine dynasphere. In a hopeless situation reliance on God's Word is the only solution. God alone can *solve* hopeless problems; man *copes* with problems in humility and watches the deliverance of the Lord (Ex. 14:13).

The perception of doctrine is an academic function, but it is also a spiritual function requiring the interlock of the first four gates of the divine dynasphere. *Learning* under the grace apparatus for perception demands the filling of the Holy Spirit, objectivity, and enforced and genuine humility. Likewise, *applying* doctrine in gate four is also a spiritual function, demanding the interlock of all the gates of God's system. The divine commands to establish and increase your spiritual momentum summarize all the mandates related to the love complex.

Walk in love [the love complex]. (Eph. 5:2*a*)

Keep walking in it [the love complex]. (2 John 6*b*)

You perpetuate your momentum in two ways: through the perception of doctrine and the application of doctrine. Perception comes in Bible class; application comes in the problems of life, the momentum tests. No believer can advance without both functions of gate four of the divine dynasphere.

SUFFERING AS BLESSING OR DISCIPLINE

Gate seven of the divine dynasphere includes eight categories of testing and their solutions, but the suffering involved in any category of testing is designed for one of two purposes. You suffer either for *divine blessing* or for *divine discipline*. All causes of suffering and all forms of testing fall within these two categories, and when you come under pressure, the first question to resolve is whether you are suffering for discipline or for blessing.

	Suffering for Discipline	Suffering for Blessing
Issue	Sin	Grace
Status	Cosmic System	Divine Dynasphere
Characteristic	Unbearable	Bearable
Viewpoint	Subjectivity	Objectivity
Solution	Rebound	Application of Doctrine

CLASSIFICATION OF ALL CHRISTIAN SUFFERING

When you suffer for discipline, the issue is sin, human good, or evil. You are under pressure because you have made bad decisions from a position of weakness and are residing in Satan's power system. You cannot claim that "the devil is after me"; *you* have pursued the devil. You have chosen to sin. Only God can convert divine discipline, or self-induced misery, into blessing, and this He has done by providing rebound for reentry into the divine dynasphere. When you are suffering for discipline, the issue is sin, but when suffering for blessing, the issue is grace. God is graciously testing you in order to stimulate your application of doctrine. You store the Word of God in your soul; He magnanimously expedites your progress toward supergrace.

The distinction between these two general categories of testing is that suffering for punishment is unbearable, whereas suffering for blessing is bearable. You cannot endure divine punishment or self-induced misery because you are in a position of weakness, slavery to the power system of Satan. But you can handle suffering for blessing through the power of the divine dynasphere.

> Testing [for blessing] has not caught up with you except the
> human kind; moreover, God is faithful, who will not permit
> you to be tested beyond your capabilities, but with the
> testing He will also provide a way out [the faith-rest drill in
> the divine dynasphere] so that you can endure it [cursing
> turned to blessing]. (1 Cor. 10:13).

When you are suffering for discipline, your viewpoint is arrogance and subjectivity; you blame others for your misfortune or feel sorry for yourself. When suffering for blessing, however, your attitude is humility and objectivity. You are using the doctrinal rationales of the faith-rest drill. You are teachable and alert to learn from the crisis. Rebound is the solution to suffering for punishment; the application of doctrine is the solution to suffering for blessing.

If you have persevered in the divine dynasphere under normal circumstances, then when pressure arrives you will *continue* to function honorably. Sometimes the pain and the pressure are so intense that you may feel you are going down instead of up; right decisions may appear to set you back; compromise of God's truth seems to be the route to quick advance or relief from pain. But by continuing to utilize God's system, all testing is effectively resolved, and a higher plane of spiritual growth achieved.

STRENGTH IN THE DIVINE SYSTEM

In the cosmic system not only are you unable to tolerate suffering, but you will continue to fail. You will become subjective, vacillating, untrustworthy, and you will drag others into your misery. You will impose on your friends or pastor, demanding their time and attention, seeking their sympathy. But no amount of counseling will avail. The best advice in the world falls on deaf ears when that person under pressure is in the cosmic system. Commiserating with such a person will not help. He resides in a sphere of power—Satan's power—that he can escape only by his own volition. Before any doctrine is usable to him, he must leave the cosmic system and reenter the divine dynasphere. Unless he is willing to make this decision, he will continue to drain his friends and family emotionally, physically, mentally, and often financially. Inside the cosmic system, no one can keep the truth organized. That is why *believers* fall apart, become psychotic, go on criminal binges, commit suicide.

There are eight basic momentum tests, and for each test God has provided a solution. The objective application of Bible doctrine operates only inside the interlocking system of love. God has given us a system; His power is available to us only inside that system. We must obey His mandates in order to pass the momentum tests and forge ahead in the Christian life. God's promise to ''not

Test	Solution
1. Old Sin Nature	Rebound
2. People	Impersonal Love
3. Thought	Doctrinal Rationales
4. Systems	Impersonal Love and Doctrinal Rationales
5. Arrogance Complex	Divine Dynasphere
6. Hatred Complex	Divine Dynasphere
7. Disaster	Faith-Rest Drill
8. Prosperity	Genuine Humility and Perception of Doctrine

TESTS OF SPIRITUAL MOMENTUM

permit you to be tested beyond your capabilities'' applies only within the sphere He has provided.

> The love [the love complex] endures with fortitude under pressure. (1 Cor. 13:4a)

The Greek verb *makrothumeo* means to be longsuffering, enduring, patient; to endure with courage and steadfastness; to exercise forbearance under provocation; to be undisturbed by obstacles, delays, failures; to be able to bear the stress and strain of pressure. Fortitude belongs to the love complex because God knew that we would need endurance for accelerated spiritual momentum in the devil's world. Stubbornness is not strength; stubbornness is weakness and inflexibility. A false code of honor is always inflexible, subjective, and arrogant, whereas perseverance in the divine dynasphere is flexible, leading to integrity in changing, unpredictable circumstances.

> And [the love complex] functions in integrity. (1 Cor. 13:4b)

Integrity demands objective thought. When God commands you to persevere in the love complex, He is ordering you to *think* divine viewpoint. Right thinking leads to right motivation, and right motivation leads to right action. All the gates of the love complex function together as integral parts of the whole when doctrine is being correctly applied.

The fundamental conflict between the divine dynasphere and the cosmic system, between the bearable and the unbearable, is emphasized in the first momentum test. If you control your old sin nature properly, you assure that you do indeed reside in the love complex and stand in a position of strength, ready to meet any challenge.

THE OLD SIN NATURE TEST

TEMPTATION VERSUS SIN

The old sin nature is the source of temptation but not the source of sin.[65] Sin, human good, and evil are the products of the sin nature when it controls the soul, but they are caused by human volition. Regardless of what you do in thought, word, or deed, you do it because you want to do it. You are responsible for all your thoughts, motives, and actions, whether sinful or honorable. Ignorance is no excuse; insanity is no excuse. What you do, you choose to do. You must take responsibility for your personal decisions in order to find solutions to your problems.

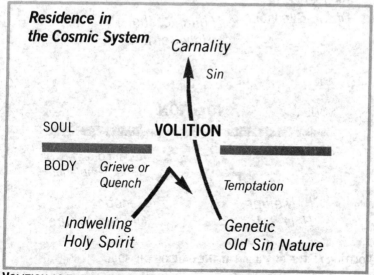

VOLITION AS THE SOURCE OF SIN

---

65. See Thieme, *Integrity of God*, pp. 75-77.

Volition is the guardian at the gate of the soul, protecting the soul from the old sin nature, Satan's inside agent headquartered in the body. Only your consent allows the old sin nature to take control of your soul. You alone convert temptation into sin. When you succumb to the solicitations of the sin nature, you automatically enter the cosmic system, entering via some variation of mental attitude arrogance. Mental attitude sins are motivational evils that lead to functional evils. Mental attitude sins are expressed in verbal and overt sins and contribute to human good and evil.

In contrast, when you are residing in the divine dynasphere and resist temptation, you remain inside the divine dynasphere. You remain filled with the Spirit. Gate two of God's system, which includes basic impersonal love, insulates you against the old sin nature. Freedom from mental attitude sins is an inherent quality of impersonal love directed toward all people, which is not only the highest Christian virtue but also your primary line of defense against failing the sin nature test. Temptation is not sin; you do not lose your fellowship with God simply because you are tempted to sin. Your love for God in the divine dynasphere gives you the strength and wisdom to resist or avoid temptation.

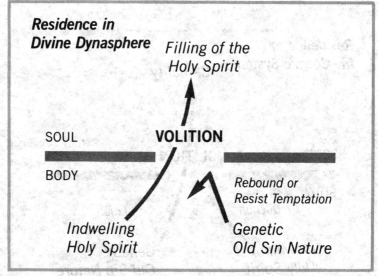

Residence in Divine Dynasphere

Filling of the Holy Spirit

SOUL   **VOLITION**

BODY

Rebound or Resist Temptation

Indwelling Holy Spirit   *Genetic Old Sin Nature*

VOLITION AS THE GUARDIAN AT THE GATE OF THE SOUL

Sin has no place in God's game plan; nevertheless, we all sin. Even the most mature believers fail from time to time. When you do slip into the arrogance complex through mental attitude sins, the solution is no longer resisting temptation. It is too late for that. The answer is immediate rebound. Everyone in the cosmic system is a loser; you must quickly move back into the sphere of God's plan in order to be on the winning side again. Rebound is tantamount to recognizing that you are responsible for the decision that took you out of the divine dynasphere and that now it is your responsibility to get back in through the grace system God has provided.

The rebound technique both reinstates you in the divine dynasphere and solves the problem of suffering for discipline. Suffering is unbearable only because you have rejected God's grace system for dealing with suffering. The inner strength of the divine dynasphere makes suffering bearable. In the cosmic system you are arrogant, subjective, and self-centered, which complicates your life and makes any difficulty intolerable. But the love complex gives you the ability to "endure with fortitude under pressure," not with gritted teeth but in the confident serenity of your fellowship with God. Personal love for God motivates impersonal love toward man and circumstances.

When you suddenly find yourself in adversity, how do you know if you are suffering for discipline or for blessing? In the cosmic system, you are being disciplined; in the divine dynasphere, blessed. But how do you determine which dynasphere is controlling you? The issue is sin. If you are sinning or have unconfessed sin in your life, you are under the control of the sin nature in the cosmic system. If you have no unconfessed sins, you have passed the old sin nature test, at least for now. You can then be certain that you are filled with the Spirit and that gate one of the divine dynasphere energizes the entire divine system.

THE REBOUND RATIONALE

Rebound is an extremely simple application of doctrine. If you keep short accounts with God, if you do not permit unconfessed sins to accumulate, then you need only a moment to name your sins privately to God. Restoration to fellowship is instantaneous, but the rebound technique is backed up by an entire structure of basic truths.

Rebound is easy for us because it was hard for Jesus Christ; it cost Him the Cross. In the perception side of gate four, you have concentrated on learning the salvation doctrines of propitiation, redemption, and reconciliation, as communicated by your pastor; now in the application side of gate four, you reverse your concentration to bring these pertinent doctrines to mind in a logical rationale. The rebound rationale ultimately leads to doctrinal conclusions that enable you to forget your failure and move on in confidence. Thus, rebound employs the three stages of the faith-rest drill.

In stage one of the faith-rest drill, your faith reaches out and claims a promise.

> For this reason, many among you are weak [warning discipline] and sick [intensive discipline], and a number sleep [sin unto death]. But if we judged ourselves rightly [rebound adjustment to the justice of God], we should not be judged. (1 Cor. 11:30, 31; NASV)

> If we confess [name, cite, acknowledge] our sins, He [God the Father] is faithful and righteous [justified] with the result that He forgives us our sins [known sins] and also cleanses us from all unrighteousness [unknown sins]. (1 John 1:9)

You claim these promises by doing what they command: name your sins. As a member of the royal family of God, you are your own priest, representing yourself as a private individual before God. When you cite your sins privately to God, He keeps His promise to forgive you and cleanse you from all your sins, known and unknown. How you feel about your sins is not an issue. There is no reference to your feelings in the rebound promises. Emotion is never a criterion of spiritual status. What counts is God's attitude toward your sins. Your emotion adds nothing, and a guilt complex is just another sin.

In stage two of the faith-rest drill, your faith reaches out and follows a logical rationale. According to the doctrines of salvation, specifically the doctrine of the first judicial imputation, your personal sins were imputed to Christ on the Cross and judged.[66]

> He [God the Father] made Him [Christ], who knew no sin, to be sin on our behalf [in place of us; Christ was our substitute], that we might become the righteousness of God in Him. (2 Cor. 5:21)

Reverse concentration recalls the doctrines that explain why rebound works every time and why the procedure is so simple. The sin has already been judged on the Cross, and the judicial verdicts of God are perfect, final, and irreversible. You can add nothing to a legal case that God has closed. By naming your sins, you are accepting the finished work of Christ on your behalf for the forgiveness of your sins, just as you accepted His work for your salvation. In both salvation and rebound all that remains for you to contribute is nonmeritorious positive volition. You merely accept what God has done. Rebound does not depend on you. That is why it works every time, and that is why, under the principle of grace, God receives all the credit. Your emotions, guilt, worry, and remorse are intrusions that stand in the way of your recovery and continued spiritual advance.

66. See Thieme, *Integrity of God*, pp. 77-86.

In the third stage of the faith-rest drill, faith reaches doctrinal conclusions. You conclude that the sin in question has been paid for in full, that you are now back in fellowship with God inside the divine dynasphere, that you have escaped the cosmic system and are controlled once again by God the Holy Spirit. In the energy of the Spirit and obeying the mandates connected with the other gates of God's system, you have regained control of the situation. Pressure and suffering may continue, but what was intolerable has now become bearable in the dynamics of the eight gates of God's game plan.

PEOPLE TESTING

REACTION AND ATTRACTION

When you fall victim to injustice, you can become bitterly impatient. "How long will my enemy triumph?" (Ps. 13:2*b*). Periodic opposition from people is inevitable because the majority of people in the world live exclusively in the cosmic system, and in the devil's kingdom nothing is fair. Only God's integrity is fair, giving you the divine system for survival and happiness in all circumstances. God provides divine establishment, logistical grace, Bible doctrine, the divine dynasphere, whereas people often give you nothing but vacillation, antagonism, misunderstanding, slander, and disappointment. Under such testing there is no excuse for becoming discouraged or cynical. Suffering for blessing is always positive: a mature believer's integrity is revealed not only in his personal virtues but also, to use the old phrase, you can tell a person's character by who his enemies are.

You can be distracted away from the momentum line to maturity if you react to those who naturally rub you the wrong way. A personality conflict, if uncontrolled, can develop into a deep-seated hatred, revenge motivation, or the arrogance of complete insensitivity. Hostile subjectivity has no place in the plan of God.

But your antagonists are only one category of people who can distract you from your spiritual growth. Your momentum can also suffer through those whom you love. Many a growing believer is led astray by someone he finds fascinating and attractive.

Personal love can magnify weaknesses, create vulnerabilities, and obliterate objectivity. Hence, personal love for another member of the human race, no matter how romantic, is not a virtue. Such personal love is virtue-dependent, depending on the true virtue of impersonal love, which itself depends on the virtue of personal love for God. Furthermore, personal love for God is erected on the foundational virtue of genuine humility, the teachability factor that enables you to learn Bible doctrine. Humility develops motivational virtue toward God;

motivational virtue toward God sustains functional virtue toward man, which sustains virtue-dependent personal love toward man. Impersonal love is an individual's integrity, and integrity gives strength and stability to personal love.

If your personal love is not reciprocated, or if the person you love becomes a disappointment, then reaction sets in. Without impersonal love you enter the cosmic system through the mental attitude sin of arrogance and quickly interlock with iconoclastic arrogance, the arrogance of unhappiness, or discouragement.[67] All the tremendous energy of personal love is now expressed in disillusion, depression, bitterness, implacability, self-pity, vindictiveness, or guilt reaction. The pain and confusion generated by personal love is a test of your spiritual momentum.

RELYING ON IMPERSONAL LOVE

People testing is generated by those you love or those you dislike, but the solution to both categories is impersonal love. Whether involved in personal love or personal hatred, the believer's attitude must revert to impersonal love. When someone you love disillusions you or rides roughshod over your feelings, you switch your emphasis from that person to your own character. In gates two and six of the love complex, you maintain your love and your own equilibrium and avoid bitterness.

When you switch from personal love to impersonal love, you are actually falling back on the virtue that sustains your personal love for people. Impersonal love and personal love run parallel: one a virtue toward God, the other a virtue toward mankind. Impersonal love is the *virtue* of loving all and is also the *capacity* for loving a few people with personal love. No matter what may be the ups and downs of a personal love relationship, the capacity of impersonal love is always there. The foundation is consistent: your understanding of Bible doctrine, which builds your Christian integrity.

When personal love falters and one of the select few who are the objects of your personal love suddenly becomes less attractive to you, you still have the foundation of impersonal love. This becomes the mechanics for solving people problems. You do not demand that the object of your love change his personality to suit you or regain the qualities that attract you. Instead, you shift your emphasis from personal to impersonal love. If personal love is not working at the moment, you maintain your own stability. Your emphasis on impersonal love permits the object of your love the grace and freedom to be a person. He does not and cannot always live up to the high expectations you cherish in the objects of your personal love.

---

67.   See below, pp. 163-65.

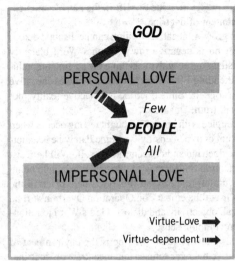

Virtue-Love →
Virtue-dependent ⇢

**THE BELIEVER'S PERSONAL AND
IMPERSONAL LOVE**

We are all imperfect, and from time to time each of us is living proof of the total depravity of man. Periodically we need to be tolerated with impersonal love just as our loved ones need to be graced occasionally by our impersonal love. Impersonal love is the only means of survival for personal love.

Likewise, when you are tempted to enter the cosmic system through hatred, you must switch to impersonal love. Instead of indulging in vituperation, you must treat the offensive individual on the basis of who and what you are, not on who and what he may be. Impersonal love for all people fulfills the principle of live and let live. In social life impersonal love insures civilized behavior, poise, and graciousness. In business life impersonal love maintains your honor and professionalism when dealing with people you may personally loathe. In spiritual life impersonal love enables a completely incompatible variety of believers to assemble in harmony in one local church to hear the teaching of Bible doctrine. Without impersonal love you cannot sustain your happiness and growth in the devil's kingdom in close proximity with other people, each of whom possesses his own weaknesses, eccentricities, and old sin nature.

THOUGHT TESTING

POSITIVE VOLITION VERSUS NEGATIVE VOLITION

Momentum in the Christian life demands thought. What you think is what you are (Prov. 23:7), and in order to grow up spiritually you must think Bible doctrine in both learning and applying. In thought testing the issue is positive versus negative volition toward doctrine. In the arrogance complex of Satan's cosmic system, negative volition makes an issue of self; in the hatred complex, negative volition opposes the content of doctrine.[68]

As a distraction to spiritual growth, negative volition can be a subtle detour from the truth. Not everyone who is negative toward God's Word blatantly rejects the message. Some Christians agree with everything the pastor communicates and may be tenacious in attending Bible class but are nonetheless negative because they think only in terms of self. Bible doctrine is objective reality, not subjective. Arrogance distorts all truth.

For a believer who is preoccupied with himself, thought testing occurs when a particular doctrine strikes a point of hypersensitivity. Immediately he is tempted to shift his attention from the doctrine and concentrate on self. Will he resist the temptation and focus his attention on learning the doctrinal principle being presented? Will he seek to accurately understand this doctrine's place in the whole realm of Biblical truth? Or will he embark on Operation Overthink? If he indulges his arrogance he loses all objectivity and distorts God's Word to rationalize conclusions that defy even common sense.

God is logical, not illogical; knowledge of doctrine is the environment of true thought. But the hypersensitive believer refuses to concentrate on doctrine, frequently going off half-cocked, straining to apply what he does not adequately understand. Only *epignosis* doctrine can be used for application, the construction of the edification complex, and spiritual growth. When a believer tries to apply *gnosis* doctrine to his life, he becomes shallow, relying on his own prejudices, subjective instincts, and stubbornness.

Stubbornness may pass for positive volition, but the two are not the same. Stubbornness is a flaw that can exist in a stupid person or a smart person. His preoccupation with himself is the weakness that makes him stick with Bible class. He has no genuine interest in or love for the truth. He is locked into inordinate concern for what others think of him, so that he continues to attend even though he has never benefitted from the pastor's message.

A believer also faces thought testing when a point of doctrine runs counter to his personal opinions. His prejudices and preconceived notions are challenged, but instead of reacting with subjectivity, he reacts with antagonism against the doctrine itself.

THE NEED FOR A FRAME OF REFERENCE

In the process of growing spiritually, you develop a doctrinal frame of reference. The more you know, the more you can learn; doctrine is built on doctrine. When a principle is taught that is more advanced than your current frame of reference can accommodate, obviously you will not understand it. You may hear

---

68. See below, pp. 160-63.

that rebound requires nothing more than privately naming your sins to God. If you were reared in a legalistic home, the doctrine of rebound may shock you at first. You have spent all your life doing penance, trying to work up a feeling of remorse, promising God you will never commit that sin again, and suddenly you are told that your effort was in vain. Indeed, you are dogmatically taught that all your human works to earn restoration to fellowship with God have been blasphemous. Your immediate inclination is to reject the entire concept of rebound by grace.

The problem is your ignorance. Your frame of reference lacks the doctrines of redemption, reconciliation, propitiation, the principle of the judicial imputation of all personal sins to Christ on the Cross, and an understanding of the privileges of your royal priesthood. There is no way that the accurate doctrine of rebound could possibly fit into the erroneous frame of reference of your religious upbringing. As a result you are tempted not only to oppose rebound but even to denounce the pastor as apostate.

If you flunk thought testing on the issue of rebound, you will never take the first step toward spiritual maturity. In order to pass this test, you must reserve judgment. You may not be able immediately to accept a particular point of doctrine at face value, but you must be humble enough to realize that you still have a lot to learn. Just as, when eating fish, you would place the bones to one side of the plate, you also set aside the doctrines you cannot accept. You do not throw out the entire spiritual meal. Eventually, as you continue to learn doctrine, you will construct the frame of reference that enables you to understand and accept these doctrines.

You pass the thought test by objectively concentrating on what the pastor is saying so that you can comprehend the concept, whether you believe it or not. Receptive comprehension in the left lobe precedes full understanding in the right lobe. As your frame of reference expands, you will be able to integrate doctrines that seemed difficult at the time with other doctrines that you have learned in the interim.

Throughout your life as a believer, you will always have questions about various points of doctrine. All of God's Word is meant to be understood; it is *revelation,* not obscurity. Therefore, if you set aside for later the concepts you do not understand and continue to take in doctrine, eventually those questions will be resolved. But then, other questions will take their place. You will never run out of things to learn. Spiritual growth is the dynamic process of increasing your *epignosis* frame of reference and integrating doctrine with doctrine.

THE COHESIVENESS OF TRUTH

A believer can also flunk thought testing by attempting to reconcile doctrine with his favorite academic subject. This is the same problem as having a limited doctrinal frame of reference, but now the believer has a secular rather than a religious background. Contemporary theories of psychology, sociology, anthropology, biology, or even the physical sciences may run counter to the teachings of the Word of God. The conflict exists either because doctrine itself is misunderstood or because the scientific theory is incomplete.

Actually all truth fits together as one coherent whole under the omniscience of God; apparent contradictions are based on arrogance or ignorance in the minds of men. A believer may have been taught in college certain tenets of philosophy that do not mesh with his current understanding of God's Word. If he clings to the erroneous philosophy, he either rejects doctrine or distorts the truth to fit the mold of the false.

During the first century A.D., the philosophy of Gnosticism presented a devastating thought test for the early Church. Many believers were lured away from spiritual momentum in the divine dynasphere. Gnosticism incorporated Christian vocabulary but completely twisted the truth, advocating as morality everything from sybaritic debauchery to austere asceticism. By mixing spiritual truth with philosophical and mystical notions and appealing to the lust patterns of nearly everyone, the Gnostic religious philosophy seduced many early Christians.

Your defense against thought testing is the faith-rest drill with emphasis on the rationales—the essence-of-God rationale, the plan-of-God rationale, the logistical-grace rationale. Loyalty to the truth is Christian integrity, and only a believer with integrity can successfully resist falsehood. This solution demands that you exercise your freedom and personal initiative to habitually take in doctrine.

When doctrine is ignored or treated casually, then doubt becomes another form of thought testing: you lack a fresh inventory of truth with which to ward off false ideas. Doctrine in the soul becomes rusty when not maintained by daily intake based on self-motivation. The faith-rest drill cannot operate when the rationales have deteriorated through a lack of doctrinal perception.

Reverse concentration of the faith-rest drill copes with thought testing because the logical delineation of doctrine exposes the inconsistencies of false thinking and defeats its influence. Thinking the truth is the only defense against thinking what is false. The conflict of the divine dynasphere versus the cosmic system is the battle of thought versus thought. This warfare is waged in your soul: divine viewpoint is pitted against cosmic-influenced human viewpoint. Satan's evil counterfeits attack the reality of God's plan.

Satan's genius is far superior to any human rationalism or empiricism. Our only hope of passing thought testing, since we face such a superior enemy, is to rely on faith. Empiricism and rationalism are cheap substitutes compared to faith. God's Word outshines miracles, which change nothing, and surpasses all human philosophies, which resolve nothing. Through faith we must depend on all categories of God's truth: establishment, the Gospel, and doctrine. Only Bible doctrine in your soul, recalled to mind through the faith-rest drill, can withstand the subtle, attractive, chameleon propaganda of the devil, whose objective is to halt your spiritual momentum.

SYSTEM TESTING

UNFAIRNESS IN THE DEVIL'S WORLD

Many a weak individual has failed in an organization because of his own ineptitude or inefficiency only to falsely blame prejudice, politics, or unfairness in the organization for obstructing his promotion. Making an issue of self in self-pity or self-righteousness is superficial. Such a subjective individual is disorganized in his soul and is incapable of administration, executive thinking, or even reliable obedience to company policy. He is no asset to any organization, and he is easily distracted from progress in the plan of God.

On the other hand, genuine unfairness does exist in human organizations and systems. Sooner or later every believer on the momentum line will fall victim to an unfair system. You may be preyed upon by a criminal only to discover, when the case comes to trial, that our present judicial structure favors the criminal over the law-abiding citizen. You may be a superior employee and yet be passed over for an important position, which is given instead to a less capable person who has played politics with the boss. You may be an officer in a metropolitan police department that is run by bureaucracy instead of leadership and find yourself abused, reprimanded, or suspended for an action that actually should be commended. As a military officer, you may face pettiness and unfairness from career-minded senior officers who would be incompetent to command even a platoon under the pressure of combat. A rotten system creates rotten people and makes victims of those who are honorable. This is what I mean by system testing.

A bad system often includes good people, but when they are abused by the system, their attitude, motivation, and integrity need not be destroyed by the unfairness they suffer. The advancing believer need not allow system testing to contribute to his own failure.

If you are a good employee but are fired by an unfair boss, what should you do? Should you become bitter or vindictive and vent your wrath to anyone who will listen? Should you take vengeance or seek to vindicate your sullied honor? Should you threaten to sue? Or fall into worry or self-pity? Indeed not. As a member of the royal family of God, possessing the power sphere that sustained the Lord Jesus Christ, you were never intended to behave as unbelievers do, or as believers behave in the cosmic system. Even though you have been handed a reversal, you still have the opportunity to turn it into a substantial victory.

But if you allow this momentum test to lure you into a pattern of cosmic reaction, you miss your opportunity; you act like a spiritual peasant. Failing the system test means failure to advance at this particular stage of your spiritual life. No testing of the growing believer ever comes as an accident. If you are treated unfairly, God has a purpose in it. He has a reason for bringing pressure into your life. His objective is to accelerate your growth.

When an organization implies that you have failed when actually the system itself, not you, has failed, you have an occasion to advance that does not exist under conditions of success. We can always learn from our failures; rarely do we learn from our successes. At one time or another everyone fails or is considered a failure. But it is your attitude in failure that determines your mettle, not your attitude in success.

Anyone can conduct himself with dignity and poise under agreeable circumstances, but when difficulties abound, especially when the misfortune is unfair, then a person's true character is illuminated. What you really are is what you are under pressure. In other words, paradoxically, failure is the making of a person. No one can succeed without overcoming failure. In disaster he forges the virtues that lead him out of failure into success. Hence, system testing should be the challenge of the believer, not the destruction.

You have no excuse for being shocked when you are treated unfairly. Who ever told you the world was fair? Satan rules this world through his cosmic system, and no facet of his system is fair, just, or honorable. The devil's system is totally unfair because Satan has something missing from his character. He is the most beautiful angelic creature ever to exist; he is the most personable, most erudite, most accomplished genius to come from the hand of God (Ezek. 28:12b–17). Yet by his own free will Satan lacks integrity. Integrity comes from truth, Bible doctrine in the soul, which Satan opposes. As the enemy of truth, Satan can only be unfair. But in the very quality he lacks, we find our strength to deal with his injustices. In Bible doctrine and the integrity of living in the divine dynasphere, we have the solution to system testing.

SOCIAL LIFE WITH MAN, SOCIAL LIFE WITH GOD

In principle, the solution to system testing is our social life with God. In specific application, the answer is the combination of implementing impersonal love and using the faith-rest drill.

Anyone with discernment and sufficient humility to possess common sense limits his social life. He reserves his personal love for just those friends who are not only honorable and stimulating but are also compatible with his personality, interests, and objectives in life. Beyond that inner circle are many acquaintances whose company he may enjoy on a limited basis. You choose your friends by their virtues; you like their approach to life and value their observations and opinions. Because of their integrity you respect their opinions and, therefore, you care what they think.

When you become the victim of an inequitable system, you may be embarrassed to face your friends. System testing often brings the corollary pressure of peer ostracism. You may imagine that your friends condemn you, so you avoid them and cut out your social life altogether. But such a reaction is strictly preoccupation with self. You have fallen into the arrogance, subjectivity, and self-pity of the cosmic system.

But you may also react by going out of your way to explain yourself. You may devote tremendous energy to justifying yourself so friends will not assume the worst. But people will think whatever they wish to think. Your subjective attempts to control their opinions merely confuse the issue and suggest that the worst is, in fact, true. You are wasting your time and theirs.

Whether you retreat from your friends or try frantically to explain yourself to those who ostracize you, you have flunked the system test. By your own volition you have converted an unfair situation into a personal failure.

When you have been rejected, fired, or censured by an unfair organization, there will always be people who will look down on you. Gloaters are never hard to find, especially if you have excelled in the past. When your reputation and good name come under attack, you may lose some friends, but they were not true friends in the first place. If they forsake you, you are all the better for it. Genuine friends are revealed under pressure; the fact that you have become *persona non grata* in a certain organization means nothing to them and does not affect their loyalty in the least. Hence, momentum testing has the added benefit of winnowing your social life.

In the final analysis, your social life with God is far more important than your social life with people will ever be. Your relationship with God is your stability. He is not upset because you have been treated unfairly. He desires that you be occupied with Him, and He knows that system testing can accelerate your progress toward that goal.

We normally call our fellowship with God "spirituality" or "worship" or "the Christian way of life," but these often fail to communicate. "Social life with God" more aptly describes our fellowship with Him. We enter into social life with people because we desire companionship, sharing, humor, intellectual stimulation, and because we *enjoy* our friends and acquaintances. We can also enjoy *God* during our lives on earth. Through Bible doctrine and the function of the interlocking systems of love, we can find pleasure in Him.

Our social life does not depend on being able to see, touch, or hear God; the Word of God is a much "more reliable witness" than our human senses (2 Pet. 1:19). When we make our relationship with God our most important social life, that *is* spiritual momentum. This is the interlock between Bible doctrine in gate four of the divine dynasphere and personal love for God in gate five. If your social life with Him is right, then no failure or alleged failure in life can cause you to use your own volition to destroy yourself in the satanic system.

Based on your rapport with God, the specific solution to system testing is twofold. Since the challenge to your spiritual momentum involves both people testing and thought testing, the solutions to these separate pressures must combine. The believer must utilize impersonal love to deal with the people in the system and must use the faith-rest drill to cope with the injustices of the system itself.

DIRECT ATTACKS OF THE COSMIC SYSTEM

SATANIC CONTROL OF THE SOUL

Satan has no integrity. In eternity past he received maximum love and generosity from God, which he repaid with ingratitude and treachery. Ruthlessly ambitious to advance himself, Satan promises happiness and prosperity he cannot produce. His policies appear to be noble, elevated, and enlightened, "and no wonder, for even Satan disguises himself as an angel of light" (2 Cor. 11:14). But his apparent truths always have a dark side. If you are not alert to his sinister lies, you become his slave.

> If therefore the light [satanic deception] that is in you is darkness, how great is the darkness! (Matt. 6:23*b*, NASV)

Satan is a menacing foe, "like a roaring lion, seeking someone to devour" (1 Pet. 5:8). He is singleminded; he knows his objective—to discredit God and establish his own utopia on earth. He is well organized. He has a system for achieving his goal. To gain *control* over the kingdom he now *rules*, the devil manipulates mankind in the cosmic system. You as a believer in the Lord Jesus Christ are Satan's quarry. Satan is an insidious genius who would deceive us all were we not protected by truth in the divine dynasphere.

A magnetic leader, Satan commands vast forces of fallen angels or demons; Earth and fallen mankind belong to his realm. In the Bible Satan's kingdom is called the *kosmos*, usually translated "world." *Kosmos* refers to a system, an orderly, cohesive organization with a purpose, policy, and structure of authority. When the Bible declares that someone loves the world (2 Tim. 4:10; James 4:4; 1 John 2:15) or lives according to the standards of the world (Rom. 12:2; Eph. 2:2), that individual resides in the satanic system of power. He enslaves himself to Satan's authority, executes Satan's policy, and fulfills Satan's purpose.

The cosmic system employs two dynaspheres, which pose the fifth and sixth momentum tests. The *arrogance complex* leads the believer into apathy toward Bible doctrine, while the *hatred complex* parlays that indifference into antagonism toward doctrine.

Worldliness is individual involvement in the cosmic system. Satan encourages superficial definitions of worldliness to camouflage his evil strategy. Legalistic believers mistakenly assume that worldliness consists of gambling, carousing, dancing, drinking, or any behavior that shocks them personally. But while such activities may reflect poor judgment and may indeed involve sin in one category or another, they are not the essence of what the Bible describes as worldly.

Worldliness is what you *think* inside the cosmic system, not just what you *do*. Satan's ultimate weapon is evil thought—the subtle distortions, half truths, and lies he uses to control man's thinking. This ultimate weapon is called *demon influence*. When you embrace satanic ideas, you are the dupe of Satan. Your sincerity does not protect you; ignorance is no excuse. You become your own worst enemy. When you believe 'the father of lies'' (John 8:44), the content of your own soul prevents spiritual growth and prohibits divine blessings.

> But that same Spirit [the Holy Spirit] explicitly communicates that in later periods of time some [believers] will fall away from doctrine [become apostate], paying attention to deceitful spirits [evil teachers] and concentrating on doctrines of demons. (1 Tim. 4:1)

"Doctrines of demons" enter your inventory of ideas when your volition operates without truth—without divine establishment, the Gospel, and Bible doctrine. This absence of truth, this vacuum in the soul, is called in the Greek *mataiotes,* "emptiness, vanity." The vacuum draws in false doctrines, filling your soul with arrogance and antagonism.

> For bombastically speaking arrogant words from the source of emptiness [the *mataiotes* vacuum], they [false teachers] keep enticing by lusts, by lasciviousness, those who barely escape from those who live in error [from believers living in the cosmic system]. (2 Pet. 2:18)

Man is weak not strong. We borrow strength—for good or for evil—from two antithetical sources: the divine dynasphere or the cosmic system. If you refuse the power of the divine dynasphere, then you are controlled by the tyrannical cosmic system. When you reject Bible doctrine, you *receive* the alternative, satanic doctrine, with destructive effect.

If anyone teaches a different doctrine and does not concur
with sound doctrine, namely those doctrines of our Lord
Jesus Christ, even to that doctrine pertaining to godliness
[doctrine leading to maturity], he has received arrogance,
understanding nothing. (1 Tim. 6:3, 4a)

When human volition presents any opportunity, Satan seizes the initiative;
the individual "receives arrogance." If the unbeliever refuses protection in the
divine dynasphere through faith in Christ or obedience to the laws of establishment, if the believer fails to rebound and continue in doctrine, arrogance intensifies. False doctrine and evil ideas infiltrate the soul until he can no longer make
good decisions. Spiritual "blindness" blacks out his soul (John 12:40; 2 Cor.
4:3, 4); he develops "hardness of heart" or scar tissue of the soul (Ex. 7:22;
8:15, 32; 9:34).

Unknowingly or deliberately, you fall victim to satanic influence by your
own volition. You choose to submit to "the spirit that is now working among the
sons of disobedience [negative volition]" (Eph. 2:2). Through active or passive
consent, you create an opening for demon doctrines to enter your soul. You may
actively pursue evil, as in idolatry or Satan worship, or you may *passively* render
yourself vulnerable through drug addiction or through attitudes of self-
righteousness, self-pity, anger, guilt reaction, or disrespect for establishment
authority. Sin is not just sin; sin triggers the power of the cosmic system.

PROFILE OF SATANIC POLICY

Both dynaspheres of the cosmic system exploit your bad decisions, impris-
oning you in a labyrinth of satanic deceit. By definition a dynasphere is a system
of power in which man is controlled by a power greater than himself. God designed one dynasphere to bless man; Satan invented two dynaspheres to enslave
man. You cannot change these three dynaspheres. You can only recognize their
existence and choose between them. The divine dynasphere produces winners in
life; the two cosmic dynaspheres manufacture losers.

Satan uses the cosmic system as:

1. the vehicle for administering his rulership of the world
    (Eph. 2:2),

2. a repository or classroom for the transfer of cosmic
    doctrine to man (1 Tim. 4:1, 2),

3. a tactical trap for enslaving mankind (2 Tim. 2:26),

4. a factory for producing losers (Heb. 4:1, 2).

In the *arrogance complex*, or *cosmic one*, man is preoccupied with himself. Because he exaggerates his own importance, he cannot appreciate divine grace, nor can he enjoy the blessings of God's plan for his life. By overestimating himself, he becomes his own worst enemy. He emphasizes self instead of God.

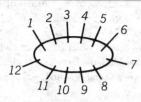

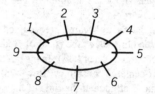

COSMIC 1 *Arrogance Complex, Interlocking System of Arrogance*	**COSMIC 2** *Hatred Complex, Interlocking System of Hatred*
Preoccupation with self	Antagonism toward God and plan of God
Own enemy	Enemy of God
Fighting self	Fighting Bible doctrine
Emphasizes self instead of God	Emphasizes human viewpoint instead of divine viewpoint
Satan's mental attitude at his fall	Satan's mental attitude after the fall of man
Philosophy of Satan in the prehistoric angelic conflict	Philosophy of Satan in the historical extension of the angelic conflict
Philosophy of Satan as the ruler of fallen angels	Philosophy of Satan as the ruler of the world
Inculcation with the philosophy of Satan before the creation of man	Inculcation with the philosophy of Satan after the fall of man
Enslaved to self	Enslaved to Satan

THE TWO DYNASPHERES OF SATAN'S COSMIC SYSTEM

In the *hatred complex,* or *cosmic two,* man is antagonistic toward God and the plan of God. A person who rejects, disputes, contradicts, or ridicules the Word of God creates his own frustration by fighting against the truth. The *hatred complex* emphasizes human viewpoint rather than divine viewpoint.

The arrogance and hatred complexes reflect the history of Satan's personal career. Originally he was the most powerful, intelligent, and personable of all angels; he was the anointed cherub, the exalted, aristocratic guardian of the throne room of God (Ezek. 28:14, 15). But, savoring the admiration of other angels, Satan became preoccupied with himself (Ezek. 28: 16a, 17a). He regarded himself as the equal of God, and for this blasphemous arrogance he fell from grace (Isa. 14:14). In his fall Satan lured one-third of all the angels into his self-centered conspiracy (Rev. 12:4). The *arrogance complex* duplicates in man Satan's attitude at the time of his own fall.

Two cosmic dynaspheres exist because Satan intensified the strategy of arrogance that he used originally against angels. When God created man to resolve the angelic conflict, the devil counterattacked, expanding arrogance into deliberate, vehement opposition toward God. In bitter antagonism Satan contrived the fall of man. The *hatred complex* duplicates in man Satan's attitude beginning with the fall of man.

The *arrogance complex* represents the philosophy of Satan in the prehistoric angelic conflict; the *hatred complex* his philosophy in the human extension of the angelic conflict. When anyone lives continually in the *arrogance complex,* he is inculcated with the thinking of Satan as the ruler of fallen angels before the creation of man. Anyone who remains in the *hatred complex* is inculcated with the thinking of Satan as the ruler of the world after men became his minions.

Each of Satan's dynaspheres creates human slaves. The gates of the *arrogance complex* interlock to enslave man to his own bad decisions; the *hatred complex* enslaves man to Satan. The arrogance and hatred complexes explain the sin, human good, evil, and misery in the human race, just as the love complex explains virtue and capacity for love and happiness.

The cosmic system continually threatens your spiritual momentum. Gates from the arrogance and hatred complexes interlock in myriad combinations, attacking each believer's personal weaknesses and areas of blindness.

> Be of sober spirit, be on the alert. Your adversary, the devil, prowls about like a roaring lion, seeking someone to devour. But resist him, firm in your faith [doctrine]. (1 Pet. 5:8, 9a; NASV)

> Wear for yourselves the full armor from God [the divine dynasphere] that you may be able to hold your ground against the tactics of the devil. (Eph. 6:11)

The devious "tactics of the devil" are exposed in the gates of the cosmic system, but you cannot resist the cosmic system in your own power. Only divine viewpoint thinking can defeat the sinister force of demon influence in your life. You must understand the mandates of the divine dynasphere and obey these principles as a guide to using your own judgment and spiritual common sense.

SUMMARY OF THE ARROGANCE COMPLEX

The arrogance complex is like quicksand. You may enter by any gate, but once in the system, you are in a position of weakness. In a state of weakness you cannot make good decisions. If, as a believer, you do not escape through immediate rebound and application of doctrine, you sink into new weaknesses, succumb to new sins that never before tempted you. Arrogance affects every facet of your soul; demon influence eventually alters your personality. Although one gate drew you into the system, many gates will pull you down until you are buried in cosmic involvement.

There are twelve gates in the arrogance complex:

1. Attitude arrogance
2. Negative volition
3. Authority arrogance
4. Self-righteous arrogance
5. Sexual arrogance
6. Criminal arrogance
7. Psychopathic arrogance
8. Arrogance of unhappiness
9. Iconoclastic arrogance
10. Rational and irrational arrogance
11. Arrogance of Christian service
12. Client nation arrogance

Gate 1, Attitude arrogance. Mental attitude sins are motivational evil, leading to the functional evils of all other gates of the cosmic system. When you are proud, jealous, vindictive, afraid, bitter, angry, implacable, or immersed in self-pity and guilt, you "give the devil an opportunity" (Eph. 4:27). No other category of sin is as destructive to your spiritual momentum, for as a man "thinks within himself, so he is" (Prov. 23:7*a*). You must guard yourself against mental attitude sins, rebounding quickly and restoring the relaxed mental attitude of gate two of the divine dynasphere.

Gate 2, Negative volition. Preoccupation with self leaves you indifferent to Bible doctrine. You may concede that doctrine is truth, but your priorities are faulty. You ignore the Word of God, and although not antagonistic, you render yourself defenseless in the spiritual conflict. Satan manipulates you when you cannot wield the "sword of the Spirit" against false doctrine (Eph. 6:17).

Gate 3, Authority arrogance. In pride man duplicates Satan's original sedition against God and the devil's subsequent tyranny over man. Arrogant people *under* authority despise their leaders and conspire to overthrow or undermine them (Ps. 12:2-4); arrogant people *in* authority abuse their power (1 Kings 18:40; 2 Sam. 12:1-9). An arrogant, *successful* person assumes that the organization in which he excels depends on him, but in reality he depends on the organization for the opportunity and environment for success. The arrogant, *unsuccessful* individual blames the system for failures caused by his own inefficiency, ineptitude, or laziness.

Gate 4, Self-righteous arrogance. The devil incorporates all possible good into his cosmic system (2 Cor. 11:14), attempting to establish his own Millennium and prove himself "like the Most High [God]" (Isa. 14:14). Satan distorts the virtue-morality ordained by divine establishment into self-righteous arrogance. The self-righteous, legalistic Christian believes his experiences and achievements give him special standing with God, but "there is no partiality with God." God deals with all mankind by the same standards of justice (Rom. 2:11). Self-righteous people often become crusaders, imposing their prejudices on others. Haughty and vain, they judge anyone less perfect than themselves (Matt. 7:1, 2).

Gate 5, Sexual arrogance. When not harnessed by virtue in the soul, normal desire for sex becomes a powerful distraction to spiritual momentum (2 Sam. 11:2-4; 1 Cor. 7:9, 33-35). Self-centeredness demands self-gratification. Driven by lust, which is desire out of control, sex ceases to be an expression of love between husband and wife. An unbridled quest for self-gratification *uses* rather than *loves* another person. Sexual arrogance destroys capacity for romantic love and leads to boredom, misery, impotence, perversion, and degeneracy (1 Cor. 6:18). Sex becomes ritual without reality, a frantic search for happiness, not an expression of happiness and love that emanates from the soul.

Gate 6, Criminal arrogance. Criminality is an arrogant way of thinking (Prov. 24:1, 2). Despising all authority, the criminal *chooses* to become a criminal. His own arrogance, not his environment nor his upbringing, leads him to the criminal presumption that he is superior to the rights, privacy, and property of others. Instead of improving himself, he continually tries to prove himself, using and hurting others to demonstrate that he is in control. Other people exist only for his convenience. He prides himself in being above the law and regards himself as a good person. By his own volition, the criminal is unteachable. God ordains capital punishment for duly convicted criminals (Ex. 21:12, 23; Num. 35:30; Rom. 13:4).

Gate 7, Psychopathic arrogance. Apart from certain chemical imbalances in the brain that are physiological not sinful, psychosis illustrates the self-destructive power of human arrogance. Bad decisions limit future options; believer or unbeliever divorces himself from reality through his own volition (Rom. 1:21, 22). His subjective decisions evolve into a pattern of distorted thinking, which creates a fantasy world in his mind. He does not recognize this imaginary world as unreality and hence has no desire to remedy his illusions. Stubborn, intolerant, insecure, sometimes violent, he cannot relate to other people. This locked-in subjectivity often leads to suicide.

Gate 8, Arrogance of unhappiness. Happiness is a personal achievement attained through obedience to divine mandates. Happiness results from virtue and truth in the soul translated into good decisions. In the divine dynasphere consistent good decisions create an environment for happiness in the soul. The arrogant person, however, expects circumstances, possessions, or other people to make him happy. When he is frustrated in these demands, he blames others. He wallows in self-pity, compensating for his bad decisions with further bad decisions in a frantic search for new stimulation. Misery does not love company; misery *demands* company. The unhappy person with a martyr complex spreads a pall of gloom over all in his periphery in order to control people and have his own way. The arrogance of unhappiness is subjective preoccupation with self.

Gate 9, Iconoclastic arrogance. Historically, in eighth and ninth century Byzantium, an Iconoclast or "image breaker" was a fanatic who destroyed religious images or objects of veneration and worship. Illustrating cosmic inflexibility in personal relationships, an iconoclast is a person who is subjectively preoccupied with others: he builds up a perfect image of someone, then, discovering his idol's human flaws, attacks this person he fatuously worshipped. Worship is a virtue only when directed toward God (Ex. 20:1-6). The arrogant person idolizes someone he should at most respect or admire. Inevitably the iconoclast discovers his idol's feet of clay, suffers disillusionment, and reacts bitterly, destroying the idol he alone created.

Gate 10, Rational and irrational arrogance. Whether ignorant and stupid or educated and brilliant, the arrogant fancy themselves rational when disputing or superficially interpreting the Bible. I call this *rational* arrogance, although no distortion of doctrine is ultimately rational. God is rational, and He reveals Himself to the humble, the teachable, those with positive volition. Doctrine cannot be reconciled with human philosophy and science; man's thinking must reconcile itself to doctrine. *Irrational* arrogance is emotional revolt of the soul.[69] God

---

69. See Thieme, *Integrity of God,* p. 18.

designed emotion to be governed by truth in the mentality; Satan exploits uncontrolled emotion.

Gate 11, Arrogance of Christian service. Satan lures sincere Christians into the arrogance complex by weaving normally legitimate deeds into a fabric of legalism. While performing Biblically mandated activities, these believers are oblivious to Satan's manipulation, unaware that their spiritual momentum has come to a halt. God commands Christian service, but prayer, witnessing, giving, teaching, administration, and donations of time, assistance, and expertise to any field of Christian work can also be performed in the cosmic system. True Christian service is motivated by Bible doctrine in the power of the divine dynasphere. Service performed to earn divine approbation, impress other Christians, or stave off divine discipline is "wood, hay, and straw" fit for burning, not for eternal reward (1 Cor. 3:12, 13).

Gate 12, Client nation arrogance. Satan rules the world, but Jesus Christ controls history. Our Lord selects certain nations to be His agents. These client nations have established governments that protect the freedom, privacy, and property of their citizens and, under the concept of separation of church and state, permit the Gospel and Bible doctrine to be taught. These nations also allow organizations to initiate and support missionary activity to other countries. The client nation is also a haven for the Jews, a place of refuge from anti-Semitism and persecution in other parts of the world. Israel was the original client nation, God's chosen people, whom Christ the Messiah will regather and restore to client status at His second advent. During the Church Age, however, God blesses the entire human race through Gentile client nations.

Believers residing in a client nation are the "salt of the land," the preservative of the nation (Matt. 5:13), also called the "remnant" (Rom. 9:27; 11:5). Although unheralded in the annals of history, anonymous believers determine the uptrends and downtrends of civilization as Christ directs the course of history to bless or discipline His own. Therefore, to subvert the nations, it is Satan's strategy to attack the integrity of believers (Rev. 18:23; 20:3, 8). When a majority of believers within a client nation become arrogant, rejecting divine establishment and Bible doctrine, these believers are guilty of client nation arrogance, hastening divine judgment against their nation (Hosea 4:1-6).

SUMMARY OF THE HATRED COMPLEX

The gates of the arrogance complex interlock with the gates of the hatred complex. Your pride intensifies into stubborn antagonism. When illusions of self-importance are exposed and challenged, you react with resentment. When divine establishment, the Gospel, or Bible doctrine contradicts your self-righteous delusions, you take offense at the truth. You rationalize your sins and defend your conceit by denying and attacking divine viewpoint thinking. To justify your evil, you despise the good. You become the ally of Satan in his unrelenting hatred of God and the plan of God.

> If the world [the cosmic system] hates you [in the divine dynasphere], be aware of the fact that it hated Me [Christ] before it hated you [Christ was first to reside in the divine dynasphere]. . . . He who hates Me also hates My Father. . . . They have seen [demonstrations of Christ's Messiahship] and hated both Me and My Father. (John 15:18, 23, 24)

> When anyone hates his fellow believer, he is in the darkness [the hatred complex], and he walks in darkness, and he does not know where he is going because the darkness has blinded his eyes. (1 John 2:11)

In these passages "hatred" is more than an isolated mental attitude sin; hatred is a satanic system, a dynasphere of interlocking gates whose power can be resisted only in the greater power of the divine dynasphere.

Your antagonism toward the plan of God increases as the gates of the hatred complex interlock with each other. Negativism spreads to every area of life. Work, politics, entertainment, and friends all become targets of your unconstructive criticism. Having destroyed your own relaxed mental attitude and capacity for divine blessings, you become a chronic complainer. Circumstances and people are never right; you are never satisfied. Enslaved in demon influence, you make yourself and those around you miserable.

You can never afford to succumb to any of the nine gates of the hatred complex:

1. The old sin nature
2. Negative volition
3. Degeneration
4. Antiestablishment
5. Demonism
6. Cosmic panaceas
7. Religion
8. Anthropocentric academic speculation
9. Evil

Gate 1, The old sin nature. As Satan's inside agent the sin nature within man executes the devil's sinister policy of hatred and antagonism. Aquired by Adam at the Fall, the old sin nature exists genetically in the human body, "waging war against the principle of [the] mind" where Bible doctrine, "the law from God," is received, retained, and recalled (Rom. 7:22, 23). By tempting man to commit sin, this inherent distorter of human life continually opposes the divine plan for blessing man (Gal. 5:17).

Gate 2, Negative volition. In the arrogance complex, negative volition ignores God through preoccupation with self, but in the hatred complex negative volition attacks God, the plan of God, and Bible doctrine. Unbelievers who adhere to divine establishment but then react to the Gospel with negative volition will begin to oppose the truth they formerly believed. As a result, "the last state [of negative volition] is worse for them than the first" (2 Pet. 2:20). Each rejection of truth by believer or unbeliever intensifies negative volition until an individual has locked himself into antagonism toward God (Ex. 9:34, 35).

Gate 3, Degeneration. Degeneracy is the abuse of freedom that weakens a nation from within, inviting enslavement by a dictator or foreign conquerer. When individual citizens compromise their integrity, the national character declines, the quality of life within the nation deteriorates. Because of negative volition and prolonged arrogance, "God has delivered them over in the lusts of their right lobes to an immoral status,...to passions of dishonor" (Rom. 1:24, 26), to rampant crime, violence, sexual perversion, and drug addiction. Degeneration is *disorganized evil* in contrast to political or religious tyranny, which is *organized evil.* A dictator monopolizes evil as he restricts freedom and controls the populace; degenerate himself, the despot suppresses degeneracy by forcing strict morality upon the people. To secure power, organized evil attacks disorganized evil *and* persecutes Christianity; disorganized evil does not persecute but coexists with Christianity. Degenerate unbelievers and believers may be evangelized or exposed to Bible doctrine by Christians in the divine dynasphere, who are the preservative of a nation, the "salt of the land" (Matt. 5:13).

Gate 4, Antiestablishment. An *arrogant* individual contributes to the decline of society and the nation, but a rebellious, resentful person who *hates* divinely delegated authority makes direct attacks against the divine institutions—human freedom, marriage, the family, and the national entity.[70] These institutions are essential for the perpetuation and prosperity of mankind, but individuals in the hatred complex subvert human freedom by denouncing its inherent components: volition, privacy, property, and authority. They ridicule the virtues of marriage and reject parental authority. They excoriate, obstruct, and commit treason against the government. Malcontents obsessed with their own anger never offer

---

70. See above, pp. 64-74, 166.

realistic alternatives but desire only to demolish the authorities under which they live.

Gate 5, Demonism. Satan commands vast armies of fallen angels or demons who execute his strategy for controlling mankind.[71] Certain echelons of demons operate *covertly* behind the scenes; others create a diversity of *overt* effects. Demons can indwell the bodies of unbelievers, called demon possession, or influence their souls with "doctrines of demons" (2 Tim. 4:1). Demons cannot possess believers, who are protected by the indwelling Holy Spirit (1 Cor. 6:19, 20), but the subjectivity, confusion, and false ideas from demon influence effectively neutralize the believer.

Gate 6, Cosmic panaceas. After aggravating the difficulties of life, Satan entices man with solutions apart from truth. Human viewpoint supplants divine establishment, the Gospel, and Bible doctrine. A panacea is an oversimplified, supposed cure-all prescription guaranteed to remedy a complex problem. Panaceas captivate the ignorant, those who resent truth and arrogantly cling to false premises. A prevalent historic panacea is human equality, yet equality cancels freedom, the key to human life. Socialism, communism, and altruism all claim to accomplish good but belong to the cosmic system. Although compassion and generosity are Christian virtues practiced by individual believers in the divine dynasphere, Christianity is not a program of social action (John 12:8). Christianity is not a crusade to eradicate evil from the devil's world but a system of personal spiritual growth. Understanding and applying the truth provides genuine solutions to life's problems.

Gate 7, Religion. Satan's most insidious ploy against the human race is religion. Christianity is not a religion. *Religion* is man by man's efforts striving to gain the approbation of God (2 Tim. 3:5); *Christianity* is man's relationship with God through faith in Jesus Christ (Rom. 8:38, 39). In *religion* man seeks God through personal merit and works (Eph. 2:9); in *Christianity* God seeks man through the saving work of Christ (Eph. 2:8). *Christianity* nurtures capacity for happiness when the believer turns over the control of his life to God through obedience to divine mandates. *Religion* breeds unhappiness when the proselyte surrenders control of his life and custodianship of his happiness to a hierarchy of human beings who enforce ritualistic systems of asceticism or lasciviousness. Christians who work for divine blessing distort Christianity into legalism. They elevate themselves above Christ by emphasizing Christian service above His perfect, finished work on the Cross. Legalists exalt human production above obedience to divine protocol.

Gate 8, Anthropocentric academic speculation. "Anthropocentric" means "centered in man; considering man to be the most significant fact of the uni-

71. See Thieme, *Demonism* (1974).

verse; assuming man to be the measure of all things; interpreting the world in terms of human values and experiences.''[72] If not seduced by religion, man can be deceived by philosophical, academic criticism to dismiss the Word of God as absolute truth. When philosophical assumptions give central importance to man instead of God, academic research can amass persuasive yet fraudulent evidence against divine viewpoint. Because human rationalism and empiricism cannot prove Biblical truth, the pseudo-intellectual rejects truth and ''advances in knowledge out of bounds and does not remain on the field of play by means of the doctrine of Christ'' (2 John 9). No one becomes a winner in life by running brilliant, intellectual touchdowns out of bounds, ignoring the mandates of the divine game plan. Life must be interpreted in terms of God's plan not man's experiences.

Gate 9, Evil. Evil is Satan's self-destructive policy as ruler of the world. The cosmic system is his vehicle for administering this sinister policy. God warns against evil (Rom. 12:9, 21; 1 Pet. 3:9) and restrains evil in human history through timely divine judgments (Gen. 6:13; 15:16*b*; Matt. 23:37, 38; 24:22). God will ultimately destroy all evil, but to discredit Satan, God permits the devil's policy to run its course in human history. Although Satan labors to establish a perfect kingdom to rival the prophesied Millennium of Christ, the devil is incapable of enlightened rule. Evil excludes integrity (Heb. 5:14). Evil, also called ''good and evil'' (Gen. 2:9), includes much apparent good, along with deceit, violence, terror, and confusion. Evil is the manifestation of Satan's arrogant, distorted genius in opposition to Bible doctrine, which is the manifestation of God's grace.[73]

This summary of the arrogance and hatred dynaspheres forces us to one conclusion: for your own happiness, avoid the cosmic system! In genuine humility you must recognize that you are no match for Satan, now or ever, and must never give him an opportunity to exploit your weaknesses. Regardless of your level of spiritual maturity, his strategy appeals to your weaknesses. Human weakness can never defeat cosmic strength. You can successfully pass these momentum tests only by learning and obeying the divine system. You can follow Christ as a spiritual winner only in the strength of the divine dynasphere.

DISASTER TESTING

The believer's reaction to intense suffering can divert him from the momentum line and into the two cosmic systems. Loss of a loved one, a crippling

---

72. *Webster's Third New International Dictionary,* s.v. ''anthropocentric.''
73. See Thieme, *Integrity of God,* pp. 12-13.

accident, dismissal from a long-secured job, sudden disappearance of financial security, terminal illness—these major distractions can cause the believer to focus on himself and his problems to the exclusion of objective reality. Even in the most dreadful circumstances, the believer must remain in control of his life, retain his personal sense of destiny, and make good decisions from a position of strength, the divine dynasphere. If he permits himself to become enmeshed in mental attitude sins, he surrenders to spiritual inertia and refuses to take the responsibility for his attitude and actions. He has entered the cosmic system and failed the disaster test.

The solution to disaster testing is *thinking* by means of the three stages of the faith-rest drill. In particular, the shock of the crisis must be neutralized by claiming Biblical promises in stage one of the drill. Promises are concise statements of God's faithfulness and power, reminders of His plan for your life.

Self-pity and fear are often the immediate reactions in a disaster, and the believer controls his subjectivity and fear by reaching out with his faith to claim a divine promise. Promises refocus attention on God instead of self; they clear the decks for action, establishing the inner peace of the relaxed mental attitude. Without the relaxed attitude of impersonal love, no one can concentrate on the logical rationales of stage two of the faith-rest drill.

Mental sins like self-pity, fear, and worry cut off thought; they obscure reality; they eliminate common sense. In a crisis the believer must reduce complexity to simplicity. He must remember promises, which clarify his eternal relationship with God, instead of being overwhelmed by the complications that beset him (Ps. 61:2). When divine promises have calmed his fear, then with a clear mind he is able to concentrate on God's provisions and reach doctrinal conclusions.

After concluding that "if God is for us, who is against us?" (Rom. 8:31), the believer can then approach the complexity of his current problems from a position of strength, not a position of weakness and reaction. Testing can come as personal disaster in which the believer faces a devastating situation in his own life, or it can take the form of historical disaster. Even the dangers and uncertainties of economic depression, social degeneration, and military defeat cannot destroy the believer's blessings under the plan of God. The believer inside the divine dynasphere applies the logistical grace rationale. He knows that God will support and bless him as long as the divine plan calls for him to remain in this life. He knows that Jesus Christ controls history and that no divine blessing will be denied to any advancing believer except by his own negative volition. Historical circumstances never hinder God from blessing mature believers. The believer residing in the divine dynasphere faces national and worldwide disasters with the same confidence in God and courage toward circumstances that he maintains in a personal crisis.

PROSPERITY TESTING

THE MOST DANGEROUS TEST

Disaster obviously challenges the believer's equilibrium en route to gate eight of the divine dynasphere, but a much more subtle and dangerous test is posed by prosperity. Historically, no nation has ever survived its own prosperity; individually, very few Christians successfully pass the prosperity test. Whether in national or personal prosperity, a believer is usually oblivious to the fact that he is confronting the gravest of all obstacles on the road to spiritual maturity. Prosperity tends to blind the believer to the source of his blessings and the importance of Bible doctrine. This causes more spiritual casualties than does any other momentum test.

God's objective is to bless the believer on earth with spiritual, temporal, social, historical, and even dying blessings "exceeding abundantly beyond all that we ask or think" (Eph. 3:20). Phenomenal divine blessings are in store for you, not just in heaven but here in the devil's world. This supergrace prosperity requires great capacity of soul. The accoutrements of happiness that many people struggle to acquire bring only complications and disillusion for those who have not developed the faculty for appreciating and using them.

Neither wealth, status, promotion, fame, social life, sex, possessions, nor any other attainment automatically brings happiness. You must acquire the capacity for life, for love, for happiness. Such capacity is one of the mature believer's spiritual blessings, which protect him so that other, temporal blessings do not distract him from his continued spiritual growth. Prosperity is always a test of character, self-discipline, concentration, and capacity. That is the reason the greatest blessings of the Christian life are reserved for mature believers or are given as a momentum test to believers who are just reaching the threshold of maturity. From the point of salvation onward, logistical grace provides what may be considered to be wonderful blessings, but the truly exceptional blessings are reserved for those who have developed capacity through consistent residence and function inside the divine dynasphere.

Because of your faithfulness to the mandates of the Word of God, you *will* be prospered. God invented the divine dynasphere as His game plan for blessing you, and His game plan *works*. God keeps His word; if you follow His plan, you *will* be blessed. In social life you may find a wonderful new friend or may be invited into an exclusive circle that you have admired from the outside for a long time. In business you may be promoted into a prestigious position of confidence that carries great authority. Economically a particular investment may make you wealthy in a relatively short period of time. There is an infinite variety of blessings that God can give; God prospers each believer individually with a different combination of blessings.

Perhaps your most recent divine blessing may be the fulfillment of personal love for a member of the opposite sex: you have found romance. You marry this ideal person, and you are enormously happy. In the midst of your pleasure and enthusiasm, you cannot imagine that anything could go wrong. But if you forget your personal love for God, which motivates your impersonal love for man, which in turn sustains romantic love, and if you forget the source of your capacity for personal love, Bible doctrine, then *everything* will go wrong. Not only will you fail to enjoy your marriage, but that relationship will multiply your own unhappiness and frustration. Any form of prosperity without capacity leads to stagnation and unhappiness.

CAPACITY FOR PROSPERITY

No matter what your particular blessings may be, that prosperity becomes a test of your capacity. Will you become so preoccupied that you forget the source? Will you complain about what you do not have rather than appreciate what you have? Will you forget that God gave you everything you possess and that He alone sustains you in this life? Many believers never pass the sophomore stage of their spiritual lives because they lose their perspective in the midst of the wonderful life that God has given them. Even with the relatively routine blessings of logistical grace, they fail to pass the prosperity test.

Spiritual prosperity in the soul is the basis for enjoying all the temporal prosperity that God can provide. The easiest thing in the world, however, is to lose your capacity. Your spiritual prosperity can disappear even though you still possess all the overt accoutrements of happiness. If you neglect Bible doctrine, that is all that is necessary for your capacity to evaporate. You will fail the prosperity test if you assume that your spiritual momentum alone will sustain you. If you assume that since you have already advanced so far you no longer need to take in doctrine every day, you will fall into the cosmic system. Momentum must be continually maintained; no believer can afford to neglect the perception of doctrine.

But doctrinal perception is not merely a means to an end, a system of perpetuating your capacity for overt prosperity. Truth is its own reward. Doctrine in the soul is the fountainhead of happiness; temporal blessings are never the source of happiness. Your happiness from your social life with God inside the divine dynasphere overflows into the realm of overt blessings. When your daily worship and fellowship with God through doctrine are forgotten, then whatever overt prosperity you may still possess becomes ritual without reality.

The secret to the prosperity test is genuine humility, which enables you to learn capacity and appreciation. Genuine humility motivates obedience to the divine mandates to faithfully absorb the Word of God. The perception of doctrine in gate four not only produces love for God but also creates and maintains capacity for the blessings that He desires to pour out upon us as the demonstration of His power and integrity in the angelic conflict.

VIII
Gate Eight, The Winner's Gate

STRATEGIC AND TACTICAL VICTORY

Every believer is a *strategic* winner in the plan of God, but few achieve *tactical* victory. Christ won the strategic victory on our behalf; the Cross separates all believers from unbelievers, who remain strategic losers and will spend eternity in the Lake of Fire.

Our Lord has placed us in a position of supreme advantage over our archenemy, Satan, just as a brilliant general decides the outcome of a battle by choosing the terrain on which his forces will engage the enemy. At salvation Christ places us in a position of maximum strength, the divine dynasphere. Although His strategic victory guarantees us eternal life and a resurrection body, there is no guarantee of tactical victory in this life or eternal rewards in heaven. We secure tactical victory on the battlefield of our own souls only through continued function in the divine dynasphere. Our objective is to become double winners, to seize and hold the high ground of spiritual maturity in gate eight of God's power sphere.

The strategic winner glorifies Jesus Christ once by making a single decision to believe in Christ for salvation; the tactical winner not only believes in Christ but makes thousands of decisions to obey the mandates of the divine system. The believer advancing to maturity maintains his perspective and organizes his life based on right priorities: mandates first, virtue first, Christ first, grace first, momentum first, doctrine first.

The strategic winner is one of the ''all'' in phase two of God's plan who receives only divine impersonal love; the believer who is also a tactical winner is among the ''few'' recipients of divine personal love.[74] The greater blessings of time and eternity are reserved exclusively for double winners. Although the single winner will receive a resurrection body in heaven, he loses all eternal rewards.

Strategic Winner Only	Strategic and Tactical Winner
One decision glorifies Christ	Many decisions glorify Christ
All believers	Few believers
Divine impersonal love	Divine personal love
Suffering for discipline	Suffering for blessing
Self-induced misery	Shares God's happiness
Fears death	Fears nothing
Will glorify God in eternity	Glorifies God in time and eternity
Makes wrong decisions	Makes right decisions
Lives in the cosmic system	Lives in the divine dynasphere

TWO CATEGORIES OF WINNERS IN THE PLAN OF GOD

Logistical grace sustains the strategic winner even though he lives in the cosmic system. In contrast, the tactical winner has exploited logistical grace in his advance to maturity so that now he is blessed by logistical grace *and* super-grace. No adversity can disturb his inner tranquility; any suffering he endures is intended for blessing and accelerated growth. The believer who is only a strategic winner, however, is upset by the most mundane problems and suffers unbearably under divine discipline. In all circumstances he creates his own misery, which is relieved only by intermittent stimulation that he mistakes for happiness. In similar circumstances the tactical winner manufactures his own happiness from Bible doctrine and shares the happiness of God.

The Christian who fails to exploit his strategic victory fears death and dies under maximum divine discipline, the sin unto death.[75] The tactical winner fears nothing in life or death. The believer in the cosmic system is a strategic winner but a tactical loser; after salvation he will not glorify God again until entering the eternal state. The believer in gate eight of the divine dynasphere is a strategic and tactical winner; he glorifies God in time and eternity. The cosmic believer may

---

74. See above, pp. 49-50.
75. See Thieme, *Christian Suffering*, p. 183.

be a permanent winner, but after salvation he makes wrong decisions from a position of weakness. The believer who exploits the power of the divine dynasphere establishes a habit of making right decisions.

John delineates both categories of victory and declares that only our Lord's strategic victory places us in position to win the tactical victory.

> For this is the love for God [motivational virtue], that we may continue observing His mandates [advance to tactical victory in the divine dynasphere], because every category of humanity which has been born from God [strategic winners] overcomes the cosmic system [strategic victory as the basis for tactical victory], and this is the [initial] victory which has overcome the cosmic system, our faith. Who is this person overcoming the cosmic system? No one else but he who has come to believe that Jesus is the Son of God. (1 John 5:3–5)

As Peter was writing his second epistle, he knew that he would soon die and be present face to face with the Lord (2 Pet. 1:14). This impulsive apostle, who had overcome many obstacles on the road to spiritual maturity, concludes his dying words with a mandate to maintain momentum and achieve tactical victory.

> You therefore, beloved, knowing this beforehand, be on your guard lest, being carried away by the error of unprincipled men [without virtue], you fall from your own steadfastness [secure position in the divine system], but grow in the grace [logistical grace] and knowledge of our Lord [tactical victory] and Savior [strategic victory] Jesus Christ. To Him be the glory, both now and to the day of eternity. Amen. (2 Pet. 3:17, 18; NASV)

Peter had earlier outlined the system for developing spiritual momentum. The first three gates of the divine dynasphere support the intake of Bible doctrine in gate four, and the tactical victory of gate eight is a result of faithfulness in learning and applying the Word of God.

> Therefore, putting aside all malice and all guile and hypocrisy and envy and all slander [mental and verbal sins are eliminated by gates one, two, and three of the divine system], like newborn babes, long for the pure milk of the word [Bible doctrine], that by it you may grow [tactical victory] in respect to salvation [strategic victory], if you have tasted the kindness of the Lord [and you have]. (1 Pet. 2:1–3, NASV)

THE COMPLETED STATE OF HAPPINESS

The believer who passes the momentum tests accelerates his growth and enters the winner's gate. Many blessings belong to gate eight, all of which contribute to the *completed state of happiness* in which the believer shares the happiness of God. This final gate is the culmination and intensification of all the other gates. The inner strength of stabilized maturity is the ultimate objective of God's game plan for the royal family.

Throughout the First Advent, Jesus Christ resided in gate eight of the love complex. In His Gethsemane discourse, the night before He was betrayed, Christ spoke concerning the power sphere that He would soon turn over to His royal family. He stated that happiness is the ultimate goal of the Christian way of life.

> Just as the Father [the source of the love complex to Christ] loves Me, so also I have loved you. Reside in My love [complex]. If you keep [fulfill, execute] My mandates, you will reside in the sphere of My love [complex], just as I have fulfilled the mandates of My Father and I reside in the sphere of His love [complex]. I have taught you these things in order that My joy [the happiness of gate eight] might be in you and that your happiness might be completed [fulfilled]. (John 15:9–11)

The Apostle John identifies Bible doctrine as the source of the believer's happiness.

> In fact, we write these things [Bible doctrine] in order that our state of happiness might be completed. (1 John 1:4)

The state of happiness is the divine dynasphere. There are degrees of happiness in the divine dynasphere, from minimum for the immature person who occasionally resides in the system, to maximum for the faithful believer who perseveres in his intake of doctrine to maturity and beyond. Each gate contributes to the happiness of the one functioning in the system.

In this regard the divine dynasphere is also the unbeliever's environment for happiness. There is no happiness for anyone outside God's system. The unbeliever can enter the love complex through gate three, enforced and genuine humility. All true happiness is based on truth, and the authority orientation and common sense of enforced and genuine humility are related to the truth of the divine laws of establishment.

From gate three, the unbeliever can interlock with gate two in the sense that the humble unbeliever limits the influence of his old sin nature by resisting temptations to commit mental attitude sins. By using his volition to control his own life, the unbeliever can maintain that relaxed mental attitude of basic impersonal love. This is the basis of virtue, honor, and integrity in the unbeliever. An unbeliever who has integrity and genuine humility has greater capacity for life than does the believer who resides in the cosmic system. The virtuous unbeliever can sustain romantic love and can achieve a far more successful marriage than can a legalistic, arrogant Christian (Eccl. 9:9). The honorable, humanly mature unbeliever treats others from his own integrity and can enjoy the wonderful rapport of a few compatible friends, who also have high standards of personal integrity. The unbeliever can live by the principle that virtue precedes love, virtue precedes happiness.

If this is the limited, temporal happiness available to the unbeliever in a few gates of God's system, the temporal and eternal happiness of the mature believer who functions in all the gates is far stronger. God designed us; He created us. He "knows our frame" from eternity past (Ps. 103:14). He knows a great deal more than we do about what makes us happy. The complete love complex is the environment for complete happiness.

The tragedy is that people assume they can find happiness through their own devices outside God's system. This attitude is the common denominator of all arrogance. Satan, who is utterly unhappy and frustrated in the angelic conflict, observed Jesus in the prototype divine dynasphere. Satan despised our Lord's constant inner happiness, stability, poise, and courage, which under varying circumstances had an entire spectrum of expressions but was never broken. Even the death of His friend Lazarus, when Jesus wept (John 11:35), the decline of His nation (Luke 13:34), and the anticipation of His suffering on the Cross (Matt. 26:39; Luke 22:42) elicited expressions of Christ's tremendous capacity for life, which included His constant, underlying happiness in the plan of God.

Christ's happiness was stabilized by the truth. He understood the doctrine of divine decrees, which explains how all things fit into God's overall viewpoint of time and eternity.[76] But Satan rejects all truth. Totally arrogant and desperate, Satan tried to destroy our Lord's happiness. But no antagonism, opposition, injustice, or violence could destroy the power of Christ's "completed state of happiness." Failing in his attack against Christ, the devil now concentrates his genius against the believer and unbeliever by counterfeiting the happiness that only the divine dynasphere can produce.

---

76. See Thieme, *Integrity of God*, app. B, "The Doctrine of Divine Decrees," pp. 257-81.

FALSE HAPPINESS VERSUS TRUE HAPPINESS

PSEUDO-HAPPINESS IN RELIGION

Satan has no happiness to share. He therefore creates a pseudo-happiness to lure people away from God's plan. As the ruler of the world, Satan has the power to provide pseudo-prosperity. He presents the attractiveness of wealth, fame, sex, and power as if they were happiness in themselves, but Satan's most subtle and effective deception is religion.

Christians have the impression that they will be happy if they are performing certain "spiritual" functions, avoiding certain "worldly" activities, or receiving the approbation of others in the congregation or community. Because pastors and other religious leaders often encourage this fallacy as a way of life for happiness, believers are tempted to fake happiness in order to vindicate their religious beliefs. True Christianity is not a religion; the Christian life is residence in the whole divine dynasphere. Religion is Satan's ace trump. The pseudo-happiness of Christians outside the love complex is just as short-lived and ultimately destructive as the high from a drug.

The Greek noun *chara,* found in both passages quoted in the previous section, is usually translated "joy." But as generally understood by Christians today, the word *joy* represents a distorted concept. As part of religion, joy has come to connote the overt display of some exuberant feeling that is supposedly a sign of being spiritual. Spirituality, however, is residence and function inside the divine dynasphere. Spirituality emphasizes not emotion but thought, thinking Bible doctrine. Emotion without true thought is involvement in Satan's system, not God's.

Many cults promote an aggressive, effusive "joy" as a means of enslaving and controlling their members. Emotion is used as a tool for breaking down the common sense of new converts. Often, joy is integrated with illegitimate forms of ecstatics connected with "speaking in tongues."[77] Even in respectable, formal denominations it has become fashionable for ministers and members to exhibit joy as they perform their magnificent but empty rituals. The superficial, hypocritical displays of emotion so common in Christian circles today have nothing whatever to do with God's plan for spiritual royalty. Such "joy" is an evil, satanic substitute for the genuine inner happiness of the mature believer.

This is not to condemn legitimate expressions of emotion nor to advocate a stern, dour facade of puritanical inflexibility. We are exploring a word found in the Bible, and in order to discover the accurate meaning we must scrape away the barnacles of religion. Gate eight of the love complex is not devoid of emo-

---

77. See Thieme, *Tongues.*

tion, but emotion is in response to an entire frame of reference of doctrinal thought. Genuine happiness depends on truth.

HAPPINESS AS A BY-PRODUCT OF TRUTH

Although happiness is the ultimate objective of God's game plan, happiness is strictly a by-product. God's plan calls for us to pursue truth in gate four of the divine dynasphere. There is no shortcut to gate eight. The shortcut to happiness is the long road to misery.

> Consequently, we pursue [spiritual momentum from gate four of the divine dynasphere] those things [Bible doctrines] related to prosperity [the blessings of spiritual maturity at gate eight] and those things [Bible doctrines] related to the edification of each other. (Rom. 14:19)

"Edification" refers to erecting a structure in the soul, the believer's inner strength which is completed upon reaching gate eight.[78] All believers share the common objective of spiritual maturity and under the royal family honor code are bound to avoid what would distract another believer from reaching the goal.[79]

Happiness comes to those who keep faithfully learning and applying Bible doctrine.

> Seek ye first the kingdom of God [Bible doctrine as the believer's highest priority], and all these things [the blessings and happiness of gate eight] will be added unto you. (Matt. 6:33, AV)

In contrast, those who seek happiness itself, whether in wealth, power, religion, or any other system of pseudo-happiness, find only frustration, disappointment, and misery. A frantic search for happiness merely intensifies the unhappiness that motivated the search in the first place, as illustrated by addiction to drugs. Since the word *joy* has been used so indiscriminately by Christians today, we will translate the Greek noun *charis* appropriately as "happiness."

The Greek verb in 1 John 1:4, which the King James Version renders "may be full," is the perfect passive subjunctive form of *pleröo*. *Pleröo* has a number of related meanings: to fill up a deficiency, to fully possess, to fully influence, to fill up with a certain quality. In 1 John 1:4, the concept of *pleröo* is comple-

---

78. See below, pp. 183-88.
79. See below, pp. 129-32.

tion: "that our state of happiness might be completed." The perfect tense of the verb indicates completed results from past action. Prolonged residence and function inside the divine dynasphere brings about the completed state of happiness. Every gate of the system works at maximum capacity for the mature believer.

The passive voice of *pleröo* indicates that such happiness receives the action of the verb rather than produces the action. John makes it clear that doctrine brings us to this completed state of happiness. Supported by the first three gates, gate four provides the spiritual momentum that results in gate eight. Truth precedes happiness. If we seek happiness apart from God's plan, we will always be unhappy. God's game plan calls for us to seek truth, since happiness comes as a natural consequence of learning and applying the truth. The subjunctive mood of *pleröo* means that the completion of our happiness is a potential, the fulfillment of which depends on our decisions over a long period of time to keep residing and functioning in God's power system.

John reiterates the importance of Bible teaching in the second epistle, in which he repeats the same form of *pleröo* as in 1 John 1:4.

> Although having many [doctrines] to write to you, I do not
> wish to do so with paper and ink, but I anticipate coming to
> you and teaching face to face, that our state of happiness
> might be completed. (2 John 12)

COMPONENTS OF COMPLETED HAPPINESS

DIVINE HAPPINESS AND TRUE INDEPENDENCE

The mature believer's "completed state of happiness" in gate eight of the divine dynasphere includes sharing God's happiness, becoming spiritually self-sustaining, completing the edification complex of the soul, receiving supergrace blessings, and being appointed to the highest order of royal family knighthood.

Sharing God's happiness has nothing to do with circumstances or the details of life. Sharing the happiness of God is a result of knowing God and being inculcated with His thinking. God always has perfect happiness; when the believer shares the thinking of God, as revealed in Bible doctrine, he shares God's happiness.

> For the joy of the Lord is your strength. (Neh. 8:10)

> Now therefore, O sons [believers], listen to me [Bible doc-
> trine personified is speaking], for happiness [comes] to
> those who guard my ways. Concentrate on doctrinal teach-

ing so that you will be wise, and do not neglect it. Happinesses to those who listen to me [Bible doctrine], assembling daily at my gates [the place of doctrinal teaching], waiting [mental attitude of eager anticipation] at my doorpost. (Prov. 8:32–34)

As the believer resides and functions inside the divine system, he is strengthening his soul. He is making himself spiritually self-sustaining so that he can think, decide, and act for himself without seeking advice or approval from others. The more we know about God, the more we love Him, but, in addition, as we come to understand His mandates and His plan for our lives, the problems of divine guidance become matters of spiritual common sense.[80] We discover that we can make good decisions from our own inventory of Bible doctrine and can take full responsibility for our own lives. Personal independence is found in subordination to God's system. The divine dynasphere is our position of strength. The better we understand how God deals with us through a *system*, the more stabilized is our happiness and the more meaningful our lives become.

God is perfect; He never disappoints; He has never let anyone down. As you learn about Him, you realize how wise He is, how faithful, how entirely wonderful. You come to depend on Him, and in doing so you gain a better perspective of people. With your confidence grounded in God, you can successfully handle any human relationship. No one can disturb, upset, or depress you; this is the strength of impersonal love, gate six, based on the strength of your occupation with the Person of Christ, gate five. The combined power of these two gates contributes to your strength in gate eight, and that is as strong as anyone can be in this life. Such strength has nothing to do with physical muscle; it has everything to do with thought.

THE DIVINE DYNASPHERE AND THE EDIFICATION COMPLEX

FOUNDATION AND FIRST FLOOR: THE SPIRIT AND THE WORD

The Bible depicts this strengthening of the soul in terms of erecting a structure or constructing a building in the soul. This process is called edification. An edifice is a building, and the Greek verb *oikodomeo,* "to edify," is a compound from *oikia,* "house," and *domeo,* "to build." The believer attains spiritual maturity when he completes the construction of the edification complex in his soul and lives in the penthouse, the completed state of happiness.

---

80. See Thieme, *Divine Guidance* (1973).

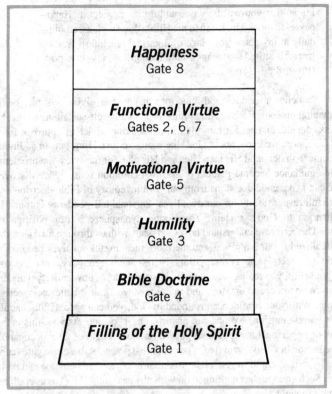

Happiness
Gate 8

Functional Virtue
Gates 2, 6, 7

Motivational Virtue
Gate 5

Humility
Gate 3

Bible Doctrine
Gate 4

Filling of the Holy Spirit
Gate 1

THE EDIFICATION COMPLEX RELATED TO THE GATES OF THE DIVINE DYNASPHERE

The divine dynasphere, which is the Christian way of life, and the edification complex, which is the inner result of obeying God's mandates, merge at the ultimate objective. From the foundation to the penthouse, the floors of the edification complex correspond to the gates of the love complex.

The foundation of the inner structure of the soul is the unseen support of the filling of the Holy Spirit. All Christian dynamics, strength, and growth are based on the power of the Energizer. The first floor of the structure corresponds to gate four of the divine dynasphere. Spiritual momentum in the love complex equals the construction of the edification complex.

For I say, through the grace which has been given to me, to everyone who is among you, stop thinking of self in terms of arrogance [*huperphroneo*] beyond what you ought to think [*phroneo*], but think [*phroneo*] in terms of sanity for the purpose of being rational without illusion [*sophroneo*], as God has assigned to each one a standard [of thinking] from doctrine. (Rom. 12:3)

This verse contrasts two Greek verbs: *huperphroneo*, "to overthink, to think too highly of oneself, to think in terms of arrogance" and *phroneo*, "to think objectively." Objective thinking is the first floor of the edification complex; the standard or criterion for objective thought is Bible doctrine. Paul combines yet another verb with *phroneo* and *huperphroneo* in order to amplify the contrast between right thinking and arrogance. The purpose of the believer's objective thinking is that he be sane and rational. *Sophroneo* is a multifaceted verb that means "to be in one's right mind, to be sane, reasonable, sensible, serious, to keep one's head." I have translated these two positive verbs— *phroneo* and *sophroneo*—with an expanded phrase that brings out their full connotation: "think in terms of sanity for the purpose of being rational without illusion."

The believer who is "rational without illusion" can face all the vicissitudes of life without falling apart, without being disturbed, without withdrawing into neurosis or psychosis. He has learned enough Bible doctrine to graduate beyond the superficial thinking that is so common among believers today, and he has developed the common sense of divine viewpoint in his daily life. When properly understood, doctrine in the soul is normal, sane thinking.

SECOND FLOOR: HUMILITY

The second floor of the edification complex is genuine humility, which corresponds to gate three of the love complex. Built upon the sane, objective, rational truth of Bible doctrine, genuine humility represents the successful transition from authority to freedom in life. The authority orientation of the advancing believer is built on understanding and obeying the principles of doctrine and divine establishment.

For even if I should boast somewhat freely about our authority [the authority of the pastor in teaching doctrine], which the Lord gave for edification [building up the believer through doctrine] and not for destroying you [arrogance is destructive], I will not be ashamed of it. (2 Cor. 10:8)

For this reason I am writing these things while absent, in order that when I am present I may not use severity in accordance with the authority that the Lord gave me for the purpose of edification and not tearing you down. (2 Cor. 13:10)

If the Corinthian believers were humble, they would benefit from Paul's authoritative epistle; if they were arrogant, they would be unteachable and would continue toward their own destruction. Humility represents teachability and forms the basis for the next floor of the edification complex.

Knowledge [*gnosis*, not *epignosis* understanding of doctrine] puffs up, but love edifies. (1 Cor. 8:1*b*)

THIRD AND FOURTH FLOORS: MOTIVATIONAL AND FUNCTIONAL VIRTUE

The third floor of the edification complex is the motivational virtue of personal love for God. Personal love emphasizes the object of love, and we come to know who and what God is through learning Bible doctrine. Personal love requires integrity in the one who loves. The third floor of the edification complex is built on the foundation and first two floors: integrity precedes love.

The fourth floor is the functional virtue of impersonal love, the basic Christian virtue. For the immature believer impersonal love is the relaxed mental attitude at gate two of the love complex, where he resists temptation to commit mental attitude sins and utilizes rebound when necessary. The immature believer obeys the divine mandates for basic Christian modus operandi as a result of his respect for God's authority. But in order to develop into integrity at gate six, impersonal love must be strengthened by the motivational virtue of personal love for God.

Hence, mature impersonal love, as the fourth floor of the structure in the soul, is built upon the ministry of the Holy Spirit, momentum from Bible doctrine, teachability from genuine humility, and the motivational virtue of personal love for God, as well as upon the objectivity of basic impersonal love. Impersonal love is also one of the standard techniques for passing momentum tests, so that impersonal love occurs in gates two, six, and seven of the divine dynasphere.

FIFTH FLOOR: HAPPINESS

The penthouse of the edification complex, the royal residence of the mature believer, is the state of happiness of gate eight of the love complex.

Happiness to the man who finds wisdom [*chakmah* in the Hebrew corresponds to *epignosis* in the Greek] and the man who gains understanding. (Prov. 3:13)

Be happy in the Lord, O righteous one [the believer possesses God's righteousness], and give thanks for the memory of His holiness [divine integrity]. (Ps. 97:12)

But now I come face to face with You [Christ addresses the Father in prayer], and these things [Bible doctrine] I am communicating in the world that they [believers] might keep having My happiness [in the prototype divine dynasphere] having been fulfilled in themselves [in the operational divine dynasphere]. (John 17:13)

Great resources of doctrine are required to construct the edification complex in the soul. God's Word in the believer's soul—the "standard of thinking from doctrine" described in Romans 12:3—provides the relationship between the function of the divine dynasphere and the construction of the edification complex. Ephesians 4:11 has stated that edification is one of God's purposes in giving the spiritual gift of pastor-teacher. The context continues in Ephesians 4:14–16 to demonstrate the relationship between the divine dynasphere and the edification complex.

In order that we no longer be immature [the communication of doctrine brings us to maturity at gate eight], being tossed here and there by the waves [Satan's counterfeit systems that oppose God's plan] and being blown here and there by every wind of [false] doctrine face to face with their cunning methods of deception, but by the teaching of doctrine in the sphere of love [gate four of the love complex] you [pastors] may cause them to grow up by the all things [of doctrinal teaching] with reference to Him who is the Head [the absolute authority], even Christ, from whom all the body [the royal family with its variety of spiritual gifts] being joined together and taught categorically by every joint of supply [logistical grace supplies pastors who provide Bible teaching], according to the operational power [the filling of the Spirit at gate one of the divine dynasphere], in measure one for each part [God provides a right pastor under which every positive believer can learn doctrine], resulting in an edification complex belonging to himself in the sphere of love [the love complex]. (Eph. 4:14–16)

THE BEGINNING OF SUPERGRACE

The happiness of the mature believer with a completed edification complex is the beginning of supergrace. The immature believer has limited capacity, which becomes maximum capacity when his spiritual momentum has carried him to maturity. Each gate of the divine dynasphere contributes to the believer's happiness; happiness exists in varying degrees until completed happiness is stabilized in gate eight. Consistently sharing the happiness of God belongs to the first category of supergrace—spiritual blessings. Spiritual blessings are the prerequisite for the other five categories of supergrace blessings: temporal blessings, blessings by association, historical impact, the special blessings connected with undeserved suffering, and dying grace.[81]

When the believer has come to share the happiness of God through Bible doctrine, he does not require or depend on overt blessings to sustain his happiness. His state of happiness does not hinge on money, success, promotion, marriage, or the approbation of others. Whether people appreciate him or not is inconsequential to his happiness.

> I have come to know how to get along with humble means,
> and I also know how to live in prosperity; in any and every
> circumstance I have learned the secret of being filled and
> going hungry, both of having abundance and suffering need.
> (Phil. 4:12)

Since the believer who enjoys a mature relationship with God does not need any other special blessings, God can give such blessings to him. God can prosper the happy believer precisely because he will not base his happiness on the prosperity that God gives him. The details of life will not distract the mature believer from his first priority—his personal love for God through the intake and application of Bible doctrine. At least, the details of life will not distract him *if* he continues in the divine dynasphere.

> But I hold this against you: you have abandoned [forsaken,
> deserted] your most important love [the Lord Jesus Christ].
> (Rev. 2:4)

---

81. See above, pp. 57-58.

Prosperity is the most difficult test for anyone to pass. In contrast to adversity, which forces a person to draw upon his inner resources of doctrine in order to weather the storm, prosperity tends to deceive the believer into letting down his guard. The prosperous believer may struggle to secure the blessings he has; he loses his momentum by emphasizing security instead of freedom. He takes his eyes off the source of his prosperity. God in His perfect justice gives the blessings of supergrace only to the mature believer who has already attained maximum happiness without reference to circumstances.

Anyone who prospers without capacity, whether through the laws of establishment in the business world or by some satanic system of pseudo-prosperity, is no happier because of his achievement. That is why the Psalm says, "Do not be envious of evil men" (Ps. 37:1b). God can make anyone an instant millionaire; sometimes He uses vast wealth or promotion as a means of divine discipline to show a believer his true spiritual poverty. The story of King Midas, who thought he would be happy if everything he touched would turn to gold, is the classic illustration of personal disaster wrought from prosperity without capacity.

THE SUPREME HONOR: FRIEND OF GOD

Every Church Age believer is a member of the royal family of God, but even among royalty there is no equality. Volition makes the difference. By our own decisions we advance spiritually and attain supergrace and the other blessings of gate eight of the divine dynasphere, or we retrogress into reversionism. The inequalities among the spiritual nobility of the Church Age will be most dramatic at the Judgment Seat of Christ. There, the mature believer will be rewarded with tremendous eternal blessings (2 Tim. 4:7, 8; James 1:12; Rev. 2:7, 10, 17, 28), while the immature believer will be admitted to heaven "as if by fire" without rewards of any kind (1 Cor. 3:12-15; 2 Tim. 2:11-13).

The superiority of the mature believer is not restricted to eternity future. On earth the believer who reaches gate eight of the divine dynasphere and perpetuates his spiritual momentum is invested into the most exclusive order of royal family knighthood. He is called the friend of God.

The mature believer's investiture into the royal order of the friend of God is the ultimate honor in this life. Few believers have ever attained this order of knighthood. In the entire span of history recorded in the Old Testament, only two men were called the friend of God: Abraham, the father of the Jewish race (2 Chron. 20:7; Isa. 41:8; James 2:23), and Moses, the father of the Jewish nation (Ex. 33:11a). These two great believers did not have the advantage of the divine dynasphere.

Now, inside the divine dynasphere, every member of the royal family has an unprecedented opportunity to attain this supreme honor from our Lord. Even the believer who seems to you most unlikely to succeed has a far greater opportunity to become the friend of God than did Abraham, Moses, David, Elijah, Daniel, or any other outstanding believer of past dispensations.

The friend of God ceases to be merely the object of divine impersonal love; he now becomes the object of God's complete personal love. At salvation all believers receive God's righteousness, which not only completes their salvation but also gives them potential for all the special divine blessings of time and eternity. In our study of divine personal and impersonal love, we noted that God can love personally only what His righteousness approves.[82] When salvation is the issue, God loves us with personal love the moment we receive His absolute righteousness. But when the issue is the Christian way of life, God cannot love us with personal love until we learn Bible doctrine and reach maturity.

Every believer receives logistical grace as the constant demonstration of God's faithfulness and impersonal love, but very few believers in any dispensation fully exploit logistical grace. Few even begin to fulfill the tremendous potential of imputed righteousness. As members of the royal family, we possess the same divine righteousness that Abraham and Moses received, but our logistical grace is far superior to theirs. We have the complete divine dynasphere to sustain our spiritual advance. We may have many reasons, but there is no excuse for failing to attain the maximum blessings of gate eight.

This, then, is the final goal of the divine dynasphere—not only that we be occupied with the Person of Christ and enjoy maximum social life with God but that He can love us with maximum personal love and accept us into the exclusive circle of His friends. The supergrace advantages of being the friend of God are phenomenal. This is our purpose in life, our spiritual destiny.

THE TEST OF THE DIVINE DYNASPHERE

We have now developed all eight gates of the divine dynasphere. In summary, God the Father gave a sphere of power to the incarnate Christ to sustain His humanity in the devil's world. This was the prototype divine dynasphere; Christ was the test pilot. For thirty-three years our Lord functioned inside God's love complex, and despite continual temptations, beyond any we will ever know, Christ resisted every satanic attack and perfectly fulfilled the plan of God. After accomplishing His mission in the First Advent, Christ turned over His power system to us. He ran the divine dynasphere through a complete checkout and then gave the entire system to us so that we, too, can fulfill the plan of God for our lives. As the royal family of God, we have a power system greater than has existed in any previous dispensation.

---

82. See above, pp. 39-42.

When our Lord was about to be betrayed, He gave us a mandate: "Reside in My love" (John 15:9b). This is tantamount to a test pilot saying, "Fly it." Christ had wrung out the system completely and reported "All systems go." The design was perfect. For us to obey that simple divine command, we must know and obey many other divine mandates.

When a pilot receives orders to fly a mission, that one order incorporates many other instructions. He is implicitly ordered to check his instruments, to taxi to the end of the proper runway, to set his flaps for takeoff, to handle the throttle in a certain way, to follow a prearranged flight plan. There are literally thousands of functions implied in the command to fly a particular aircraft, all of which the pilot learned step by step.

Likewise, the divine order to "reside in My love" is a single command that involves many other commands, but all of them interlock into one complete system. The New Testament frequently refers to love and divine power, but we cannot possibly obey our instructions if we fail to understand that love is a system. Christian love is not a nebulous emotion encouraged by a collection of unrelated Bible verses; Christian love is a cohesive *system* of power. The realm of power in which we must conduct our Christian lives is comprehensive; we obey the order to "fly it" by properly operating in all of its eight gates.

Many believers try to live the Christian way of life in only one or two gates. Some make an entire modus operandi out of gate one, distorting the ministry of the Spirit by "speaking in tongues." Other believers seek to apply personal love to all mankind without understanding the doctrine of impersonal love; they sentence themselves to a life of frustration.

Likewise, some believers take witnessing, giving, church attendance, and prayer out of the overall system. When properly motivated, these are legitimate Christian responsibilities of the royal ambassador. They fit into the divine dynasphere as applications of doctrine in gate four. However, when believers emphasize these legitimate activities in isolation from the system, then witnessing or prayer become illegitimate programs of legalism. Such believers go through the motions of serving God in order to impress other Christians or to impress God and earn His blessings. No one can earn or deserve God's blessings, and anything less than the entire love complex distorts God's plan and incurs His discipline.

God designed the entire system. The system as a whole is far superior to any of its parts. Each gate is legitimate in itself, but all the gates must function together as the Christian way of life. Only the believer who resides and functions in the love complex as a complete, balanced system obeys our Lord's command to "reside in My love."

IX
A New Approach To Christology

THE TEST OF TRUTH

The eight gates of the divine dynasphere work together in the believer without fanaticism, without exaggerating, misapplying, or overlooking isolated truths. All the pieces fit. This categorical doctrine gives you a balanced approach to your Christian life, enabling you to execute the plan of God as one consistent, orthodox system of protocol. You know when you are in God's system; you know when you are out. You understand the requirements of gaining and maintaining spiritual momentum. Foremost in your priorities is "the author and perfecter of our faith" (Heb. 12:2), Jesus Christ, who tested the prototype of the system. You become occupied with Him as you obey the very mandates He obeyed, molding your life with positive decisions similar to His steadfast decisions.

The divine dynasphere enables you to fulfill God's purpose for keeping you alive, but this new categorization of the Christian way of life also answers longstanding questions concerning the Person of Christ. The doctrine of the divine dynasphere has special significance in systematic theology.

Christology is the Biblical study of Christ our Savior, the God-Man. Christology is the heart of Christian theology, for this doctrine reveals the character and personality of "the prince of life, the one whom God raised from the dead" (Acts 3:15), "the one whom God exalted to His right hand" (Acts 5:31). Christology is the touchstone of accurate Bible teaching.

> By this discern [apprehend, learn to recognize] that per-
> sonality [which is] from God. (1 John 4:2*a*)

The Greek noun *pneuma*, usually translated "spirit," refers here to a "personality," the teacher, the communicator of Bible doctrine.

> Every personality [honorable minister] who teaches that
> Jesus Christ has come in the flesh is from God. (1 John 4:2*b*)

The test of the orthodox Bible teacher is his emphasis on Christology and
soteriology, the doctrines of the Person and saving work of our Lord. Regardless
of how eloquent or persuasive a pastor may be, no matter how moral his life, he
is a false teacher if he misrepresents our Lord and presents a false Gospel. All
other doctrine is anchored to the correct understanding of the Person and work
of Jesus Christ. The accurate communicator "teaches that Jesus Christ has come
in the flesh," that He is both God and man.

Paul, too, identifies Christology as the pivotal doctrine. When other doctrines had been distorted and abused by the subjective Corinthians, sparking
quarrels and dissentions (1 Cor. 1:11), Paul reaffirmed the precedence of Christ
and salvation.

> For I determined to know nothing among you except Jesus
> Christ, and Him crucified (1 Cor. 2:2, NASV)

Who is Jesus Christ? Who is this Person who saved you? Our study would
be incomplete if we failed to illuminate the divine dynasphere in the life of our
matchless Lord Jesus Christ. The study of Christ, or Christology, includes every
aspect of who and what He is, from His preincarnate existence in eternity past
to His ultimate glorification in eternity future. Three essential doctrines included
under Christology pertain to the divine dynasphere and the spiritual life of the
royal family: the doctrines of the hypostatic union, kenosis, and impeccability.

THE HYPOSTATIC UNION

THE UNIQUE PERSON OF THE UNIVERSE

The hypostatic union designates who Jesus Christ is. The term "hypostatic"
is derived from the Greek *hupostasis*, "essence, substance." Jesus Christ is
"the exact image of [God's] *hupostasis* or divine essence" (Heb. 1:3); He *is*
God. Christ unites in Himself the essence of God and the essence of man, form-
ing a new *hupostasis* or essence, the hypostatic union, the God-Man.

At the virgin birth the second Person of the Trinity took upon Himself true humanity and became a new Person, the unique Person of the universe. He is different from God in that He is man, different from man in that He is God. He is unique because He is God, infinitely superior to man, and because He is impeccable humanity, superior to sinful humanity. The uniqueness of Christ alerts us to the truth that He is our only way to God, the only way of salvation. He is the "one mediator between God and man" (1 Tim. 2:5).

The hypostatic union is the complete Person of Christ, His two natures combined in one personality. As stated in theological phraseology:

> In the Person of the incarnate Christ are two natures inseparably united but without mixture or loss of separate identities, without loss or transfer of properties or attributes, the union being both personal and eternal.

Because He is a man does not make our Lord less than God, nor does His being God prevent Him from being truly a man. His two natures, though united, retain their separate identities. His divine attributes always adhere to His divine nature; His human attributes belong to His human nature. Deity remains deity; humanity remains humanity.

The infinite cannot become finite; the immutable cannot be changed. No attribute of deity was altered by the Incarnation. To rob His divine nature of a single attribute would destroy His deity, and to rob His perfect human nature of a single attribute would destroy His humanity. Our Lord is *both* God *and* man, not some absurd hybrid that is *neither* God *nor* man.

There is no contradiction in this union of God and perfect man. Only *fallen* man violates God's norms and standards, but Christ was not fallen man. No moral failure is implied in our Lord's physical weakness, fatigue, hunger, thirst, indignation, or death. Indeed, man in his perfect state is compatible with the essence of God, as Adam was created before the Fall and as Christ, the Last Adam, was virgin born (Rom. 5:14; 1 Cor. 15:45).[83] Man was created in the image of God to have fellowship with God (Gen. 1:27).

Christ's humanity does not compromise the absolute standards of divine integrity (Ps. 8:4-6). God can love only what His integrity approves. Proof that Christ's humanity is compatible with His deity is that, just as God loved Adam and the woman before the Fall of man, so also the Father and the Holy Spirit love the *entire* Person of Christ—both God and man—with infinite divine love (John 15:9, 26).

---

83. See Thieme, *Integrity of God,* pp. 48-54, 77-79.

PERSONAL AND ETERNAL

The hypostatic union is personal. A new personality, a unique *hupostasis*, came into being at the virgin birth. Jesus as a man was not merely in harmony or sympathy with God. Nor did the second Person of the Trinity indwell or possess our Lord's humanity, as the deity of Christ indwells us, members of the royal family (John 14:18-21; Rom. 8:9, 10; 2 Cor. 13:5; Eph. 3:17-19; Col. 1:27; Rev. 3:20).[84]

Each Church Age believer is "in Christ," but our union with Christ is not a hypostatic union. "If any man is in Christ, he is a new creature" (2 Cor. 5:17) because that individual is reconciled to God, reborn from spiritual death into spiritual life, having "received adoption as sons through Jesus Christ" into the royal family of God (Eph. 1:5). Salvation gives Church Age believers a privileged position in Christ,[85] but we are not both God and man in one Person as is Christ.

The hypostatic union is eternal as well as personal. Christ as eternal God will never cease to also be a member of the human race. He is "the same yesterday, today, and forever" (Heb. 13:8). At this moment Jesus—as a *man*—is seated in royal glory at the right hand of God the Father (Acts 5:31; Heb. 1:3). Our Lord's deity is omnipresent and does not sit; only His *humanity* sits. At the Second Advent the *humanity* of Christ will return to earth (Zech. 14:1-11; Rev. 1:7), and as King David's *human* heir Jesus will eternally reign over Israel (2 Sam. 7:8-17; Ps. 89:20-37).

Our Lord is both undiminished deity and true humanity forever. We specify *undiminished deity* because false doctrines have claimed that Christ became less than God when He was born "in the likeness of sinful flesh" (Rom. 8:3) or that somehow He was unequal in His divine essence with the essence of the Father. We say *true humanity* because sects and cults down through the centuries have denied that Christ was truly a human being. But our Lord possesses a body (Heb. 10:5*b*; 1 Pet. 2:24), soul (Matt. 26:38), and spirit (Mark 2:8; Luke 23:46)—without sin (1 John 3:3; Heb. 4:15)—just as Adam in the Garden was created with these three essential components of man. The Bible teaches that Christ is God and that He is man.

God is revealed in the Bible, not in human theories. Basic issues concerning the unique Person of Christ, which have led to false speculation, are clarified by the doctrine of the divine dynasphere.

> How could the creator become a creature, a human being,
> without compromising His deity?

---

84. See Thieme, *Integrity of God*, p. 115.
85. See Thieme, *Integrity of God*, pp. 105-12.

> How could sovereign, immutable God become a servant yet remain God?
>
> How could the unglorified humanity of Christ remain perfect, acceptable to God as a blameless sacrifice for our sins, while living in Satan's kingdom?

These questions may overtax the inventory of doctrinal ideas in your soul, but the answers are not conjecture or speculation; they are *history*. The historical life of Christ in hypostatic union on earth proves that God resolved these issues. The answers to these questions reveal the dynamics of our Lord's integrity; as you learn these doctrines you expand your capacity to know and love Him. "How blessed is the man who finds wisdom . . . and gains understanding" of the Lord (Prov. 3:13). The divine dynasphere, correlated with the doctrines of kenosis and impeccability, is the frame of reference for understanding how Christ solved these problems, purchasing your salvation and pioneering your life as a spiritual winner.

KENOSIS

VOLUNTARY RESTRICTION OF INDEPENDENT FUNCTION

The doctrine of kenosis takes its name from the Greek verb *kenöo*, "to deprive oneself of a rightful function, to debase oneself." Kenosis explains how the supreme God of the universe condescended to become a man and suffer the humiliation of the Cross. Although Jesus Christ "was rich, yet for your sake He became poor, that you through His poverty might become rich" (2 Cor. 8:9).

In eternity past God the Son, who is coequal and coeternal with God the Father and God the Holy Spirit, voluntarily subordinated Himself to the plan of the Father. Complying with the Father's plan for the Incarnation, Christ voluntarily deprived Himself of the independent exercise of His divine attributes from the virgin birth until His resurrection.

At no time did Christ surrender any attribute of His divine essence or "empty Himself" of His deity, as alleged by a false doctrine of kenosis. God can never become less than God. He did not divest Himself of His deity because in Christ "all the fullness of deity dwells in bodily form" (Col. 2:9).

The Father's plan called for our Lord to be the Messiah, the Anointed One, who would come to save fallen mankind (John 11:27). For the First Advent this plan required our Lord to "take on the form of a slave, being made in the likeness of men" (Phil. 2:6, 7), serving both God and man. Christ served God by revealing God to man (John 1:18) and served man by redeeming mankind, purchasing man's freedom from slavery to sin (John 8:31-36; Eph. 1:7; 1 Pet. 1:18, 19). To become a servant Christ had to veil his preincarnate glory, "the glory which [He] ever had with [God the Father] before the world was" (John 17:5). He was called upon to enter into hypostatic union with unglorified humanity and restrict those expressions of His deity that would prevent Him from executing the plan of the Father. As the lowest degradation, Christ had to suffer divine judgment for the sins of mankind (Phil. 2:8).

The second Person of the Trinity voluntarily accepted this messianic mission. In eternity past He was appointed to be "the Lamb slain," the sacrifice for our sins (Rev. 13:8). Throughout His first advent Jesus Christ in hypostatic union continually refused to exercise the attributes of His deity apart from the mission given Him by the Father.

As deity Christ remained omniscient, but as humanity He was born ignorant and learned Bible doctrine "precept upon precept, line upon line, a little here, a little there" (Isa. 28:10; Matt. 24:36). As God, Christ remained omnipresent, existing equally in heaven and on earth (John 3:13), while as a man He endured long journeys on foot, subordinating Himself to the primitive technology of His day. He refused to relieve His human fatigue by supernaturally transporting Himself or depending on His deity's simultaneous presence at His destination. Nor did His deity tell His humanity about automobiles or airplanes. When He was hungry, Christ resisted the satanic temptation to turn stones into bread (Matt. 4:3, 4) while His omnipotence held together the universe, including all the bread on earth (Col. 1:17). Sustaining the universe did not jeopardize the Father's plan for the Incarnation; materializing bread for His own sustenance would have compromised His mission as a servant.

During the Incarnation Jesus Christ did not exercise His divine attributes to benefit or glorify Himself. Instead, the Father's design of the prototype divine dynasphere assigned to God the Holy Spirit the mission of sustaining and glorifying Christ (John 8:56; 16:14). Upon the foundational virtue of genuine humility, Jesus as a man exemplified the motivational virtue of confidence in God just as we, who do not possess divine attributes, are commanded to trust in God. We could never turn stones into bread, but in our trials and temptations we rely on the same power system than sustained Christ when tempted to violate kenosis.

This self-imposed limitation of kenosis ended with the glorification of Christ—His resurrection, ascension, and session at the Father's right hand—after His mission for the First Advent was accomplished (John 19:30).

SOVEREIGN YET SUBORDINATE

Sovereignty is divine volition, absolute free will in the eternal, infinite essence of God. Each Person of the Godhead is sovereign, subject to no one, dependent on no one, answerable to no one. No Member of the Trinity is ever coerced or forced into a course of action; He does only what is His pleasure to do (Isa. 46:10). To be less than sovereign is to cease being God, which is impossible, for God is also immutable and cannot change.

The pleasure of God the Father was to author a plan to reconcile fallen man to Himself; the pleasure of God the Son was to execute this plan of grace, to "always do the things that are pleasing to [the Father]" (John 8:29). By His independent, sovereign will our Lord elected to subordinate Himself to the Father, expressing His own desire "for all to come to repentance" (2 Pet. 3:9*b*) and demonstrating perfect confidence in the essence of the Father, which is identical to His own.

God can accomplish all He *wills* to do, but He may not will to accomplish all He *can* do. He chooses to follow certain policies; He chooses not to take certain actions. God the Son did not cease to be sovereign when, rather than retain the independent function of His divine attributes, He decided to obey the authority of the Father, securing our salvation. The sovereignty of the Son aggressively upheld, seconded, affirmed the sovereignty of the Father. Kenosis was an offensive not defensive divine strategy, aimed at ultimate victory in the angelic conflict. Christ accepted the challenge to wield the most powerful weapon ever designed, the divine dynasphere.

From His omniscience in eternity past, the second Person of the Trinity knew every detail of the Father's plan, including the design of the divine dynasphere. Aware of the tremendous divine dynamics—identical to His own —that would support and sustain His humanity, He could agree to deprive Himself of independent function, subordinate Himself to the plan of the Father, and become the God-Man without compromise to His own divine essence. Since the divine dynasphere met the absolute standards of God the Son in eternity past, we can place our confidence in the divine dynasphere as our Christian way of life.

Each Member of the Godhead loves His own integrity with subjective divine love and the integrity of the other two Members with objective divine love. Christ was absolutely confident in the equal divine essence of the Father and the Holy Spirit. He knew they would uphold Him. As He faced the ordeal of becoming man and bearing our sins, God the Son trusted implicitly in the integrity of the Father and the Holy Spirit. Kenosis is the most dramatic demonstration of objective divine love of the Members of the Godhead for one another.

This reciprocation, this expression of absolute trust, confidence, and love within the Godhead proves that obedience to legitimate authority is not demeaning. Even within the Godhead freedom and authority coexist, uncontaminated by arrogance, jealousy, inordinate competition or ambitiousness. Although Jesus Christ "eternally existed in the essence of God, [Christ] did not think equality with God a profit to be seized and held" (Phil. 2:6). Omnipotent God Himself is the pattern of humility as a virtue.

THE EXAMPLE OF GENUINE HUMILITY

The doctrine of kenosis is expressed most concisely in Philippians 2:5-8. This classic passage reveals the thinking of Christ not in an abstract theological discussion but as an example of genuine humility for us to follow. All doctrine, including Christology, is ultimately intended for application.

God the Son voluntarily submitted to the mandates of God the Father and, as a man, demonstrated an attitude we are commanded to emulate.

> Keep on thinking this within yourself, which was also resi-
> dent in Christ Jesus, who though He eternally existed in the
> essence of God, did not think equality with God a profit [a
> gain] to be seized and held, but He deprived Himself [*kenöo*,
> of the independent function of deity] when He had received
> the form of a slave, when He was born in the likeness of
> mankind [but without the sin nature]. In fact, although He
> was discovered in outward appearance as a man, he humbled
> Himself by becoming obedient to the point of death, that is,
> the death of the Cross. (Phil. 2:5-8)

The doctrine of the divine dynasphere clarifies the doctrine of kenosis by showing what Christ voluntarily chose to *do*, not just what He voluntarily chose to *restrict*. From the perspective of deprivation, Christ voluntarily *restricted* the independent exercise of His deity, but from the positive point of view He voluntarily *obeyed* all the mandates of God that define the gates of the love complex. Christ "abided in His love " (John 15:10).

The divine dynasphere explains kenosis because humility does not stand alone in the system. Humility is the foundation of all other virtues. The combined dynamics of all the gates add up to a way of life far greater than the sum of its component parts. Christ was not merely humble; He possessed all the confidence, courage, strength, capacity, and happiness of the entire system. Jesus could become a servant or slave because the deity of God the Holy Spirit, the Energizer of a powerful *system*, sustained Him. Our Lord's accomplishments as a servant demonstrated the ministry of God in His life.

IMPECCABILITY

FREEDOM FROM THREE CATEGORIES OF SIN

The effectiveness of the love complex is demonstrated by the third doctrine connected with Christology, the doctrine of impeccability. Our Lord's complete and uninterrupted reliance on the divine dynasphere is manifested in the sinless perfection of His life.

Christ remained free from all three categories of sin in the human race: the old sin nature, Adam's original sin, and personal sins. The *old sin nature*, the "sin" that "reigns in your mortal body" (Rom. 6:12), is passed down genetically from father to children, but Christ did not have a human father. The virgin birth of Christ enabled Him to enter the human race free from the inherent sin nature that corrupted the human race when Adam sinned (Rom. 3:23; 1 Cor. 15:22).

The *sin nature* and *Adam's original sin* always go together. An affinity exists between them: Adam's original sin created the sin nature. As an expression of perfect divine justice, God completes this affinity in each individual when, at the moment of physical birth, He imputes Adam's original sin to every human being who possesses an old sin nature. The result of this imputation is spiritual death, "for the wages of [Adam's] sin is death" (Rom. 6:23a). We are born physically alive, spiritually dead. In the humanity of Christ, who possessed no old sin nature, there was no home or target to which Adam's sin could be imputed. Because He did not receive the imputation of Adam's original sin, Christ was born physically and spiritually alive.[86]

The first two categories of sin were already eliminated from our Lord's life by the time He was born. Free from the old sin nature and Adam's sin, He faced life having to contend only with avoiding *personal sins*. To be qualified to die for our sins, Jesus had to be "unblemished and spotless," free from personal sins Himself (1 Pet. 1:19). Were He a sinner, He would be condemned. He would have to bear the punishment for His own sins and would be unqualified to substitute for mankind. Only someone not sentenced to death can take the place of the condemned.

PERFECT GOD, PERFECT MAN

To appreciate how our Lord avoided personal sin and remained impeccable, we must remember who Christ is. He is the God-Man, the hypostatic union. He is perfect as God and as man. These two aspects of His impeccability are capsulized in two Latin phrases, *non posse peccare* and *posse non peccare*.

Non posse peccare, meaning "not able to sin," describes the deity of Christ. God is perfect righteousness and cannot tolerate sin or imperfection. He is omniscient and, therefore, cannot be deceived or tricked into sinning, as the woman was deceived by the serpent (Gen. 3:4-6). God is uncompromising justice and can only judge and destroy sin. Indeed, God cannot even be tempted to sin. No sin appeals to Him in the least, and as a result He never tempts us to commit sins.

---

86. See Thieme, *Integrity of God*, pp. 77-79.

> Let no one say when he is tempted, ''I am being tempted
> from God,'' for God cannot be tempted from evil. Further-
> more, He Himself does not tempt anyone. (James 1:13)

The second Latin phrase, *posse non peccare*, means "able not to sin." This statement refers to the humanity of Christ, who possessed the ability to resist sin. As a man Jesus could be tempted and could have sinned, but He did not.

> For we have not a High Priest [Jesus Christ] unable to sym-
> pathize with our weakness, but having been tempted in all
> points in quite the same way [as we] but apart from sin.
> (Heb. 4:15)

As God, our Lord was neither temptable nor peccable; as a man He was both temptable and peccable. This adds up to the true conclusion that as the God-Man, Christ was temptable but impeccable. In the hypostatic union Christ could be tempted, but He could not sin.

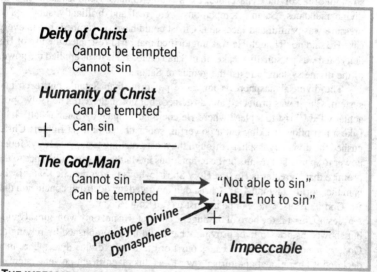

THE IMPECCABILITY OF CHRIST

When I learned the doctrine of impeccability in seminary, I recognized this to be the only accurate conclusion, yet all the questions concerning Jesus Christ's perfection were not resolved. Only the prototype divine dynasphere explains the impeccability of our Lord. As a man He lived for thirty-three years in the love complex, the environment of virtue. Although tempted in every way that we are, as well as in unique temptations that no one else will ever face (Matt. 4:1-4), He never violated kenosis but consistently relied on the power of God the Holy Spirit, gate one of the divine dynasphere. As long as Jesus remained in the divine power system, He could not sin (1 John 3:5).

The humanity of Christ received as a gift from the Father an interlocking system that assured His impeccability. The divine dynasphere empowered Him to reach the Cross fully qualified to bear our sins. The plan of the Father assigned our Lord a mission, a destiny, to purchase the salvation of mankind, and the Father provided all the support necessary for Christ to accomplish that mission. God does the same for us.

THE CHALLENGE TO POSITIVE VOLITION

"Able not to sin" emphasizes the free volition of Christ's humanity. In the strength of the divine dynasphere, He was *able* to make right decisions to obey divine mandates. Satan's temptations were real and brilliantly subtle. The pressure was painful and incessant. Christ could have succumbed, but in every case He said no. Though He was unglorified man, had restricted the use of His deity, and was personally weaker than Satan (Heb. 2:7), Jesus applied the power of the divine system to resist the genius of Satan.

The divine dynasphere is far more powerful than Satan's entire cosmic system. Christ was protected and sustained, but not sheltered. The Holy Spirit actually led Christ to a place where He could be tempted by Satan (Matt. 4:1). Like a test pilot checking out a powerful, sophisticated new jet fighter, Christ pushed the divine dynasphere through the most gruelling tests, yet always found power to spare. The results of the temptations in Matthew 4 give substance to the promise that "greater is He [the Holy Spirit] who is in you than he [Satan] who is in the world" (1 John 4:4). Christ demonstrated the doctrinal conclusion that "if God is for us, who can be against us?" (Rom. 8:31).

Jesus Christ is the hero of the angelic conflict. He not only won our salvation but showed us how to live, proving what could be accomplished by relying on God. For more than three decades our Lord tested the divine dynasphere then declared it operational and turned over to us this magnificent power system.

> And everyone who keeps having this hope in him [the mature believer at gate eight anticipating eternal rewards] purifies himself [continues to grow in the divine dynasphere] just as that unique Person [Jesus Christ] is pure. (1 John 3:3)

We cannot be impeccable as Christ was impeccable, but by resisting temptation and using rebound whenever we sin, we can live in the same environment of virtue in which He lived. We can acquire wisdom, making decisions from a position of strength; develop capacity for love and happiness, having complete control over our own lives; and achieve Christian integrity with a personal sense of destiny. By our decisions to obey God's mandates, we follow our Lord in the divine dynasphere. As we execute God's game plan, we join in the glorification of the Lord Jesus Christ and, as did our Lord, become winners in this life and forever.

Subject Index

Scripture Index

OLD TESTAMENT

NEW TESTAMENT

1 CORINTHIANS

NOTES

NOTES

NOTES

NOTES

NOTES